Congressional Populism and the Crisis of the 1890s

Congressional Populism and the Crisis of the 1890s

Gene Clanton

University Press of Kansas

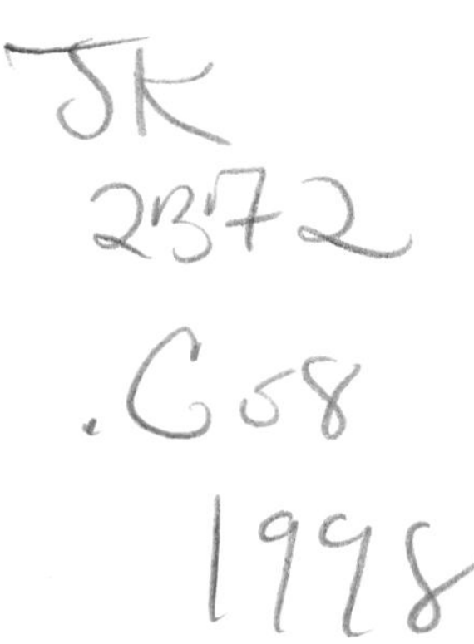

Published by the University Press of Kansas (Lawrence, Kansas 66049), which was organized by the Kansas Board of Regents and is operated and funded by Emporia State University, Fort Hays State University, Kansas State University, Pittsburg State University, the University of Kansas, and Wichita State University

Library of Congress Cataloging-in-Publication Data

Clanton, O. Gene.
Congressional populism and the crisis of the 1890s / Gene Clanton.
p. cm.
Includes index.
ISBN 0-7006-0913-X (cloth : alk. paper)
1. Populism—United States—History. 2. United States—Politics and government—1893–1897. 3. United States—Politics and government—1897–1901. I. Title.
JK2372.C58 1999
320.973—dc21 98-20605

British Library Cataloguing in Publication Data is available.

Printed in the United States of America

10 9 8 7 6 5 4 3 2 1

The paper used in this publication meets the minimum requirements of the American National Standard for Permanence of Paper for Printed Library Materials Z39.48-1984.

For My Parents
Orval Elmer (1905–1963) and Verl Anne (1909–1993)

Truth reveals itself in degrees, and we can progress from an incomplete to a more and ever more complete comprehension of truth. Truth is not a thing, not an object which we either have in its entirety, or have not at all. Truth is a matter of spiritual growth, and the development of truth on earth is not more than the progress of the human race.

—Goethe

Contents

Preface

This is an examination of the People's or Populist party in Congress. From 1891 to 1903, beginning with the Fifty-second and ending with the Fifty-seventh Congress, fifty individual Populists representing sixteen states and one territory served in the national legislature. They claimed their seats at a very special point of transition in the rise of modern America—in truly an epochal decade—and they saw themselves as the bearers of a reform message vital to the nation's future. It was a message that has often been misconstrued if not simply ignored and buried in the voluminous and underexplored record of Congress. The purpose of this study is to reconstruct the record of that episode as completely and objectively as possible, with special attention to what the Populists were saying and advocating. In doing so, I relied extensively on the *Congressional Record.*

To avoid confusion, I must also point out that my frame of reference does not include that voguish, ahistorical, generic rendition of "populism" that continues to be employed, quite cavalierly, primarily by political pundits and journalists. It needs to be understood that Populism was considerably more than just a "heightened expression . . . of a kind of popular impulse that is endemic in American culture," as Richard Hofstadter put it more than forty years ago; likewise, it was more than a "language" or a "persistent yet mutable style of political rhetoric," as Michael Kazin argued quite recently.[1] A better understanding of the "old radicalism" in America and a closer examination of the phenomenon at the congressional level should help in dealing with this confusion.

It is indeed true, as I have readily conceded from the beginning of my involvement with this subject, that political styles of those positioned on the fringes of the political spectrum share some common ground: to begin with, a propensity for conspiracy theories, a pronounced tendency to confuse accusation with proof, an affinity for simplistic analysis and outrageous hyperbole, and a disposition toward self-righteous certitude. This is familiar terrain historically, especially among those driven by an evangelical personality or psychology. For that reason, what Hofstadter identified as the "paranoid style" in American politics has merit and should be retained as an analytical tool. But at the same time, writers need to ensure that an extra effort is made to avoid leaping to a similar conclusion regarding substance. Style is one thing; substance quite another. A flat-line, left-to-right continuum must be retained and employed as a way of distinguishing the extreme Left from the extreme Right and shades in between. In content there has always been a world of difference between the two poles, and unless writers ground themselves much more thoroughly on the substantive side of the original Populist revolt—especially as revealed at the national level—they would surely be well-advised to find more appropriate terminology to describe whatever demotic phenomenon momentarily captures their fancy.

Acknowledgments

Over the years a good many students and several colleagues have contributed in significant ways to the creation of this study. Among the many graduate students I have been privileged to work with, a special thanks is due to Ronald Fahl, Thomas Riddle, Lawrence Stark, Janice Miller, Peter Dunlop, Gregory Harness, and Susan Vetter. The ten truly outstanding graduate students enrolled in the final edition of my Rise of Modern America class offered during the fall of 1996 all deserve great praise for having worked their way through much earlier versions of manuscript chapters as part of an unusual—and no doubt highly intimidating— class assignment. Among my departmental colleagues, Richard Hume, for a second time, went far beyond the call of duty, graciously volunteering to read the study in its entirety and offering many valuable suggestions for improvement. For that I am deeply indebted and very appreciative. No doubt had I acted upon more of his advice this study would be much the better for it.

Several notable field specialists also assisted me in this project as it slowly made its way into final form. R. Hal Williams, Bruce Palmer, James E. Wright, Worth Robert Miller, and Walter T. K. Nugent, in different capacities and in varying portions, reckoned with the manuscript in a very constructive manner. In the same vein, my thanks also go out to the two anonymous reviewers employed by the press. Their comments and critical suggestions have been especially helpful: For sure this would be a far better piece of work had I been able to remedy all the shortcomings highlighted by their careful reading. I would also like to express my special appreciation to Peter H. Argersinger, who has been involved with this subject nearly as long as I have and from whom I have learned a great deal over the years.

At an earlier stage, Cynthia Miller, then with the University Press of Kansas, persuaded me to renew my association with my former publishers. I truly appreciate the encouragement and contagious enthusiasm she displayed for this subject.

My appreciation also goes out to Fred Woodward, Michael Briggs, and especially to Nancy Scott Jackson, who sustained that interest. One could not have asked for a more professional and dedicated group of people with whom to work.

I am pleased to also mention the Department of History, the College of Liberal Arts, and the Graduate School at Washington State University for the support I have received over the years as a member of the faculty. This work certainly would not have been possible without the travel assistance, research grants, and leaves of absence granted to me throughout my tenure at that fine institution.

Finally, I would like to thank the good folks at Interstate Aviation in Pullman, Washington—Felix Moran, John Michels, Adam Nelson, and Chris Davis, flight instructors extraordinaire—who somehow managed to teach this old history professor how to fly an airplane during the same period of time that most of this study was being written. Flying has been a wonderful diversion, savior of my piece of mind, and the fulfillment of a lifetime dream. Precisely the kind of activity that made the long hours of writing more bearable and more productive.

Introduction

Early in 1897 the Kansas legislature, controlled by Populists and "Popocrats" (Populist-Democratic party hybrids), elected William Alexander Harris to the Senate of the United States, thus ending William Alfred Peffer's senatorial career. Talk about a world turned upside down: here was a state whose vast majority of citizens had for years taken special pride in claiming to have perhaps the highest percentage of Union veterans per capita, the self-proclaimed "jewel in the crown" of the Republican party, voting to send an ex-Confederate and longtime Democrat to Washington, D.C., to replace a former Republican with vintage Unionist credentials. Despite their sharply differing backgrounds and factional differences, however, the two Kansans were forever linked in history, both having been catapulted to prominence by the Populist revolt.

William Peffer was Populism's first senator. Throughout his single term he was a favorite target of hostile cartoonists, guaranteeing that he would be known primarily as that political freak with the long beard—"Whiskers" Peffer—rather than the foremost champion on Capitol Hill of unadulterated Populism.

For certain, life was a deadly serious business for William Peffer; he was nothing if not a dedicated man. Six years of remarks on the Senate floor had produced precious few—if any—humorous diversions from the business at hand. His zealotry on behalf of the cause, apparently made more offensive to some by his austere, no-nonsense demeanor, accounted for the intensity of the assault by caricature. Convinced that their side would benefit by the tactic, fervid anti-Populists were even fond of suggesting that the eponym "Pefferism" was a synonym for Populism.

Considering Peffer's unyielding defense of Populist principles, one could easily write off his rejection after 1896 as the product of deconversion at the grass roots or the result of conventional political maneuvering, but at least two additional factors were at work, reflecting on the man himself. The first he could neither change nor ultimately even hide beneath an unusual beard—a shortage of charisma that was in no way mitigated by a proclivity for wordy prose. The other, more symptomatic and far more troublesome, stemmed from a deep-seated disdain for Democrats, especially southern Democrats. On top of all that, there was that undeniable link between Peffer's uncompromising defense of the original Populist program and his rejection by more pragmatic Democrats and Populists—elements of an informal reform coalition in Kansas, that, incidentally, had played an important role in his election. But considering how soon Populism's first senator returned to the camp of anti-Populist, unrepentant Republicanism after being defeated, one should pause to ask what had prompted his earlier commitment to Populist principles. The shadow cast by the Civil War and Reconstruction was indeed long. Inextricable as these two factors no doubt were, one suspects that his antipathy toward Democrats may have been nearly as fundamental as his commitment to Populism. Apparently, constancy recommended itself in his case as much by its separable qualities as by its correspondence with principles.

Peffer was a Pennsylvania native who, as a young man—initially as a public school teacher and then as a farmer—became part of the nation's massive westward migration, a bona fide rank-and-file member of what has been called "the antislavery-expansionist coalition." After a move from Missouri to Illinois, reportedly induced by hostility to his outspoken opposition to slavery, Peffer enlisted as a thirty-one-year-old private with an Illinois regiment and served to the war's end, advancing to the rank of lieutenant. While in the military, he became an adjutant and judge advocate, thereby managing—with the aid of independent studies—to prepare himself for a postwar career in law, which he practiced for a time in Tennessee and Kansas. Approaching age forty, "the judge," as he was sometimes called, launched yet another, and apparently more agreeable, career as an editor, sequentially, of several small-town, rural newspapers in southeastern Kansas. From 1874 to 1876, the new Republican editor also served in the Kansas senate. His most important position in journalism would come later as editor of Kansas' leading agricultural weekly, the Topeka *Kansas Farmer,* a position he held when he was elected to the U.S. Senate in 1891.[1]

As a loyal Republican, Peffer had thus staked out a claim for himself in the lower to middling ranks of an old, rural middle class. For him, as for many others, severing party ties was especially traumatic, and he was slow in joining the third-party reform effort, coming directly to the People's-Farmer's Alliance cause from the GOP, the state's One-Party Dominant. His Republican affiliation dated from the origins of the party and included a brief residence as a lawyer in postwar Tennessee, which no doubt contributed nothing to his reconciling with the southern Democracy. During the Populist revolt, it is likely that he continued to think of himself as a "true" Republican (possibly with a small *r*), following in the revered footsteps of Abraham Lincoln.

William Harris's political roots were just as firmly planted on the other side of the Mason-Dixon line. He also came belatedly and directly to Populism, in his case, from the camp of Democrats, leaving his bridges unburned. He no doubt thought of himself as a genuine Democrat (possibly with a lowercase *d*), acting consistently within the tradition of Jefferson and Jackson. He had already been twice nominated and once elected to Congress as an at-large candidate by Populists and Democrats. A resident of the state since 1865, which gave him an earlier Kansas connection than Peffer, Harris was the son of a former Virginia Democratic congressman, the "scion of an old family whose Virginia landholdings derived from a grant made by William and Mary," according to one source.[2] He was also the beneficiary of the best education the South could provide and served as an officer in the Confederate army, attaining the rank of colonel before his twenty-fifth birthday (the highest rank achieved in the regular forces by any of the fifty Populist congressmen to be elected).[3] His move to Kansas came as a result of his employment as an engineer for the Union Pacific Railroad. For several years he also worked as an agent representing various railroads with land to sell in Kansas. Years later, he became a rancher and developed a successful purebred cattle operation near Linwood, about ten miles northeast of Lawrence. Through substantial investments in land and business ventures and by farming and ranching, possibly boosted by an inheritance, he had built an impressive estate by the mid-1880s and, in the process, had made a name for himself as a breeder of shorthorn cattle.

If Harris had indeed been pushed out of an old southern upper class, in Kansas the Virginian managed to establish a foothold in the forward echelon of an old middle class with ties to the nation's emerging new middle class. His profile was that of a progressive or liberal Democrat rather than a genuine Populist, and his political activities consistently bore that out.

After his election to replace Peffer, Harris addressed a joint session of the Kansas legislature. One of the themes he chose to emphasize at that rare moment of recognition pertained to the abuse of corporate power in America. Even though Peffer and Harris differed substantially regarding solutions to that particular problem, they were in accord regarding the injustice of the preferential position corporations had come to enjoy in the Gilded Age.[4]

Harris stated the matter this way: "From the time of the Dartmouth College decision [by the Supreme Court in 1819] down to today, there seems to have been mapped out a field exclusively occupied by corporations, which to the average private citizen seems strange and mysterious. They have been endowed with rights which are wholly different from those which are exercised by the natural citizen. They have been given powers vastly in excess of his, and without limitation or restriction, are permitted to go in many directions altogether and entirely beyond the rights accorded to natural citizens."[5]

In expressing alarm regarding the rights of artificial versus natural persons, Harris immediately connected with a tradition of human rights considerably older than himself—indeed, one with its major roots in the soil of his native Virginia. And the perception of corporate rights as "strange and mysterious" was surely the case with a great many Americans.[6]

Three years later, the person who would become the last Populist congressman, a lawyer transplant from the land of Lincoln and another Civil War veteran, William Neville of Nebraska, drew even more extensively on that same tradition to denounce imperialism. In a debate in the House of Representatives, Neville indicated that his anti-imperialism was determined by a concern for "human rights." He emphasized that he was proud to be associated with a party that was still firmly committed to the "principles" of the Declaration of Independence. It was, he said, "a real consolation to believe in the common brotherhood of the human family; to believe that when God made man and woman as the source of human development, class distinction was not decreed." Human rights were transcendent and universal. "No government," said Neville, "can claim the dignity of being a government by the people when a portion of its people are subjects not having equal rights before the law."

Then, after chastising House Democrats for their willingness to deny fundamental human rights to black Americans and twitting Republicans for their willingness to do the same to brown people in areas the American government had annexed by force, Neville stated: "The right to life, liberty, and the pursuit of happiness is as dear to the black and brown man as to the white; as precious to the poor as to the rich; as just to the ignorant as to the educated; as sacred to the weak as to the strong, and as applicable to nations as to individuals, and the nation which subverts such right by force is not better governed than the man who takes the law in his own hands."[7]

These were not esoteric notions Harris and Neville were dredging up. Their concern went to the heart of the political phenomenon called Populism. They are recalled here to highlight a vital, yet still underappreciated, energizing source of origin. From the nation's beginning, conflict had been created by discrepancies between the ideals of the Revolution and national realities. Abraham Lincoln could speak, as he did near Gettysburg, about a new nation having been created in 1776, "conceived in liberty and dedicated to the proposition that all men are created equal," yet the frame of government, the national and state constitutions, the laws, and the system of rewards all failed to measure up to the ideal. Only when practices were blatantly out of line—as in the case of slavery—did reality put ideology to the test.

In the years after the Civil War, the nation's great economic revolution created circumstances that suggested to many—especially agrarians linked to this older egalitarian tradition—that another great crisis was impending. Those of the Populist persuasion believed that the country was steadily moving toward a new form of slavery, one likely to be worse than the old bondage that had produced the country's bloodiest of wars. Although it appeared in different trappings, dependent on whether the focus was on causes or consequences, this was the crisis of the nineties, a deep-seated, primarily agrarian-born anxiety shared by all those who were truly devoted to a democratic ethos. They tapped into a brand of democratic radicalism that was at least as old as the commercial revolution in Western civilization. Its major American architects included Thomas Jefferson, Abraham Lincoln, Henry George, Edward Bellamy, Henry Demarest Lloyd, and a host of lesser lights, all of whom grounded themselves firmly on the radical egalitarian side of the philosophy advanced in justification of the new nation announced to the world in 1776: one that placed property rights in a subordinate category among those "inalienable rights" incorporated in that famous trilogy of "life, liberty, and the pursuit of happiness." At a time when an unprecedented economic revolution and the mainstream political system, in a multitude of different ways, dictated otherwise, Populists attempted to steer the nation back onto what they believed was its proper course.[8]

Years later, this same conviction prompted Vernon L. Parrington, formerly a Kansas Populist but at the time one of the country's leading cultural historians teaching at the University of Washington, to reach this conclusion: "Since the rise of the slavery controversy the major parties, allied with masterful economic groups, have persistently ignored the Declaration of Independence, and repudiated in practice the spirit of democracy." The object of third-party movements from the 1870s on, he insisted, was to end that "treason to our traditional ideals" by creating a political system that would make it possible for "democracy to withstand the shock of the Industrial Revolution."[9] The Populist phenomenon of the 1890s was, simultaneously, the culmination of an old and the beginning of a new effort aimed at resolving that crisis (incidentally, nothing could more clearly separate the original Populists from the"populist" pretenders of a century later). Although much studied at the state and regional levels, the record of Populism at the congressional level, unfortunately, has not received the scrutiny it merits. That is the purpose of this study.

1

Populist Congressmen and Their Agendas

The Calamity Convention at St. Louis last week, pretending to represent a great national party, was the most disgraceful aggregation that ever got together in America. Anarchists, howlers, tramps, highwaymen, burglars, crazy men, wild-eyed men, men with unkempt and matted hair, men with long beards matted together with filth from their noses, men reeking with lice, men whose feet stank, and the odor from under whose arms would have knocked down a bull; brazen women, women with scrawny necks and dirty fingernails, women with their stockings out at the heels, women with snaggle-teeth, strumpets, rips, and women possessed of devils, gathered there, and sweltered and stank for a whole week, making speeches, quarrelling, and fighting like cats in a back yard. Gray-haired, scrawny, yellow-skinned women appeared upon the stage, dressed in hideous or indecent costumes, and gave performances that disgusted the most hardened Calamityites, until even Jerry Simpson gagged, and protested that the Convention was too much of a circus. . . . The gathering was so outlandish that each delegate imagined that the others were burlesquing him. To wind up the whole thing, delegates were bought up like the hogs they were.

Sol Miller, *Weekly Kansas Chief* (Troy), 30 July 1896[1]

This mean-spirited editorial assault on the delegates to the 1896 Populist national convention contains many of the bitter ingredients that were all too frequently used by anti-Populists in their ideological war against their Populist adversaries. In the South the attack would have been similar—in an earlier time frame, at least—except that the anti-Populist editor would have been a Democrat.[2] The piece was a variation on a caricature that was frequently applied to congressional Populists. Just a few weeks later another editor from the ranks of the conservative village elite, a young Republican by the name of William Allen White, became a national figure, virtually overnight, by writing a slightly less hyperbolic anti-Populist piece called "What's the Matter with Kansas?" These images were so widely distributed and then so deeply ingrained in the public's consciousness that a number of historians who dealt with the movement at the congressional and legislative levels years later devoted much of their time to demonstrating—even while finding it difficult to accept their own findings—that the "Uncle Hayseed," Neanderthal image failed to square with the facts. Unfortunately, most of these historians made no attempt to explain how and why such an outrageous discrepancy could come have to substitute for reality. We might ask, could these questions have required answers beyond the reach of quantitative analysis?[3]

Actually, the new party had nothing to apologize for when it came to the overall quality of the people it elected to the House and Senate during Populism's decade-plus participation at the Capitol. The ubiquitous caricature would suggest, however, that these folks were older, poorly educated, inexperienced country bumpkins—an attitude, incidentally, that virtually made "dumb" a prefix to "farmer" among generations of urbanites.

WHAT MANNER OF MEN?

At the time of election, the median age of these fifty Populist congressmen was between forty-seven and forty-eight (47.5). The oldest, Jehu Baker of Illinois, was seventy-four (Baker had actually been elected to three previous House terms as a Republican, the first in 1864 at age forty-two);[4] the youngest, John Fowler of North Carolina, was thirty.

In a competent but surprisingly overlooked 1954 master's thesis focusing on the Populists serving in the three Congresses from 1891 to 1897, Richard Kottman discovered that they were significantly younger in the Senate, even with Peffer's fifty-nine years added to the mix (43.25 years, compared with the 56.8 years of a random sample of major-party senators).[5] The Populists in the House of the Fifty-third Congress (1893–1895) were also found to be slightly younger, on average, than Kottman's random sample of major-party representatives (46.5 versus 48.1 years). Thus we can conclude that age was not a significant distinguishing characteristic, although it can be said that Populist congressmen were slightly younger, overall, than their major-party opponents.[6]

Opposition caricatures invariably depicted Populism's leaders in the stereotypical garb of farmers (a not-so-lovable scarecrow or Clem Kadiddlehopper prototype), the movement's primary constituents. Indeed, a significant number of Populists elected in 1890, 1892, and 1894 were engaged, part-time at least, in agricultural pursuits, which no doubt played a large role in establishing the caricature. In 1890, eight of eleven Populist congressmen elected (72 percent) were in that category; in 1892, eight of fourteen (57 percent); and in 1894, five of thirteen (38 percent). After that, with William Jennings Bryan's presidential campaign and fusion the order of the day, the number of those engaged in agriculture declined sharply. In 1896, there were only five of thirty-one farmers in the group; the smaller delegations resulting from the fade-out elections of 1898 and 1900 included three of fourteen and two of nine, respectively. The proportion ranged from a high of 72 percent in 1890 to an 1896 low of 16 percent. Significantly, the lowest percentage was still nearly twice as high as that among all representatives over the course of the decade (8.2 percent); and this, we should remind ourselves, was in a country whose population was still around 64 percent agricultural. In total, eighteen of these individuals were at least part-time agriculturalists (eighteen of fifty, or 36 percent).[7]

Although farmers were well represented among these Populists, attorneys were most numerous. Fully 50 percent (twenty-five of fifty) had been trained in the law and had passed their bar exams. All but five of these twenty-five had practiced or were still practicing law; significantly, there were apparently no corporation lawyers among them, which certainly was not the case among lawyers associated with the two major parties. Along with these farmers, ranchers, and lawyers, one also finds eight editors or publishers, four clergymen, three merchants, and one physician; one farmer and no fewer than six lawyers were also judges.

The 50 percent figure for those trained in the law was high and sharply contradicted the popular stereotype of Populist leaders. Actually, during the 1890s, six of ten Populist members of the House of Representatives were lawyers. It would be interesting to know how many corporation lawyers there were within the major-party delegations; surprisingly, however, previous work seeking to identify modernization trends did not single out that connection.[8] The Populist 50 percent figure, which includes senators and representatives, certainly suggests that if lawyers had a special expertise needed in lawmaking, the Populists were nearly as well prepared as major-party legislators.[9]

Prior officeholding is another factor that can indicate preparation for congressional office. Coming from outsider, dissident backgrounds in greater numbers, the Populists, not surprisingly, had a higher percentage of individuals who had held no previous political offices. Whereas one-fifth of all representatives during the 1890s had held no previous office, nearly one-third of the Populists (sixteen of fifty, or 32 percent) were included in that category.

The list of those without prior experience included a few of the more capable Populist leaders. Jerry Simpson was famous and much abused for having served only as city marshal of Medicine Lodge, Kansas. His commitment to the reform cause, however, began more than twenty years before he was elected to Congress, and he had twice been an unsuccessful third-party candidate for the Kansas legislature. William Harris had made a name for himself, within his state and beyond, as a rancher and cattle breeder but had held no office before being elected to Congress as an at-large candidate of Democrats and Populists; yet he was the son of a former congressman and had lived in and around Washington, D.C., for a considerable portion of his life. William Baker, a Kansas farmer for twelve years before being elected to the first of his House terms in 1890, had a rather diversified background: after completing college in Pennsylvania, he had taught school, served as a principal, studied law, and passed the bar examination in Iowa (but did not practice), then engaged in the mercantile business back in Pennsylvania for twelve years before becoming a farmer on the Kansas prairie. John Davis of Kansas, primarily an editor, had long been involved with agricultural organizations in his state. In 1873, he had been elected president of the first farmers' convention to be held there, from which the beginning of the Kansas farmers' revolt can be dated. That group created the Farmers' Cooperative Association of Kansas with Davis as its president, and it issued a platform that launched the state's farmers into politics in much the same way as the Cleburne Demands would do for Texas farmers more than a decade later.[10] John Otis of Kansas, a Harvard law school product turned dairy farmer, had been active for years within the Grange, serving as that organization's state agent and state lecturer.

Alonzo Shuford of North Carolina, a farmer, had likewise served as lecturer in his county and district Alliance. To recommend him, Kansas minister Jeremiah Botkin had only an unsuccessful 1888 race for governor on the Prohibition ticket, a party that was, despite its alcohol fixation, committed to a radical economic program of reform. Benjamin Clover of Kansas, a farmer with only a common-school education, could merely point to his fifteen-year tenure on the state school board commission as a Republican, along with his tenure as president of the Kansas Alliance while the People's party was in the process of being organized in his state. Curtis Castle from California, the only physician among these Populists, apparently concerned himself primarily with his practice before getting involved as a leader in the California Populist party, where he headed the party's organization in his county and served on its state executive committee. Alabama's Milford Howard, who had passed the bar examination in 1881 at age nineteen, was a young attorney, a fiery speaker, and an aspiring writer but had held no office prior to his election. Freeman Knowles of South Dakota and Charles Martin of North Carolina likewise had held no previous offices, but the high plains journalist and the North Carolina attorney did not ride into the Capitol on turnip wagons and apparently were not without leadership abilities.

The résumé of Mason Peters of Kansas highlighted his law practice and his work in organizing a livestock commission business. Edwin Ridgely, also a Kansan, came to Congress from business and agriculture; he also had a lively interest in the issues as a third-party advocate, dating back to 1876, to recommend him. William Strowd of North Carolina, a farmer, could only list his participation as a delegate to his state's 1875 constitutional convention. Michigan's anomalous Albert Todd, a manufacturing chemist and apparently a latecomer to the cause of reform, could point to his unsuccessful 1894 bid for governor as the candidate of Michigan's Prohibition party.[11]

Among those with experience, the most common was the most appropriate: state legislative service. Twenty of fifty (40 percent) had served in one house or the other at the state level. William Neville, a lawyer and a judge, had labored in the Illinois house before being elected to Nebraska's legislature and in 1905 to the

Arizona house. Another of these Populists had the ultimate in previous experience, having served in Congress: Jehu Baker of Illinois, for three terms as a Republican. Baker also had the unique experience of having served in the diplomatic corps as a minister to Venezuela for six years. Seven had held judicial positions, ranging from the county to the state to the federal district level, elected and appointed.[12] As Peter Argersinger noted, Samuel Maxwell had the most distinguished judicial career among these Populists. He was one of the founders of the Republican party in Nebraska and was a longtime leader in state government. Beginning in 1872, Maxwell had been elected to four consecutive terms to his state's supreme court before moving on to Congress. There were also five former prosecuting attorneys and one deputy prosecuting attorney among them. Colorado's Lafayette Pence likely topped that list, having served as prosecuting attorney for Arapahoe County, in the locale of Denver, prior to his election to Congress. Kentucky's John Rhea, who was admitted to the bar and commenced practice in 1873 at age eighteen, had served two terms as prosecuting attorney for Logan County, more than a decade before he was elected to Congress. The Populists also counted among their number several small-town mayors, a few councilmen, and several who could claim minor state or county offices.

Although Richard Kottman dealt only with the first three of the six Congresses that included Populists—the three with the largest proportion of farmers—he discovered that the party "was represented by a reasonably high percentage of educated men in Washington." He conceded, "The group could not be classified as 'uneducated farmers.' "[13] Indeed not. The party was led at the state and national levels by a group of individuals, an impressive number of whom had received a college education at a time when only a small percentage of the overall population was able to go beyond common school.[14] Eleven of these fifty congressmen had in fact graduated from one or more colleges; counting those who attended but did not graduate, one discovers that twenty-seven of fifty (54 percent) had some college education. Of the remainder, six had advanced to the high school level, and seventeen had not gone beyond common school.[15]

Senator James Kyle of South Dakota and Representative Charles Martin of North Carolina would likely qualify as the most educated, each having graduated from three different institutions. Kyle did so from the University of Illinois in 1871, Oberlin College in 1878, and Western Theological Seminary in 1882 (in between Oberlin and Western, Kyle had also studied law). Martin, a great-grandson of Nathaniel Macon, may have topped Kyle academically, graduating from Lake Forest College in 1872, the University of Virginia in 1875, and then later studying at the Southern Baptist Theological Seminary. Primarily a lawyer who qualified for admission to the bar in 1879, Martin had also held the position of principal in several high schools, had been a professor of Latin at the woman's college in Murfreesboro, North Carolina, and then later taught at his alma mater, Lake Forest College. Martin thus qualifies as the only former college professor among the group of fifty Populists. Incidentally, Martin's great-grandfather, Nathaniel Macon, had represented North Carolina in both houses of Congress in the early days of the Republic, rising to the position of Speaker of the House (1801–1807) and president pro tempore of the Senate (1826–1827). Macon was an aristocratic plantation owner and slave master, yet he was recognized as the state's leading Jeffersonian politician and was regarded as a friend of the southern white underclass.[16]

Formal education did not always correlate with actual ability. High on the list of the least formally educated, for example, was Jerry Simpson, who left school at age fourteen to earn a livelihood at sea. Yet the Kansan would be near the top of the list of all congressmen for performance, and when it came to the ability to think and to verbalize on his feet, with or without socks, Simpson had few equals in Congress, regardless of party. In the Senate, William Peffer and William Allen, although among the less formally educated, certainly ranked higher in the area of performance than did most in the upper chamber, including a number of those who had completed their education at Ivy League colleges. As Senator Peffer himself conceded, Senator Allen "stood head and shoulders above all" the other Populists in both houses of Congress in terms of physical stature and intellectual ability.[17]

Despite his obvious attributes, Allen was a sincerely humble person and apparently totally at ease being called "Bill." One has the feeling that addressing him away from the Senate as "Mr." or "Senator" would likely draw a reprimand. As a teenager, Allen had volunteered as a private and had served with an Iowa infantry unit; he remained an enlisted man but closed out his enlistment on the staff of a Union general. Apparently, the young soldier experienced some ferocious fighting. At one point during an exchange on the floor of the Senate, Allen in a quite moving aside recalled how he had seen an unusual number of his young comrades fall around him as his unit participated in an assault.[18] Being about six inches over six feet, Allen made a large target, and one wonders how it was that fate spared him. Surely, his experiences and losses left their mark deeply etched on his psyche. Allen, like many others of his generation, came away from the Civil War with a lasting sense of purpose and dedication, along the lines urged by Lincoln in his immortal Gettysburg address. Theirs was not to be a fool's errand.

Veterans from both sides were represented among these Populist congressmen, probably more so than among the Republicans and Democrats. The party had, as its adherents liked to say, "leaped the bloody chasm"—a once easily understood reference to the bloody divide that was the Civil War. Twenty-six of the fifty were too young to have served; two were too old; six were old enough but for whatever reason listed no military experience.[19] Sixteen had served: eleven as enlisted men, five as officers. The Union cause included eight enlisted men and three officers (one colonel, one captain, and one lieutenant); the Confederate numbered three enlisted men and two officers. Colonel Harris was joined by Alabama's Captain Albert Goodwyn to complete the Populist Confederate officer corps.

According to his biographical sketch, Goodwyn completed his service as a "captain of a company of sharpshooters and was decorated with the Confederate Cross of Honor."[20] If so, that would likely make the Alabama planter-farmer the highest decorated veteran of the fifty; as if to support the point, in 1928, at age eighty-six, Goodwyn would be elected commander in chief of the Confederate Veterans of America.[21] According to William Rogers, the leading historian of Alabama Populism, Goodwyn was also a "member of a distinguished southern family."[22]

John Otis, as a member of a Kansas regiment when the war commenced, assisted in recruiting Kansas' first black regiment in 1862 and then rose to the rank of colonel as paymaster general on the military staff of Governor Charles Robinson. John Atwater, a North Carolina farmer who had the distinction of being the only new Populist to emerge from the 1898 election, proudly noted his enlistment in the army of General Robert E. Lee and his service through the surrender at Appomattox. Atwater was truly a survivor.

Among these Populist veterans, there were at least three former prisoners of war. Idaho's Thomas Glenn fought with Confederate John Morgan's Kentucky cavalry, was wounded in combat, and was taken prisoner at Mount Sterling, Kentucky. For several months, until paroled, Glenn was held at Transylvania University in Lexington, Kentucky. Although the information was not included in the *Biographical Directory,* Alabama's Albert Goodwyn was reportedly captured at the battle of Missionary Ridge and imprisoned on Johnson's Island in Lake Erie until the war ended. South Dakota's Freeman Knowles served more than three years with the Army of the Potomac and was captured during the battle of Reams Station, in the Petersburg campaign of 1864, and was incarcerated at Libby, Belle Island, and Salisbury prisons until his release near the end of the war.[23]

In the final analysis, Civil War service was not a vital factor distinguishing Populists from their old-party opponents, although two Confederate veterans turned up as Populists from the West. One doubts that any Union veterans—after Reconstruction, at least—were elected to Congress from the South; they certainly were not as Populists.[24] According to one study, the percentage of veterans among the Populists and among all representatives was virtually the same (30.8 versus 30.5 percent). The percentage of enlisted men, however, was significantly higher among the Populists, a difference of about seven percentage points (20.5 versus 13.7 percent), testifying perhaps to their more humble origins, their relative youth, and their greater affinity for ordinary people. Certainly it could not be said that theirs was a party of slackers, although it appears likely that among the six who were old enough but did not serve, one might find an artful dodger or two.[25]

The *Biographical Directory* was silent regarding the religious affiliations of congressmen, apparently a rule to avoid the appearance of breaching the wall of separation. Thirteen of these fifty Populists were Kansans, however, and they were included in a group of eighty-nine major leaders whose backgrounds were investigated; thus we are not altogether in the dark on this matter.[26] As indicated, four were Protestant clergymen, and several more had Protestant religious training. No doubt a few, like Jerry Simpson, were freethinkers. A number were certainly alienated from the established churches of their parents. Representative Jeremiah Botkin, a Kansas Methodist minister, later in the decade openly identified himself as a Christian socialist. Albert Goodwyn's granddaughter provided this rare insight into the Alabama congressman's religious views: "He was a deist. He believed that no one was really an atheist in the true sense of the word. . . . He did not attend church and disagreed with many of the doctrines of the Christian churches. He thoroughly disliked any type of religious discrimination or persecution and utterly disapproved of clergymen in politics."[27]

The rhetoric of congressional Populists, however, as in the case of Kansas Populist leaders, was highly moral. Indeed, their approach to reform was such that moral and political considerations were closely linked. A this-worldly, liberating Christianity was their choice, just as the "humane preference" was their preference (Abraham Lincoln's "man over money").[28] Christian ethics informed their analysis of society's ills, and most of them were quick with an apt biblical allusion in appropriate circumstances. But contrary to what might be supposed, they were not right-wing fundamentalists; rather, they were more like left-wing evangelicals, even though the terminology did not exist in the 1890s. In Kansas, for example, of the twenty-two out of eighty-nine Populists whose biographies noted a religious preference, five were Methodists, three were Unitarians, three were Quakers, and three were Congregationalists. The Baptist, Lutheran, Presbyterian, and Christian churches each contributed one, and there were two Spiritualists and two agnostics. Regarding Nebraska, Robert Cherny came to this conclusion in his careful study: "The skimpy data on church membership further reinforces [this conclusion:] . . . Republicans and Democrats [were] more likely than Populists to belong to the Presbyterian or Episcopal church[es], and Populists more likely than Republicans or Democrats to belong to denominations usually associated with lower social status." One would assume that the Baptist church was among the less prestigious of Nebraska's denominations, and with the eleven southerners added to the congressional mix, that category would likely be significantly enlarged.[29]

It appears that a concern about humanity, in the style of the early Baptist Roger Williams (1603–1683), was in evidence here. Certainly the Enlightenment's later emphasis on individual human dignity was manifest. Religious humanism loomed large in their thinking. They may not have been familiar with Immanuel Kant (1724–1804), but there was certainly an echo of Kant's concern with human dignity, such as when the German philosopher directed that individuals should always use the humanity in their own person and in all others as an end and never as a means (but what was Kant's famous imperative if not merely a variation on the Golden Rule?). Like Thomas Paine, Thomas Jefferson, Abraham Lincoln, and many others, they talked openly of human rights and would have agreed with the editor who declared that "no religion could call itself worthy of human commitment unless it paid more than lip service to the Golden Rule."[30]

What was said about Kansas Populist leaders and religion applies just as forcefully to these congressmen. Although a number were admittedly alienated from the established churches, Christian precepts of the humane variety maintained a strong hold on their minds. "If the Populist leadership shared a common theological outlook it would have to be ethical humanitarianism which served as a yardstick by which they judged their world." Humanism in both its secular and religious derivations was unquestionably paramount.[31]

Consequently, they could be very blunt and iconoclastic in their appraisal of existing conditions. In fact, many of them took special pleasure in punching holes in the conventional wisdom. Frank Doster, the "shabby, wild-eyed, rattle-brained fanatic" of William Allen White's famous editorial smear of 1896, but nonetheless correctly perceived and generally acknowledged by Populists (and later even by some of his former opponents) as "the intellectual giant of Kansas Populism," certainly epitomized that trait. Shortly after being elected chief justice of the Kansas Supreme Court in 1896, Doster created shock waves when he told reporters that he did not "believe in hell fire, nor human slavery, nor the gold standard, nor in millionaires, nor in the wage system." Just as quickly he added, "I do believe in the Ten Commandments and the Golden Rule, in the initiative and referendum, and evolution and woman suffrage and I am edging toward theosophy and Christian Science, and open to conviction in favor of any vagrant fad that nobody will admit believing in until enough do to make it respectable." Not long thereafter he told the press, "I have been an adherent of socialism all my life. Socialism is coming about through the socialization of what we call the public utilities." It was his contention that as soon as matters "become of sufficient public concern, either nationally or locally, they will pass into the hands of the general or local public, and some fine morning, if you live to a good old age, you will wake up to find yourself living in an almost communistic society, having gotten there by transitions so easy and natural you didn't realize their occurrence until the job was done."[32] Here also one finds a good example of how closely linked religious humanism and politics were in Populist circles.

Viewed from afar and up close, it was their concern about humanity that conditioned their response to a rapidly industrializing, highly competitive society that was, as never before, racked by poverty and troubled by a growing disparity in the distribution of wealth. In 1894, in the midst of a great depression, that mind-set prompted the son of an itinerant Baptist minister from Alabama, future congressman Milford Howard—who, like many of his generation (and earlier and later ones as well), had virtually been educated from the Bible—to write a scathing attack on Congress and the administration of President Grover Cleveland thinly disguised as a novel. The book was called *If Christ Came to Congress,* and he supposedly wrote it in four weeks. Never at a loss for words and never one to mince them, Howard wrote: The "Senate is a house of plutocrats.

Many of the senators are millionaires, and if Christ came to Congress they would not associate with him because of his poverty and lowly position." Why a book on Congress? His explanation is from the preface: "If a stream is poisoned we go to the head waters to purify it, and so the author, in this little volume, has endeavored to show some of the evil practices and the corrupting, contaminating influences, which are and have been at work here at the fountain head, and which have sent out poisonous streams in all directions."[33] The title and the approach were actually suggested by his familiarity with William Stead's *If Christ Came to Chicago,* published only a few months earlier. Stead was an English reformer and editor who employed what would soon become a popular form of exposé journalism called "muckraking," a pejorative label supplied later by the most prominent anti-Populist of them all, Theodore Roosevelt. Certainly Howard's book was in that style.

Before he claimed his seat in Congress representing Alabama's "Bloody Seventh" Congressional District in December 1895, Howard wrote yet another book of the same genre called *The American Plutocracy.* It was released in January 1896. Shortly thereafter, Charles Sheldon, a minister to a predominantly middle- to upper-income Republican congregation in Topeka, Kansas, used a similar fictional device to convey many of the same concerns in the book *In His Steps: What Would Jesus Do?* Actually, Sheldon's work emerged as a series of sermons delivered to his congregation, which were then serialized in a Topeka newspaper before being published as a book. His title posed a question that troubled many at the time and for years thereafter. Thus, *In His Steps*—more because of the answer it contained than for its literary merit, which was slight—would climb by 1933 to near the top of the all-time best-seller list. The kind of religion these Populists were comfortable espousing was represented in works like these and in the writings and sermons of ministers such as Washington Gladden, George Herron, William Bliss, Walter Raushenbusch, and others—once in full bloom, a brand of religion that came to be called the "Social Gospel." Their message might well have been stillborn except for the potency of a preexisting and more individualistic brand of religion that came to be called—more by historians than by its adherents—the "Gospel of Wealth." This alternative gospel that the Populists subscribed to preached a here-and-now, cooperative brand of religion as a counter to the mainstream version, which they believed was indifferent to the masses and much too accommodating to the new economic order and its potent new business ethic, fortified, as it seemed to be, by a voguish antisocial rendition of Darwinism. Herbert Hoover would later endorse this ethic and—according to one account—appropriately name it "rugged individualism" in a 1928 campaign speech.[34]

There was general agreement among these Populists regarding the social origins of evil, and a strong belief that the conditions of their world had pitted brother against brother and man against an immoral society in a contest stacked against society's disadvantaged legions. Consequently, in religious matters, a good many Populists would likely agree with Sam Wood, a prominent leader in

Kansas before he became a Populist, who insisted, "God should be spelled with two o's (Good); devil without a d (evil)." Moreover, said Wood, "I reject all the dogmas of the church. My religion is a sincere desire to do right—to do the most possible good in this world. I believe sincerely in the fatherhood of God and the brotherhood of man." Or they would agree with Mary Elizabeth Lease, a former Catholic, when she informed more conservative-minded defenders of the status quo that "it was not Christianity but churchanity that she assailed"; or with Congressman John Grant Otis when he declared, "Our civilization demands the recognition of the fatherhood of God and the brotherhood of man, not upon Sunday only, but upon seven days in the week, and fifty-two weeks in the year." A few might even have agreed with the message written by John Dunsmore to be read at his funeral. His "Message of Love," as the former Populist speaker of the Kansas house called it, stated that he "came into being with a mind so constituted that blind faith in any creed or dogma could never satisfy . . . [his] desire for knowledge concerning the mysteries of life and being." He followed this with the statement: "I have never been able to accept as true the dogmas and creeds of the so-called Christian system." Religion was for him "the outcome of our ideas about the universe, our response to all that we know, consciously or unconsciously, of cosmic law." If any hint of a fundamentalist strain lingered, Dunsmore took care of that by stating, "As an evolutionist, I looked upon the story of the fall of man as a myth handed down from dead and forgotten ages, and consequently, the dogma of the atonement to be both illogical and unnecessary." But an atheist Dunsmore was not, and he demonstrated that by writing that "while sin remains in the universe, God is defeated: and that everlasting punishment involves an everlasting failure; that sin never injured God, except through man. That it is the God within who is injured, rather than the God without."[35] Above all else, theirs was a religion—like their politics—with a social and economic component, something they insisted was missing from the more prestigious, mainstream churches and the two old parties.

In his highly regarded study of southern dissenters, Carl Degler seemed to be undecided whether southern Populists were nobodies or somebodies, but the distinguished Stanford history professor may have relied a bit too heavily on Sheldon Hackney's rather small sampling of leaders in the latter's study of Populism and Progressivism in Alabama.[36] In the end, Degler settled for the conclusion that they were not well known but not necessarily from the lower ranks of southern society. There can be no doubt that we need more information regarding many of these southern Populists. Thanks to a culture uniquely and heavily influenced by the lost cause and notions of white supremacy, becoming a Populist in most of the South was akin to having the local madam show up at the village church on Sunday seeking admission. Clearly, southern Populists, much more so than their western and northern brethren, were outsiders and dissenters. Make no mistake about it, breaking with the One-Party Dominant of the South was a much more difficult and deadly step for white southerners than abandoning the One-Party

Dominant of the North and West in the case of former devotees (blacks excepted) of the Grand Old Party. Congressman Milford Howard of Alabama later revealed that his father had told him that "he would rather make my coffin with his own hands and bury me than have me desert the Democratic party."[37] One could hardly confirm the gravity of the decision more vividly, unless we note the painful story of a Texas Populist who had charisma to spare.

J. H. (James Harvey) Davis was known to his contemporaries and to history as "Cyclone" Davis (as in the case of "Sockless" Jerry Simpson and a few others, his nickname attained such common currency that one might think he was born with it). This "long-tall Texan" never became a congressman in the Populist era (in 1914, he would win one at-large term as a Democrat); in fact, Texas produced no Populist congressmen, even though there were more Populists in the Lone Star State than anywhere else.[38] Davis should have won in 1894, and his 1896 defeat was also suspect. He and a number of other Populist congressional candidates from Texas, Georgia, and Alabama in particular had elections flagrantly stolen from them by an opposition not at all shy about resorting to corrupt practices and violence. Writing to Marion Butler in March 1897, in the aftermath of his second bitter defeat, Davis indicated that he was virtually without funds and was preparing to resume the practice of law "to make a living for [his] wife and four children," probably in a "warm country where the negro is not a factor in politics," such as in California, Oregon, or Washington. The situation was just too much, added Davis: "I closed the last speech I made in the last campaign with fully half doz[en] shot guns and six shooters drawn on me and in the face of these odds was compelled to take the lie or fight and I chose the latter and was finally pulled out of the turmoil by a couple of friends almost senseless covered with blood from head to foot. With my head sewed up and cordaged in several places and lying half dead the next few days I received the news of my defeat and that six thousand negro Republicans had voted the Democratic ticket."[39]

Davis never made his move to the Pacific coast but continued to lecture across the nation, thanks to Marion Butler and the national committee. His bitter disappointment following, in his words, "the loss of a cause which has cost me so much labor, suffering and financial sacrifice" did not abate over time; ironically, his attitude after 1900 regarding racial issues, as was the case with several other prominent southern Populist leaders, can be summed up by the old line "if you can't beat 'em, join 'em."[40]

In terms of their qualifications, the southern contingent definitely enhanced the overall quality of the congressional Populist delegations. Eleven of the fifty were southerners.[41] Eight (72.2 percent) had graduated from or had attended one or more colleges—a truly astonishing number, considering the state of public education and the percentage of all those more privileged white southerners who were likely to have received a college education during the middle decades of the nineteenth century. Of the remaining three, one had gone to an academy and an institute, one had an academy education, and one (the remarkably home-schooled

Milford Howard) had not gone beyond common school.[42] This is without taking into consideration that William Harris and Thomas Glenn, both of whom had college training, were actually southerners who moved west. This means that the southern Populist congressmen were much better educated than Congress as a whole and than their western Populist colleagues as well.

Thomas Watson and Marion Butler surely headed this southern contingent in ability and performance. Thanks to C. Vann Woodward's classic biography, the talent of Watson is well known. Yet Butler, in a much quieter and more dedicated but still underappreciated fashion, actually surpassed the legendary agrarian rebel from Georgia. When he entered the U.S. Senate in 1895, the North Carolinian was only thirty-two years old but had already compiled a remarkable record. After graduating from the University of North Carolina in 1885, he had taught school for three years, edited and published the Clinton *Caucasian* for six years, served in the North Carolina senate for one term as a Democrat, chaired the Populist state committee during the 1892 campaign, held the position of president of his state Farmers' Alliance for two years, and then followed that with another two years as national president of the National Farmers' Alliance and Industrial Union, in addition to being chair of his state party committee for one year. Somehow he also managed to act as a trustee and an executive committee member for his alma mater. After going to the U.S. Senate, he would be elected to the chair of the Populist party national committee, a position he would hold for the next six years. While carrying out that monumental task in exemplary fashion during a crucial and unbelievably contentious period, he managed to work occasionally as editor and publisher of his paper. By 1899, he also had completed an independent course of legal studies, commenced in 1889, that led to his being admitted to the bar.[43]

Marion Butler, Thomas Watson, Milford Howard, Harry Skinner, Albert Goodwyn, John Fowler, Charles Martin, and John Rhea were by no means nobodies, and although they were farmers and not as highly educated nor as loquacious as many of their colleagues, neither were Alonzo Shuford, William Strowd, and John Atwater.[44] On the contrary, they were somebodies who have not received anywhere near the amount of attention or credit they deserve. Apparently, that was their reward for having the audacity to break with the One-Party Dominant in the South, thereby becoming betrayers of the Lost Cause and creating a serious threat to the party of white supremacy. Is it not high time that we revise this scenario and deposit the older script in the niche for self-serving tales, along with the blackout of Reconstruction and other hoary myths?

THE NATIONAL POPULIST AGENDA

Early in 1892, while acting as spokeman for his colleagues on the floor of the House, Georgia's Tom Watson said this:

> Sir, I know that what I have said here today may be utterly thrown away. I am not addressing so much this Congress as I am addressing the future. But through the hurried pencil[s] of these stenographers . . . I will reach the American people, and we expect to stir them up all along the line, until from Maine to Georgia, and from the Lakes to the Gulf, they will ask to have this Government rededicated to the old Jeffersonian principle. Mr. Speaker, what is the essence of [that principle] . . . ? Its essence is that grand truth enunciated by Abraham Lincoln . . . at Gettysburg. . . . On that memorable battlefield he asked that this Government might be dedicated to its original principles. We ask no more. . . . We insist upon that much. We insist that this Government shall be again brought back to its foundations, so that it may be a government "of the people, by the people, and for the people."[45]

With those lines, Watson not only drew a hearty round of applause but also succinctly articulated what he and many others who rallied to the Populist cause saw as their raison d'être. And with those few simple words, "stir them up all along the line," Watson may have hit upon what would be the primary role of the Populist delegations on Capitol Hill. Their ranks were thin, but their presence and influence belied their numbers. And they were not quite the "futilitarians" that one historian insisted they were some years ago, unless we misrepresent and then discount their message.[46]

On reflection, perhaps the role of "education and agitation" was ideal for the Populists.[47] No doubt they would say that that was because "right makes might." In this same speech, Watson insisted: "The fact that we are here in a very small minority does not for one moment prove that we are not right or that we shall not eventually be the majority." As in Watson's case, they believed that they were in the vanguard of a movement whose goal was to put the nation back on a course dedicated to fundamental democratic principles. Somehow, people were to be given priority over things and impersonal marketplace forces. *In their eyes, this was the crisis of the 1890s.* It was a very tall order indeed, especially considering the extent to which segments of the public had already been co-opted by those very same forces the Populists were seeking to bring under control in the name of democracy. As David F. Noble presciently noted, technology "may aptly be described as a composite of the accumulated scientific knowledge, technical skills, implements, logical habits, and material products of people, [but] technology is always more than this, more than information, logic, things. *It is people themselves.*"[48]

Understandably, these Populists were up against huge and powerful congressional majorities, drawn from both old parties, who were just as firm in their belief that they—and most certainly not the Populists—represented the wave of the future and the correct alignment of forces that would ensure an outcome they called "progress." And with that crucial indicator of well-being weighted in favor of capital accumulation and the proliferation of industrial technology, who could doubt that the new world of factories, skyscrapers, stocks, and bonds would prove to be far more dynamic and lucrative than the world of family farms, livestock, crops, and silos, no matter how mechanized and commercialized the latter may have become? Modern technology and industrial capitalism, to quote Noble, were well on their way to "weaving a paralyzing web of instrumentality."[49] One even suspects that beneath a facade of civility one could find among these anti-Populists a large kernel of confidence inspired by the belief—cynical, but all too true—that ultimate outcomes were more nearly determined by the formula "might makes right."

As the first delegation of eleven People's party congressmen prepared to attend the opening session of the Fifty-second Congress in December 1891, their party was still very much in the process of being formed at the state and national levels. (The first People's party state apparatus in the South, for example, was not organized until August 1891 in Dallas, Texas.)[50] Preceded by two critical Farmers' Alliance national conferences in St. Louis in December 1889 and in Ocala, Florida, one year later, various reform groups met in Cincinnati in May 1891 to create a national People's party, which, in turn, devised a plan at that same conference for cooperation with another national meeting to be held in St. Louis in February 1892 of a hesitant Southern Farmers' Alliance. This second St. Louis conference then formulated what became the basic platform of the People's party and joined in the call for the party's first national nominating convention in Omaha, Nebraska, in July 1892. There, on 4 July, delegates selected James B. Weaver of Iowa and James G. Field of Viriginia to head the party's presidential ticket. Far more important than the nominees, however, was the document agreed on by the convention. Although it differed only slightly from the second St. Louis platform issued a few months earlier, it quickly acquired a special quality in the eyes of People's party adherents, who by then were being commonly identified, by themselves and in the press, as "Populists," members of the "Populist party," and advocates of "Populism."[51]

Unveiled on the Fourth of July and known simply as the Omaha platform, Populism's first formal declaration of principles became for its supporters a kind of second Declaration of Independence. For certain, it was not an ordinary political statement. For the converted, its preamble constituted a valid, ringing indictment of the course America had followed since the early 1870s, along with a call to action to rectify that situation. It set forth what was seen as a master plan to save an idealized republic that Populists sincerely believed was on the verge of destruction.

Almost immediately, this Omaha platform became the bible of 1890s Populism. As scripture, the text merits more careful attention than it has received; it also serves here as a yardstick against which to measure Populist congressional performance. We should first note that it was the culmination of a third-party battle waged against the regionally dominant Republicans (principally in the old Northwest and the new West) and Democrats (the states of the old Confederacy, augmented by several border states and territories) since the mid-1870s, and it enshrined the Farmers' Alliance demands, especially as they had been perfected after 1886. Several recent studies, incidentally, treated the origins of the party almost exclusively as the product of a farmers' movement; this is a huge error, in my opinion, guaranteed to void any effort aimed at fully comprehending Populism.[52] Although the group's program of economic reform was designed to rescue an older, predominantly agrarian America from what was seen as a devastating onslaught by urban-industrial-capitalistic America—an onslaught orchestrated with impunity, in their opinion, by an unholy alliance between "the trusts and the privileged classes"—it resonated, to an extent, beyond the camp of agrarianism.[53]

On a number of occasions before the Omaha convention, Populist leaders had avoided efforts from within to convert their cause into a crusade aimed at imposing on the nation a preferred code of behavior—the prohibition of alcoholic beverages, in particular. They did that again at Omaha, and apparently this plea from the platform's preamble was for real: "While our sympathies as a party of reform are naturally upon the side of every proposition which will tend to make men intelligent, virtuous, and temperate, we nevertheless regard these questions—important as they are—as secondary to the great issues now pressing for solution, and upon which not only our individual prosperity but the very existence of free institutions depends; and we ask all men to first help us to determine whether we are to have a republic to administer before we differ as to conditions upon which it is to be administered."

Three planks constituted the entire platform—a trilogy of reforms calling for substantial alterations in the nation's burgeoning yet still geographically confined capitalistic economy.[54] The first plank, encompassing one primary and five subordinate proposals, involved financial and monetary arrangements, treated under the heading "Money." The second concerned the nation's transportation and communication networks. The third, headed "Land," addressed land in the broadest sense, as the ultimate source of all "wealth" and as the "heritage" of all "the people."[55] Populists reasoned that these functions and resources existed—or should have existed—to benefit the entire human family. Having been usurped by corporations and privileged individuals, they had to be reclaimed and superintended by means of public agencies, owned and administered by the community at large. (Anyone enamored with the generic rendition of "populism" and possibly befuddled by recent right-wing political and journalistic applications of the term should take note that privatization was their foe, not their goal; one should also pay particular attention to the fundamenal, radical economic changes being championed.)[56]

This agenda, the sum of Populism's first national platform, was followed by ten resolutions. These were measures that most of the delegates apparently supported but that they emphatically insisted were "not . . . part of the platform of the People's party." Unfortunately, more than a few historians have misunderstood or ignored the platform and this important disclaimer, focusing instead on one or more of these nonplatform, generally noneconomic, protoprogressive reforms to illustrate the meaning of Populism, thereby creating, either wittingly or unwittingly, red herrings. The ten resolutions consisted of these measures: a secret ballot, the government's use of money derived from a graduated income tax in such a way as to reduce the "burden of taxation" on "domestic industries," pensions for Union veterans, immigration restriction, an eight-hour law for government work, an end to the Pinkerton system (private, corporate armies), initiative and referendum, one term for the president and vice president and direct election of senators, an end to subsidies to "private corporations," and sympathy for a Knights of Labor strike under way at the time.

Although this platform offered an expanded list of party sentiments, missing were the Cincinnati convention's unqualified endorsement of "universal suffrage" and the second St. Louis convention's qualified call for "female suffrage." Clearly these omissions resulted from a desire to make the document more palatable to those delegates and potential voters still under the spell of traditional patriarchal and white supremacist beliefs—especially in the case of Democrats across the land. Women's emancipation was a particular stumbling block in the North and West; in the South, it was equal treatment for blacks above all, with women's rights virtually an unraised but potentially troubling issue.[57] These were glaring omissions for a party professing to represent the people, a party that would prove to be the most supportive of women's rights during the 1890s and certainly much less obstinate than its opposition regarding the rights of black Americans. It was not an oversight but a tactical decision—the first of several apparently prompted by the nation's winner-take-all electoral system. (Chroniclers of the Southern Alliance and southern Populism have also neglected to point out that southern blacks were eager to form a People's party; if it had been up to the Colored Farmers' Alliance, one suspects that the South would truly have taken the lead in forming the new party. This is one of a number of areas in need of more attention.)

During opening ceremonies at Omaha, Louisa Lease, the youngest daughter of Populism's most prominent woman, Mary Elizabeth Lease, gave a recitation that reportedly "brought down the house." She closed her address with this adlib: "The motto of the Alliance is: 'Equal rights to all and special privileges to none,' but you are not true to that motto if you do not give woman her rights. It has been said that the hand that rocks the cradle is the hand that rules the world, but we have made up our mind that there will be no cradles to rock nor babies to put in them if you don't give us our rights."[58] We should note here that the move by southern white supremacists to disfranchise black men (sadly, a move Louisa's mother might well have supported) had not yet begun in a formal, systematic fashion by means of statutes and constitutional revisions except in Florida and Mississippi, although the rights of black people in America, regardless of age or gender, were in greater jeopardy than those of white women.[59]

The platform itself was short and consensual. Later, the right to be called an Omaha Populist was determined by one's commitment to the fundamental structural changes advanced in this platform, regardless of whether one was in total agreement with its attached resolutions. Since this document was essentially the product of the St. Louis meeting of February 1892, it is necessary to backtrack a bit before analyzing further. The document drafted there confirmed, by and large, a consensual core that had been worked out since the first major conference held there in December 1889. Positions were more clearly defined, but in only one area was there anything significantly different in the second St. Louis platform: At the 1891 Ocala meeting, the Southern Alliance's executive leadership dropped the first St. Louis platform's call for government ownership of the country's railroad, telegraph, and telephone systems, opting instead for regulation. The founding convention of the People's party in Cincinnati the previous year acquiesced in that alteration, apparently in the interest of building the party's base, but the delegates at the second St. Louis convention in Feburary 1892 restored the earlier demand for government ownership.

Evidently, northern and southern leaders had to engage in some serious logrolling to achieve that outcome. For many white southerners, public ownership of the transportation and communication networks was the epitome of a detested "paternalism and centralization," a position seriously complicated by white racial prejudices and deep hostilities to the expansion of power by the federal government. Northerners, in contrast, and probably for more orthodox, conservative financial reasons, were much less supportive of the subtreasury plan, whose goal was public ownership and direction of the monetary system, to maintain what was regarded as an adequate supply of money and credit. The return to the earlier St. Louis position of government ownership of transportation and communication systems thus reflected the stronger influence of delegates from the North and West, as well as an element of concession in the interest of retaining support for the subtreasury plan. At the second St. Louis conference, however, the subtreasury plan was presented in such a way as to make it clear that it was a means and not an end—and not even an indispensable means.[60] The second St. Louis platform stated that end clearly, and it was incorporated word for word as the first and most fundamental plank in both documents: Under the heading "money," it declared: "We demand a national currency, safe, sound, and flexible, issued by the general government only, a full legal tender for all debts, public and private, and that without the use of banking corporations, a just, equitable, and efficient means of distribution direct to the people, at a tax not to exceed two per cent per annum, to be provided as set forth in the sub-treasury plan of the Farmers' Alliance, *or a better system; also, by payments in discharge of its obligations for public improvements.*" Subordinate to this first major reform, the party called for five specific financial measures: the free and unlimited coinage of silver at the ratio of sixteen ounces of silver to one ounce of gold, an increase in the "circulating medium" to "not less than fifty dollars per capita," a graduated income tax, a statement that "all state and national revenues shall be limited to the necessary expenses of government economically and honestly administered," and the creation of "postal savings banks." The second demand was the call for government ownership of railroads, telegraphs, and telephones. The third, presented under the label "Land," merely asserted the proposition that "all the natural sources of wealth" were "the heritage of the people" and therefore "should not be monopolized" to the benefit of the privileged few. The land plank and the platform concluded with this statement: "All land now held by railroads and other corporations in excess of their actual needs, and all lands now owned by [absentee] aliens, should be reclaimed by the government and held for actual settlers only."[61]

This was the Populist national agenda fashioned by the movement as the party itself was being created. It was this program that Populist congressmen were obligated to advocate and defend—at least until superseded by the 1896 national convention.

2

"Hewers of Wood and Drawers of Water": Populist Style and Substance, 1891–1895

Mr. Chairman, my only regret . . . about this tariff debate is that no master of satire has been here to describe it. I think that Bill Nye and Mark Twain have lost the opportunity of their lives. The attraction has been so great that we have almost run from the galleries . . . the gentlemen who daily take their afternoon naps...; and the peanut-eaters have forsaken us in a body. [Laughter.]

One of the amusing things about it . . . is this: The Republicans say they are in favor of protection as a principle, yet through reciprocity . . . are trying to escape it as a practice [laughter]; while the Democrats say that "free trade" as a governmental principle is thoroughly right, . . . they do not dare to adopt it as a rule of action.

I was amused . . . at the chosen champions . . . put forth by both [major] parties. . . . They selected . . . a young man who was required to be handsome and brilliant. To fight a very old battle young warriors were wanted. The old ones were tired. On the side of the Republicans they chose Mr. Dolliver from the State of Iowa—young, handsome, and brilliant. . . . On the other hand [there] was our handsome and brilliant friend from Nebraska [Mr. Bryan], . . . the "darling" of the Democratic side of the House, the prettiest man in all the bunch, and his entire speech . . . was the sum and substance of the old Democratic position on the tariff that we will practice what is wrong while we know what is right. . . .

The third party is small on this floor, but makes up in activity what it lacks in numbers. [A member: "And good looks."] The gentleman . . . anticipates my point. [Laughter.] The third party, imitating the programme of the other parties on this floor, in using their handsomest members to conduct debate, chose me to represent them in that same capacity today. [Laughter.] Not because I possessed individual and eccentric lines of beauty not possessed by the other members of the third party, but because in the variety of good looks and general makeup of loveliness, I threw them all into the shade. [Laughter.]

Thomas Edward Watson, *Congressional Record*,
52nd Cong., 1st sess., 8 April 1892, 2838

In the House of the Fifty-second Congress (1891–1893), Jerry Simpson and Tom Watson were by far the most vocal and effective Populist spokesmen; in the Senate, William Peffer and James Kyle started slowly, but both—Peffer especially—had by the end of that Congress established themselves as capable representatives of their party. In the Fifty-third Congress (1893–1895), the Senate delegation was strengthened considerably by the addition of William Allen, who was active virtually from day one. His presence seemed to spur Peffer to even greater effort, and Kyle maintained the steady and competent pace he had already set for himself. In the House of the Fifty-third Congress, Simpson, despite being gravely ill, apparently with cardiovascular disease, and absent for more than four months in 1894, was once again the most active and effective representative, making up somewhat for the void created by Watson's departure. John Bell, Lafayette Pence, Omer Kem, William McKeighan, John Davis, T. J. Hudson, William Baker, and Haldor Boen, especially during Simpson's absence, involved themselves in the debates and were occasionally quite effective.

Even before 1894, Simpson had earned the respect of most of his House colleagues, regardless of party. Midway through his illness, Simpson attempted to return to his seat too soon, business was halted, and the Populist speaker was given a rare ovation on entry.[1] Despite an occasional tendency to shoot from the hip when personally attacked, his performance, from beginning to end, was principled, consistent, and commendable.[2] By the end of his first term, in fact, the "sage from Medicine Lodge"[3] had convinced his opponents—several of whom had to learn the hard way—that he was nobody's fool and was, despite a disarming sense of humor and extraordinary wit, sincerely dedicated to the cause for which he had been struggling for over twenty years.

Populism in the House of the Fifty-fourth Congress (1895–1897), to be treated more extensively in a later chapter, was weakened considerably by losses the party sustained in its go-it-alone elections of 1894 (the consequence of Grover Cleveland's utter repudiation in the wake of the panic of 1893 and his war against silver), especially by the loss of Simpson and a number of other western Populists. Newly elected members from North Carolina and Alabama made up two-thirds of the delegation, and none was nearly as visible nor as vocal in his first term as Simpson, Watson, and others had been earlier. During that period, John Bell of Colorado was the party's designated leader and its most active spokesman. His major backup came from William Baker of Kansas and Omer Kem of Nebraska. Primarily because of the great changes that were taking place in the wake of the depression that became nationwide in 1893, this third Congress turned out to be more transitional in nature—an intermediate stage between the more distinct early and later phases of congressional Populism. In the process, the strength of the Populists in the Fifty-fourth Congress shifted to the Senate, where Peffer, Kyle, and Allen were joined by Marion Butler. The young North Carolina senator started out slowly but became steadily more active and more effective during his six years in the upper chamber—a line of development that has gone virtually unacknowledged because of the disenchantment with the 1896 fusionist effort he directed as chair of the national committee, combined with the fact that midway through his tenure in 1898, Populism itself had begun to fade rapidly out of the picture.

UP CLOSE AND PERSONAL

To gauge the performance of these congressional Populists fairly and accurately, one must follow the daily record of Congress, in all its clutter, virtually as though one were sitting in the galleries (the challenge, of course, is to fairly represent this material without subjecting the reader to the same tedious process); the index of those proceedings does not guide one to some of the most important material.[4] The larger portion of their work and thought was captured for the record via questions and impromptu exchanges on the floor. This was especially true in the case of Jerry Simpson. Throughout his tenure, congressional dialogue was his forte. It was a style perfectly tailored to his particular talents and, as previously indicated, the small delegation's primary opportunity.

Having been ushered into Congress under a dark cloud created by a wildly distorted image as a bungling, incompetent clown, Simpson was tested early on by several bold but gullible opponents. The 1890 Kansas election had prepared him well for that kind of test. In that race, he had been subjected to extremely bitter abuse by the opposition. He was accused of being an "infidel," an "anarchist," an "atheist," a "swindler," and an "ignoramus," of being "unpatriotic" and a "lunkhead" with "simian" characteristics. They say if you throw enough mud against an object, some of it is bound to stick: In his case, the only epithet that stuck initially was "Sockless," which in short order was frequently suffixed with "Socrates." He made it through the storm, just as he had as a sailor and captain on the Great Lakes for all those years; in fact, with his keen sense of humor and unusually sharp wit, he was remarkably quick to turn abuse to his advantage,[5] which he did time and again in Congress. Several New York congressmen (possibly because theirs was the home of the great financial red dragon called Wall Street?) were among the first to act on the assumption that Simpson was an easy target. In March 1892, George Ray, a conservative Republican lawyer from Norwich, got into the following exchange with Simpson while extolling the virtues of his party's high import taxes (presented here straight from the record in order to better convey its full flavor):

MR. SIMPSON: Does not the gentleman know that after collecting from the people in taxes nearly double the original amount of the national debt, it would take more pounds of cotton, more bushels of wheat, more bushels of corn, more pounds of beef or pork, to pay that debt today than it would have taken at the close of the war?
MR. RAY: I do not know any such thing, and no sensible well-informed person would ask such a question or make such a statement. [Laughter.]

MR. SIMPSON: If he did ask such a question he would probably ask it of a gentleman capable of giving an intelligent answer.

A bit later, Simpson was once again recognized to address a question to Ray:

MR. SIMPSON: If the gentleman will allow an interruption, I would like to ask him to explain for our information how it is that Great Britain under a free-trade policy, or a policy nearly approaching free trade, pays from one-third to one-half more wages than any high-protective nation in Europe; and how it is that from 1846 to the present time she has more than doubled and trebled her commerce and increased her wealth to a greater extent than any nation on the face of the earth?
MR. RAY: Well, now, in the Forty-eighth Congress a member of this House from the city of New York arose on the Democratic side and asked me that same silly question [laughter]; and the answer that I then gave him I give to the gentleman from Kansas, which is the same in substance . . . as the Irish servant gave to his mistress. She told him if a certain person called, to give "an evasive answer." When he told her the person had called she asked him: "Did you give an evasive answer?" "Yes," said he. "Well, what was it, Pat?" "Well, I axed him was his grandmother a monkey." [Laughter.] Now, I do not mean to apply that to the gentleman from Kansas at all [renewed laughter]; I would not be guilty of that discourtesy.
MR. SIMPSON [after a short period had passed]: Now, I would like to say to the gentleman from New York, in reply to what he said concerning me, that I would rather start out with a monkey for an ancestor and, coming down, make progress and be able to ask such a question as I have asked, than to have started from a perfect pair in the Garden of Eden, and give such a foolish answer as the gentleman has given. [Laughter.][6]

On another occasion, Sereno Payne, a conservative Republican lawyer from Hamilton, who could be even testier than his colleague from Norwich, gave this response to one of Simpson's pertinent but needling questions: "If I were inclined to be rude, Mr. Speaker, I would answer the foolish query of the gentleman from Kansas, by asking him if his ancestors were monkeys." Immediately, Simpson looked Payne straight in the eye and in a calm but forceful manner stated: "In which case, I should reply as did the elder Dumas, when a French fool asked him the same question. I should say to the gentleman: 'Yes, your family ends where mine began.' "[7] Needless to say, after a few more such exchanges the word was out that it was not at all wise to take the congressman from Medicine Lodge too lightly, for he seemed to give better than he got.

With monkeys so much in vogue (possibly a product of the age's infatuation with Darwinism in all its forms; Populist farmers were frequently depicted as the missing link in the evolutionary chain), Simpson himself ultimately applied the metaphor to Congress in one of his speeches opposing the Republican party's favorite subsidy program for business:

> Mr. Chairman, I was very much gratified when I had the privilege of coming into this Hall and sitting here with the great statesmen of the country, and I can assure you that I had a very high and exalted opinion of those statemen until as time went on I came to learn more about them and their proceedings here. [Laughter.] Then there came back to my mind a story . . . of a man who had gotten a lot of monkeys and educated them to perform on the stage till at last they went through their performances just like human beings, until one day some wag in the audience threw a handful of nuts and raisins on the stage, whereupon the performers went down at once on all fours scrambling for the nuts and raisins. [Laughter.] They were no longer men but monkeys. [Laughter.]
>
> I saw here exalted statesmen advocating great policies of state, and I had an idea that they were truly interested in this great country, until all at once some special privilege was thrown upon the stage, and then they suddenly got down on all fours scrambling to see who should first get his little special privilege through this great body of lawmakers. [Laughter.][8]

On other occasions, Simpson used his wit primarily to lighten things up, but usually to make a point in the process. In the Fifty-second Congress, a bill providing for an orphan asylum in the nation's capital was under consideration with strong Populist support. Simpson took advantage of the situation to chide conservative opponents by asking: "Is it not a sad commentary upon our system of government that this great city . . . seems to be swarming with orphans and destitute people?" If the "destitution is so great here in the capital," he asked, "what must it be in other portions of our Union? It seems to me time that we had some 'calamity howlers' here in Washington as well as in Kansas."[9] On another occasion, a congressman objected to a bill sponsored by an Iowa Republican that used language specifying a pension of "$50 per month" for "those who are periodically helpless." Simpson drew laughter with this interjection: "That will let us all in."[10] On another occasion, two congressmen were discussing a comment made by a Republican leader early in the party's existence and Simpson interjected this question: "You mean before the 'robber barons' got possession of the Republican party?"[11]

Prior to his arrival in Congress, Simpson had obviously anticipated and prepared himself for the first use of the "sockless" pejorative on the floor of Congress. In May 1892, it came in a somewhat unexpected manner in a colloquy with Henry Snodgrass, a Democrat from Tennessee, with an interjection by James O'Donnell, a Michigan Republican. Snodgrass was speaking in opposition to an appropriation for the study of American Indians by the Smithsonian Institution. Simpson asked a question aimed at exposing the congressman's earlier support for a sizable appropriation to fund the Chickamauga National Park in Tennessee. Snodgrass ignored the question with this response:

MR. SNODGRASS: Mr. Chairman. . . . When I came here I expected to find an old, sturdy, sockless fellow, who would not even purchase socks under this protective tariff; but to my utter astonishment, when I got here, I looked all around . . . this Hall and asked one of my colleagues to point out to me that sturdy farmer from Kansas, and Mr. Chairman, you may imagine the astonishment I felt when my friend [Mr. Simpson] was pointed out to me, wearing diamonds, dressed in satins and cloth, and, when I saw him riding up and down Pennsylvania Avenue on a bicycle, with a cigar in his mouth, I say you may imagine the astonishment I felt at that sad spectacle.

MR. O'DONNELL: Did he wear silk stockings?

MR. SNODGRASS: And silk stockings; and he is now denominated the dude of the House. [Laughter.]

It took Simpson awhile to regain the floor, but when he did, on a note of personal privilege, he directed these lines to Snodgrass:

> Mr. Chairman. . . . Among other things, he charges me with not wearing proper apparel; he accused me of going without socks in days gone by. Now, every little red-headed editor out in my part of the country has used that sort of argument against me [laughter]; but I hardly thought the Representative of a portion of the great State of Tennessee would resort to such pettifogging tactics as that. That sort of language should be left to the mud-slinging politician . . . ; but for him to come into the House . . . , where the people of the United States are assembled in their representative capacity to consider laws in the interest of the nation, to sink so low as that, reminded me, Mr. Chairman, of Goldsmith's lines—"Ill fares the land to hastening ills a prey, Where wealth accumulates and men decay."
>
> Ah, Mr. Chairman, the descent has been rapid; it is a long distance from Andrew Jackson to the gentleman who now represents the Third District of Tennessee.
>
> Now, Mr. Chairman, in regard to my being "the dude of the House," of which the gentleman accuses me, I am willing to stand alongside of him and have gentlemen compare our wearing apparel, if they think it necessary. [Laughter.] Look at him now with his Prince Albert coat and his flaming necktie and diamond ring. [Laughter.] One thing I will say, Mr. Chairman; I may have been accused of going without socks; I may have been accused lately of being "the dude of the House," but no gentleman has accused me of being the fool of the House. [Laughter.] I wish I could say as much of the gentleman from Tennessee; for I overheard an earnest conversation between two members, and it is yet an undecided question between them, I believe, whether he or some other gentleman is the fool of the House.
>
> Mr. Chairman, I have said this much in personal defense of myself. I passed over the other day the personal remarks of the eloquent gentleman from Georgia ["Alliance Democrat" Charles L. Moses], when his gall was

> stirred because I called his attention to the fact that he had been inconsistent in some of his votes. . . . The soul of the eloquent gentleman was vexed, his gall was stirred, because I had made that remark, and he took occasion to make a personal attack on me, and now, when it is followed up by the eloquent gentleman from Tennessee, I thought the time had come to call a halt to this kind of business.

The exchange did not end there. Snodgrass understandably took exception to the assertion about his being in the running for the title of "fool of the House" and struck back by saying that he had heard it said that "the gentleman from Kansas is a mountebank and a scapeless demagogue."[12] To that, Simpson replied, "That was bad." At that moment, it was indicated that Snodgrass's time had expired. Simpson then requested unanimous consent granting Snodgrass an additional five minutes. A New York Republican suggested instead that Snodgrass be allowed to extend his remarks in the record. Simpson added, "Give him five minutes, and I will not have to bring up those two members to prove my assertion." That line essentially ended the exchange, with the reporter noting "laughter and applause" from the House. Apparently, Snodgrass and Simpson, following this exchange, developed a genuine friendship—either that, or the two developed a healthy respect for each other.[13]

Simpson on occasion was also known to challenge his colleagues, much to their embarrassment, on the basis of contradictory information provided by opponents from their home districts. He took particular pleasure in exposing those who represented themselves as farmers—or as experts on farming—but were actually employed in "farming farmers"(Simpson's favorite way of describing middlemen who were perceived as exploiting farmers) rather than working the land.[14] In January 1894, John Robinson, a Pennsylvania Republican, appeared for a moment to have turned the tables on Simpson by telegraphing Kansas to get information about Jerry's "farm" (ranch, actually) and its value. Robinson was armed with this telegram from the mayor of Medicine Lodge: "Jerry Simpson owns 800 acres of land; ten years ago it was worth $2,500, and today it is worth $5,000." Simpson's response to this piece of information was: "The facts are—and I think I am the best witness in this case—that land cost me eight years ago more than $5,000; but today, after I have put $4,000 worth of improvements upon it, the gentleman can have the whole outfit for $5,000; and I will throw into the bargain a $1,900 mortgage that gentlemen on this side of the House call evidence of prosperity [great laughter.]."[15] This was, of course, neither the first nor the last time Republican strategy would backfire in an effort to get back at Simpson.

In the age of televised sessions, Jerry Simpson's popularity would likely have been unlimited. One day in January 1894, another Republican, in defense of protective tariffs, displayed what was called an example of the kind of "shoddy" products being kept off the American market by high import taxes, compliments of his party. A few days later, Simpson appeared on the floor with a very shabby overcoat he claimed to have purchased from a farmer on the outskirts of the city. He carried the tattered and soiled garment to the floor and, in an effective show-and-tell display, demonstrated how easy it was to tear the garment into pieces. His presentation evoked such "great laughter and applause" that the chair had to make a special effort to restore order. Simpson then said: "This man from whom I bought this overcoat told me that he got up at 12 o'clock at night and drove 25 miles with the products of his farm in order to sell in this great capital city. . . . My friends, that is the garment which he wore; that is the result of the profits which the farmers of this country are enjoying under your beautiful system of protection—an old shoddy rag with which this man has shivered through the winter blasts!" Again he was interrupted by applause from Democrats and Populists, and Simpson added: "Talk about prosperity to the farmer! I can duplicate that coat by the million in the United States today on the backs of American farmers and American laboring men." As he finished, he placed the coat on the seat of a prominent Republican leader nearby and was promptly asked to remove the dirty object. Simpson obliged but stated: "Yes, sir; as you are a protectionist, you do not want to come in contact with the result of your system any more than the saloon-keeper wants to come in contact with the products of his factory."[16]

For the first two years of congressional Populism, Tom Watson's considerable talents were combined with those of Simpson in the House. Watson tended to be less spontaneous and usually not quite as lighthearted in his approach to debates as Simpson, but of course the congressman from Medicine Lodge was truly one of a kind. The Georgia congressman directed much of his attention to promoting the subtreasury proposal championed by the Populists. Throughout the Fifty-second Congress the Populist speaker refused to go along with unanimous-consent requests, no matter how trivial or important, to pressure House leaders into granting the measure consideration, and in that strategy he had strong support from John Davis and Jerry Simpson. They did succeed, finally, in getting it reported from the Ways and Means Committee, but unfavorably, thus ending any realistic chance of action on the controversial measure, short of a revolutionary turnover in the makeup of Congress.[17]

Perhaps Tom Watson's most important practical accomplishment resulted from the determined fight he waged against the use of private armies, such as those that were supplied to corporations by the Pinkerton Detective Agency for use in their bitter struggle with workers. It was an issue that Watson took up early in the Fifty-second Congress but became highly relevant in July 1892 as national attention was focused on the strike at Andrew Carnegie's plant in Homestead, Pennsylvania, where Pinkertons and steelworkers employed deadly force against one another. Early in the discussion, Watson introduced a resolution calling for an investigation of the infamous agency and spoke out forcefully on its behalf. At one point he said, "I am as much opposed to laborers having a standing army as I am to capitalists having it. I believe in law; I believe in order; I believe that when there is civil disturbance the peace should be preserved by an impartial magistracy, not by the armed belligerents on either side." That line drew applause from the House. Jerry Simpson and Senator Peffer were likewise strong and outspoken advocates of curtailing the use of private armies in industrial disputes.[18]

Watson also became an avid supporter of a system of rural free mail delivery. Toward the end of his short tenure, the Georgian actually succeeded in putting through a small appropriation to sustain an experimental rural delivery system already being tested. He was not its originator but certainly gave it important support as one of its earliest backers. It was a program that would be championed even more vigorously and successfully after 1895 by Senator Marion Butler. Since both were editors and publishers of rural newspapers, one could hardly call this particular measure a disinterested one.[19]

At times, Watson also managed to put his humor and Georgia syntax to good use, as illustrated in the quotation from the tariff debate that heads this chapter. During discussion of a bill requiring the railroads to use automatic couplers, Watson put the House on notice this way: "I will stay here till the ants tote me out of the keyhole before I will give up this fight, if the gentleman in charge of this bill will just order us to stand by and fight it out." Said Watson, "I am tired of this eternal fashion of the railroads bossing this House. We are dealing here with a question of life; we are dealing here with a question that ought to be sacred to the hearts of the American people. While this very debate has been going on, men have lost their lives by the selfish refusal of these corporations to spend money in buying these safety appliances." As in this case, Populist fervor invariably increased when it was a clear case of human lives versus corporate profits.[20]

Clearly, Watson was at his best and most courageous in the stand he took in Congress (and in Georgia) on behalf of the rights of black Americans. The occasion for this was a speech he delivered in January 1893 eulogizing Congressman Eli Stackhouse, who had died in office the previous summer. Stackhouse was an Alliance Democrat, the first president of the South Carolina Farmers' Alliance, and a Confederate veteran distinguished for having survived wounds sustained in three major battles—Antietam, Gettysburg, and Chickamauga. Watson, by then a lame duck, obviously used this speech as an opportunity to deliver a message that he believed his fellow southerners in the Democratic party badly needed to hear in the aftermath of his failed reelection bid in Georgia. In that election, according to C. Vann Woodward, Watson's opponents had used a level of fraud and violence not seen in the state since the Reconstruction era.[21] Among other things, Watson noted:

> The Farmers' Alliance of the South has been misunderstood, misrepresented, and misjudged. The fact that this man belonged to it shows that it was not a mere movement in the direction of communism and anarchy; that it did not emanate from those who failed in love to the South, in respect to the law, or in loyalty to the flag. It came from men who struck at abuses. It was a protest against the condition of things that now pertains; a protest . . . against the system which shuts out from control the great masses of the sovereigns of

> the land according to the law, and gives that control into the hands of the irresponsible and secret few; a protest against a condition of affairs which denies to 8,000,000 human beings [southern blacks] the exercise of the franchise accorded by law, and which builds to the future upon the false foundation of the sectional animosities of the past.

Watson then made these truly profound observations, far and away worthier of celebration than the better-known and much-trumpeted "New South" ideas of Henry Grady or even the soon-to-be-applauded accommodationist approach to race relations advocated by Booker T. Washington:

> No society can rest secure upon a false foundation. No section can open the doorway to progress when it denies to any large body of her citizens their rights under the law; and for this reason we have dared to say in the South . . . that the true solution of the southern question [race relations] and the very foundation on which to build up southern prosperity is to give to all of its citizens equal and exact justice under the law, and accept the aid of all in building up the prosperity of a section which we all should love. . . . I believe, Mr. Speaker, that the work of Mr. Stackhouse was in the direction of solving this question, in the direction of having every laborer understand that the cause of labor is the same everywhere; having every farmer, white and black, understand that the cause of the farmer is the same; having every producer, white and black, understand that the cause of the producer is the same; and thus have them march shoulder to shoulder to the redress of grievances, demanding laws which [will] . . . insure justice to all.[22]

This was the Tom Watson that C. Vann Woodward, one of America's great historians, so justifiably admired and immortalized nearly sixty years ago. Quite likely, however, the embitterment and illiberalism that Woodward also noted and deplored in Watson's later years had their distinct origins in the deep and bitter disappointments set in motion by that fratricidal war among the white ruling caste that masqueraded as political discourse in Watson's beloved South during the middle years of the Populist decade. If there were indeed two Tom Watsons, as Woodward suggested, the second and less admirable one likely began to emerge even before the party was, for all practical purposes, ushered off the stage at the turn of the century.

Racial issues and bitter defeats played a large role in Watson's disenchantment, but there was more involved. His conservative economic views also played a role in pushing him over the line, as would be the case with a number of Populists in the party's right wing. This has not been acknowledged as clearly as it should have been, probably because Watson was a legitimate southern folk hero on the race question. Late in 1895, the Georgia Populist wrote a private and revealing letter to Marion Butler, who by then was a senator and chairman of the national committee, that included this commentary:

> You will see from the papers that the Georgia Populists gave Coxey the cold shoulder and adopted the most conservative platform the party has ever put forth.
>
> Speaking for myself, I do not hesitate to say that I will not go a step farther toward Socialism and Radicalism than the Georgia Platform goes.
>
> It is highly desirable it seems to me, that those of us who favor this moderate & conservative course should begin to educate public sentiment in that line, in our papers, to the end that the extremists shall not control our next National Convention.[23]

The "extremists" Watson had in mind would have to include some prominent leaders in Congress such as Peffer, Allen, and Butler (although the North Carolinian's position was not yet fully formed), along with a number of others in the House who prominently championed the cause of the Coxeyites. We should also note that Lawrence Goodwyn, in treating the events that led to the Bryan-Watson presidential ticket just months after this letter, singled out Watson as the hero of the more radical, antifusionist elements and Allen as a "Populist in name only."[24] All this may prove that in history's court there is indeed no safeguard against double jeopardy.

"LIKE THE SHAKING OF A RED FLAG BEFORE A BULL"

One of the growing phenomena that Populists spoke out against with great intensity during both phases of their congressional interlude was militarism. They were determined foes of increased appropriations for the army and navy during a depression that counted four to five million Americans unemployed and without assistance other than self-help and private charity. An interesting comparison from more recent history might be injected here: Since World War II, reactionary conservatives in American politics—from McCarthy to Goldwater to Reagan and beyond—have defined themselves in clusters of beliefs that can be fairly lumped together under two headings: "pro-warfare state" and "anti-welfare state"—positions regarded by some as "populism" or by the slightly more discriminating as "reactionary populism."[25] As regards the original Populists, these positions are absolutely off base; in fact, the prototypes for the reactionary movement that has gained momentum since its feeble beginnings in the 1930s in opposition to New Deal, welfare-state liberalism can be found in the camp of the 1890s anti-Populists. The record of Congress makes this important observation abundantly clear.

Jerry Simpson, who was the Populist delegation's choice for speaker officially two of his six years in Congress and unofficially for two more, led the fight against military appropriations. In fact, within a year of his entry, an advocate of military spending from New York responded this way to Simpson's criticism of a move to increase a particular appropriation: "the mention of the United States Army or the military establishment of this country seems to act upon the gentleman from Kansas like the shaking of a red flag before a bull."[26] The matter that had provoked Simpson's opposition certainly demonstrated that he was not one merely to advocate savings in every state but his own. A Kansas Republican had moved to increase by $300,000 an appropriation for work at a number of military posts, including Fort Leavenworth in Kansas. Simpson said he was "opposed to any large appropriation for building military posts. I do not think any such appropriation is necessary at this time. We are at peace, as I understand, with all the world. . . . It is especially true that in view of the condition of our Treasury . . . we are not warranted in spending money for purposes of this kind." He went on to say that he thought "we ought . . . to take all necessary and proper measures for the purpose of securing homes for our homeless people, before we provide for building up expensive military posts throughout the country." He then reminded the House, "Not many days ago . . . a bill proposing to appropriate some millions of dollars for the purpose of buying a large tract of land to provide homes for the homeless people of the country" was rejected and the argument was made that "the lack of funds in the Treasury" would not permit it.[27]

The next month, in the debate over the pension bill, Simpson returned to this theme. With the cost of war and preparation for war much on his mind, he said:

> The way to cure this evil is to strike at the root of the disease. First teach our children by precept and example that war is unnecessary, that it is a very cowardly way to settle a dispute; stop worshipping military heroes; stop building military forts and arsenals; stop building ironclads, navies and all these things that make war possible; for these things are part of the war system and may all be resolved into preparation for war, and when you have made preparations for anything you generally get it sooner or later, and yet men who are crying out against the burdens of [military] pensions, have in this Congress voted all the adjuncts and accessories, all its furniture and equipage, all its forts, navies, armies, military displays—all going to build up its war system—that keeps alive in the minds of men this barbarous plan of settling disputes.[28]

Populists had pledged themselves in the Omaha platform to support pensions for the veterans of past wars, and they did support expenditures for that purpose while endeavoring to prevent fraudulent claims being honored, but they were not among those seeking to build up a standing army or a military force for any future wars. Simpson, in particular, seemed to be philosophically opposed to militarism. In fact, his position verged on pacificism. Most Populists were inclined to object primarily because they believed that the money could be put to better use.

In one of his speeches on behalf of the opening of the Cherokee Outlet lands in Oklahoma territory, Simpson even anticipated the famous frontier thesis that

Frederick Jackson Turner was to present to the American Historical Association four months later. After citing in great detail the huge sums that had been voted by Congress for the military, for pensions and sugar bounties, for frivolous "displays," for river and harbor improvements, and so forth, he turned to the importance of land for homesteads. It was fortunate, he said, that "after the Panic of 1873 . . . this country . . . had so much vacant land." The area encompassing "the great West was just beginning to attract the attention of the settler, and hundreds of thousands of poor people [without] . . . employment in the cities went out to the country, established themselves homes, and thereby became good, law-abiding citizens, and, instead of being tramps and beggars . . . , became wealth-producers, and contributed to that large flow of wealth that has been poured into the lap of the East from the great Northwest." Those lands served as "a safety valve" for the country, said Simpson. Now "we begin to hear the warning cry of an impending panic," and Congress had to prepare for that crisis.[29] Remarks of this kind played a large role in convincing many of his detractors that the "Sockless" label needed to be supplemented by "Socrates."

Shortly before he left Congress, William McKeighan, in what even he seemed to sense were likely to be his final remarks for the record, added his voice to the Populist fight against having a professional military. After referring to the hard times confronting so many Americans at the midpoint of the 1890s depression, the Nebraskan entered a plea for those "who earn their bread in the sweat of their brow." Do something, he urged, to assist these people. He then said, "It has been the ambition of my life to live and see the time when just and righteous laws would rule, and when millions would be spent to enlighten the world where millions are now spent for swords, bayonets, cannons, and battleships to kill and destroy thousands of God's creatures in order that a favored few may wear the mantle of wealth and ride roughshod over the rights of the many."[30]

In the Senate, Peffer worked along the same lines as Simpson, trying to realign priorities. In fact, as a result of the efforts of these two Kansans, a battleship was blown out of the water, so to speak, toward the end of the Fifty-third Congress. They managed, by amendment, to reduce the $23 million appropriation for battleships, causing the elimination of one of the vessels. Having been a sailor and captain on the Great Lakes for about twenty years, Simpson was comfortable, self-assured, and well informed in any and all debates involving maritime matters. While in Congress, he clearly described and became a supporter of a development project that would ultimately, in Dwight D. Eisenhower's time, culminate in the completion of the St. Lawrence Seaway. And for those who employed the argument that a great navy was needed to protect the nation from Great Britain and its powerful fleet—an argument that was made most often during the Venezuela boundary dispute—Simpson shot back: "Every interest of Great Britain puts her under bond to keep the peace with us. Why, Sir, if Great Britain should throw her shells into our great cities—Boston, New York, or Philadelphia—she would in all human probability destroy more property belonging to

British subjects than to American subjects." Laughter and shouts of "Oh, no!" accompanied that remark.[31]

In one of his speeches in the Senate toward the close of the Fifty-third Congress, Peffer summed up quite well the Populist position on the military. Simpson was on his way out of Congress by then and would not return until 1897, at which point Peffer would no longer be in the Senate. One senses this parting of the ways from Peffer's remarks, which included a quote from one of Simpson's commentaries in the House. First off, Peffer referred to the dismal economic situation: "25 percent of the working force of the country are absolutely idle, 25 percent working on at not more than half time, and one-half of the remainder on less than full time. While that condition prevails we are talking about adding $23,000,000 to our debt in order to increase the Navy, when we have already 75 fighting ships in condition for service, or soon will." To Peffer, it was all absurd. The "tendency of our people . . . is to adopt a military idea." And in this Congress, he said, "we have made arrangements for the use and employment of military officers in our agricultural colleges; we are authorizing the same . . . in many of our large private schools, colleges, and universities; and we are even going so far as to teach military tactics in our public schools." From somewhere deep down, said Peffer, has come a "mania for militarism, and it is pervading the social condition of the entire world." He feared that ultimately the nation was headed in the direction of using this force "to suppress rebellion and insurrection and revolution amongst the common people."[32]

During this speech, Peffer was assured by opponents that such expenditures would work their way down to the common people. Perhaps, answered Peffer, but the Populists wanted "productive" and more immediate relief for the suffering masses. William McKeighan, in one of his earlier House speeches, had even helped define and name this approach to the economy that would come to be called "trickle-down" economics, a use of terms that would not be clearly spelled out until William Jennings Bryan's famous "Cross of Gold" speech of 1896.[33]

THE ROLE OF GOVERNMENT

Although it has been argued that the Populists advocated a government of minimal scope, this simply was not the case, except as related to putting an end to the special favors already received by various manufacturing and business interests. They were not antistate conservatives; in fact, they advocated a remarkable number of positive governmental measures associated with the later twentieth century.[34] Sad to say, this aspect of Populism has not been fully recognized, largely because their performance on the one and only national stage available to them—Congress—has been generally ignored.

First, they were not under the spell of some mythical golden age. To be sure, their opponents on occasion accused them of wanting to turn back the clock.

They were quick to deny any such goal. And unless resistance to moves by manufacturing interests to do as they pleased is taken as the mark of retrogression, they must be acquitted on that charge. Their support of measures designed to apply restraints to a buccaneering, neomercantilistic, capitalistic economy and culture was readily seen by their more conservative colleagues as retrograde. Their goal, as they saw it, was to confer—and in the monetary area to restore—control over key elements of the economic system to the public, to enhance the general welfare. As Senator Peffer said in one of his early speeches, "When we look backward over the progress of this century and see how far we have come, it seems strange that we are just at the threshold of the greatest problem of all the centuries, the equitable distribution of the products of labor; that we are only beginning to learn the powers which justly belong to the government of a free people, and to see how admirably adapted to the demands of a high civilization our own Government is."[35] Speaking in an age of negative—but far from neutral—government, Peffer felt it necessary to say this: "When we speak of the Government we do not refer to some great unknown or untried power, some foreign entity separate and apart from ourselves, our institutions and our country; nor do we allude to a paternal potentate, prince or power, endowed with fatherly instincts whose watchful care directs our way and guards our interests. Paternalism is an exotic; it does not flourish in a Republic where the people are the source of power." With these words, Peffer captured sentiments that were at the very core of Populism's view of the role of government. And as Simpson put it in fewer words in one of his 1890 campaign speeches, "The government is the people and we are the people."[36]

Speaking in support of direct election of U.S. senators, Omer Kem noted that he did not see that particular reform as "a cure for all the evils complained of by the people." Yet he saw it "as a step in the direction" toward "popular government." In his view, "the true function" of government was "to protect the weak against the strong, and [to] secure to all citizens regardless of their station . . . the right to life, liberty, and the privilege of pursuing happiness in their own way so long as that way does not conflict with the same right of others."[37] The problem was, of course, that in the modern age, special obstacles appeared to thwart the fulfillment of individual rights, and they needed to be reckoned with by the people through their government in carrying out that "true function" that Kem had identified.

John Davis, more clearly than others, was quick to point out the special problem posed by a fast-emerging corporate power structure in an age still driven by precorporate, individualistic mandates. He made the following comment in defense of labor's right to organize while backing a bill mandating an eight-hour day for federal workers and for the District of Columbia:

> Let me draw you a picture of a corporation. We are supposed to be all children of one Heavenly Father. There is another creature in this country that

> God never made. It is a corporation. What is it composed of? Let us suppose a corporation of ten persons. By a charter granted them they become a legal person having the right to sue and be sued. The law can not make a conscience or a soul, and hence we have a new feature; the combined intelligence and brains of ten men, having large quantities of money, but no soul and no conscience, and we are asked now to compel individual men to compete with that new creature. It can not be done. Men must organize or go to the wall when dealing with corporations.[38]

Remember that the right of labor to organize and bargain collectively would not be explicitly recognized by Congress until the Wagner Act of 1935.

Populists were close to being of one mind on the need for government (the people in their organized capacity, as they saw it) to take steps to curtail the abuse of power by corporations. Speaking at the time of the Homestead Strike, Peffer asserted that Congress had "the right constitutionally to protect its own citizens anywhere in the country. I believe furthermore that it has a right to determine for itself when and where a private business has gone to the extent of its usefulness in that capacity and when it is time for the government to interfere."[39] And as most of them saw it, public ownership of public services was merely common sense applied to economic arrangements.

But not every Populist was quite as ready as Peffer to have the national government "interfere." Congressman William McKeighan from Red Cloud, Nebraska, one of the organizers of the Alliance in his state and a former Democrat elected in 1890 as an Independent and in 1892 as a Populist with Democratic support, was opposed to the subtreasury system from the outset and apparently was a determined foe of most prevailing forms of governmental assistance. At the time of this speech, McKeighan seemed to be a proponent of equal treatment for business, labor, and agriculture—equal in the sense of no assistance. At one point he said, "I have never been able to bring myself to believe that it is the business of the government to interfere in the regulation and adjustment of the business of our people, believing as I do that the men who are trained in the school of actual experience know better how to conduct and regulate their own business than the members of this or any other Congress." Toward the end of this speech, occasioned by his support for an attempt to get wool added to the free list in the tariff debate, McKeighan received a mixture of laughter and applause with this line: "I am not, nor are the people that I represent, advocating any system of daddy government." Shouted out one member, "Why, you are a straight Democrat." McKeighan promptly denied that he was still a Democrat and said that he was proud to belong to a party that truly believed in "equal and exact justice before the law."[40]

One historian focused on McKeighan as representative of the congressional delegation,[41] but he was not. In fact, none of the others—including William Allen of Nebraska and William Harris of Kansas, both of whom also opposed the subtreasury proposal—came close to the position voiced by McKeighan. And even this farmer from Red Cloud was more complex and reform minded than this commentary drawn from a single speech would suggest, especially after the depression became national beginning in 1893.[42] Nonetheless, there were significant differences among these Populists that should not be minimized. They were there from the beginning, and by 1897 they had coalesced in such a way in Kansas as to result in William Peffer being replaced by William Harris, as highlighted in the introduction.

Prior to 1896, however, most of these Populists would likely have agreed with the position delineated by Frank Doster, one of the party's leading intellectuals. Never a congressman, but widely recognized as an extraordinary intellect among the Populists, the Kansas judge analyzed the situation with a keener insight than most. In a major 1894 Labor Day speech, Doster spelled out the meaning of the Omaha platform and Populism this way: "The failure to adapt the legislation of the country to the strange conditions which this new life has forced upon us is the cause in greater part of our industrial ills." As a result, he said, the People's party was born, and it "proposes as the only means to the desired end to utilize the power of the social mass to bear upon the rebellious individuals who thus menace the peace and safety of the state. It says . . . the powers exercised through [monopolies and trusts] . . . are in reality the functions and agencies of government itself." Populists, he said, would have the government, which was, after all, only the people in their organized capacity, "assert their rightful dominion" in this modern situation. And as a basis for such action, said Doster, they advance two political propositions: first of all, "it is the business of the government to do that for the individual which he cannot successfully do for himself, and which other individuals will not do for him upon just or equitable terms; the other, that the industrial system of a nation, like its political system, should be a government of and for and by the people alone."[43]

At about this same time, "Topeka's Mark Twain," G. C. Clemens, another prominent leader among the Kansas Populists and a lawyer noted for his expertise in corporation and property law, defended his party's position regarding the role of government in a three-part article with the revealing title "The Philosophy of the Omaha Platform: Not Paternalism but Fraternalism."[44] The previous month, Omer Kem had already made the same point in one of his congressional speeches. Clemens argued that the prevailing "theory of government is paternalism; paternalism for the benefit of monopolists." That, he argued, was a logical product of what has practically been regarded since the beginning of time as the primary purpose of government: "protecting property against the propertyless; the rich against the poor." The Populists, he insisted, aimed at making "government the instrument, not of the rich, but of the people; its object, not the perpetuation of monopoly, but the happiness of society." After all, wrote Clemens, who was by no means a churchgoer himself but was supportive of the Social Gospel, the "teachings of Christ himself" were all in the same direction—either that or, he seemed to imply, the Gospels according to the New Testament were meant only for the next world.[45]

WHAT AILS THE NATION?

The Populist view of the role of government was closely tied to their understanding of what ailed society and why it was thus afflicted. In areas in which the voters were prevented by force or fraud from expressing their will at the polls, the problem was fairly easily understood and explained. But when the people were free to choose and proceeded to vote against what the Populists considered to be in the general interest, that led to other, sometimes conspiratorial, explanations—occasionally even to explanations that the people themselves were to blame. Early in 1894, Simpson, responding to the question of why "labor stands starving today amidst plenty," argued: "Let me say to the laboring men that this is not the fault of the monopolists, of the plutocracy, as you call them. It is the fault of the laboring men themselves." They have "voted to put into office the men who made these laws, and they are responsible for it; and until they have intelligence and manhood enough to vote for their own interests and to send their own representatives here to secure legislation that shall give to them a share of the wealth that they create they can expect no lasting benefits through any party."[46]

The failure of the country to adapt its laws and practices to the new situation created by revolutionary economic changes was one explanation for what ailed society. At times, that view took more personal forms. In one of his speeches in the House early in 1892, Watson said that he would like to convince "this House that this agricultural depression does exist. You are the custodians of the law. It is with you to say what you will do with this condition of things; it is with you to say whether . . . statutes shall be passed which recognize the claim of these people to redress of grievances and the improvement of their treatment under the law." He then talked about the history of cotton prices to take issue with the conservative argument that overproduction was at the root of the matter. "The prosperity of a people," said Watson, "lies not so much in the amount of wealth as in the distribution of it."[47]

Time and again the Populists also referred to a betrayal by both major parties of the original principles on which the nation was founded. Former Republicans readily made reference to the ideas of Lincoln and lamented the abandonment of ideals born out of the slavery crisis and the Civil War. Marion Butler on a number of occasions utilized a similar line of analysis as regards the southern Democratic party. In one of his speeches, the North Carolinian told Senate Democrats and Republicans that they had both lost sight of the principles their parties were supposed to cherish. "The People's Party," he said, "came into existence to defend and to put in practice the great, true principles of Democracy and Republicanism as represented by Jefferson, Jackson, and Lincoln, and because . . . both old parties . . . have deserted and gone over to the side of the monopolists and gold bugs."[48]

Like most Populists, William Allen seemed to have no trouble distinguishing among various human rights at issue. In an exchange with Senator Orville Platt from Connecticut in a debate over an income tax, he bristled at Platt's claim that property rights were just as sacred as human life. He said that he did not believe it. "However sacred property may be . . . , the right to live is supreme over all things." After conceding that "property under our constitution and form of government is absolutely sacred," Allen said that no Populist wished to "impair the right of property in the slightest degree." There was, however, a determination on the part of his party to see that "every man who enjoys a fortune . . . shall enjoy it as the result of honest labor . . . , and that he shall not be permitted, through vicious legislation, to reap the fruits of the labors of others, or to amass a fortune which is the result of fraudulent and dishonest practices." After alluding to the great maldistribution of wealth in the country and to the threat against even more sacred notions of human rights, Allen stated: "If a Senator . . . asserts these great truths, the batteries of corporations [and] . . . the money power are opened upon him, he is characterized as a Socialist, as a Populist, an anarchist perhaps, because he preaches the doctrine of the rights of the humble and the poor of the nation. No, sir, we would not disturb one of these fortunes. We would hold them sacred, but let no fortunes be accumulated after this which are not honestly accumulated."[49]

Congressman Ben Clover was one of those who spoke for the record very little during his one term. While in Congress, he was even subjected to ridicule back in Kansas for dozing off in the House on occasion, and it was somehow discovered that he was intimately involved with a woman who was not his wife, said to be the kind "who wore red slippers." Despite all that, one of his speeches, consigned to an appendix, contained interesting material regarding how and why many farmers, such as himself, had been "driven to the wall." After painting a picture of the disastrous consequences for the debtor resulting from the ever-worsening deflationary spiral that had gone on since the early 1870s, Clover stated: "Conspiracy is a very mild name for the persistent enactment and misconstruction of laws, in order that Shylock might have his pound of flesh regardless of the Christian blood he might shed, or the desolation of this wilderness of debt into which the people of this fair land have been driven." As he saw it, "Never since time began was a confiding people more thoroughly deceived or more cruelly wronged by their rulers than have been the American people in the last quarter of a century."

Clover then referred to a remark by a New York congressman expressing hope that the battle taking shape "be not a sectional question; that it be not made a question of the country against the city, nor the city against the country." Clover said: "Let it be not made a question of the West and the South against the

Northeast, but that it be made a national question. I do not wonder that the gentleman [from New York] pleads so eloquently and so feelingly in behalf of the section he represents. When I reflect that for lo! these many years the West and the South have been but hewers of wood and drawers of water for the monopolists of the section he represents, I do not wonder that he pleads for the continuance of a system which pours the wonderful wealth of these great sections into the bursting vaults of Wall Street and those of protected manufactures." These were the remarks, he said, "of just a farmer."[50] That they were, and they undoubtedly resonated strongly among all those who rallied to the Populist cause.

Without question, those individuals in the South and West who responded positively to Populism—and quite a number of Democrats and even a few Republicans as well—believed that in the years since the Civil War, they and their sections had been made to be "hewers of wood and drawers of water" for the industrial northeastern quarter of the nation (a parallel in our time might be those who feel that they have been consigned to a lifetime of service-related work). With fully three-fourths of American industry concentrated in that portion of the nation as late as 1900, who could say that this element of colonial dependency, together with its perception of exploitation and gold-standard malice aforethought, was absolutely without merit? All actions, we are told, have equal and opposite reactions. Such disproportionate development, it would seem, was destined to produce its own countervailing force. On the political side, perhaps it culminated in a phenomenon like a tree with a double trunk—one called Populism and another identified for a time as "Bryanism," and still later as a branch of that even more variegated reform persuasion called Progressivism.

3

"Money Is King": Grover Cleveland's Special Session

To my mind, Mr. Speaker, the causes of the condition of our people today are numerous; they did not begin yesterday or the day before, or last year or the year before. This [depression] . . . had its rise in the bad institutions of government with which we started out. We began wrong. We have failed to secure to human society and to individuals the rights that belong to them. This great nation in the course of its progress has created enormous powers, and instead of fortifying the rights of the people, has granted these vast powers to a privileged class.

Jerry Simpson, *Congressional Record,* 53rd Cong., 1st sess., 18 August 1893, 486 ff.

The story of the financial panic of 1893 and the depression that followed and endured until nearly 1898—usually only partially told—is one of an economic downturn widening and deepening to include the industrial and urban sectors of the economy. Although international in scope, the debacle on the American side actually had its origins in the hard times that passed for normalcy all over the South in the aftermath of the Civil War. This was decisively compounded, beginning about 1887, by the collapse of an expansionist boom and the beginning of hard times in much of the new West.

The fact that the economic downturn became urban, industrial, and national—and thus only then officially a depression—in such a sudden and big way certainly gave a new and unexpected twist to the nation's politics beginning in about the middle of 1893. Ultimately, the debacle produced a fundamental political realignment. Nationally, the Republicans would emerge from the repositioning as the majority party, not to be undone until the depression that followed the crash of 1929. The Democrats would find themselves in the minority, with their base weighted even more heavily in favor of the South and West. And the Populists would see whatever chance they had of becoming a major party vanish like the mists of the morning. All of this, in one of American history's premier ironies, was likely set up by Grover Cleveland's election as president in 1892, due in large part to the fact that in six western states, electoral votes were denied to Republicans by the Populist revolt. One can make this argument because, had the Republicans been in power, the economic collapse that began in 1893 would in all probability have wreaked as much or even more havoc on the GOP, and under those circumstances, a reform coalition of Democrats and Populists would have been much easier to build and undoubtedly more potent and viable. But then the gods do indeed work in mysterious ways.[1]

"THE SHADOWS OF A GREAT TWILIGHT"

By the time Grover Cleveland was inaugurated in March 1893, a "badly overextended" economy, as one historian kindly put it, had already begun to show signs of pending financial panic. Undaunted, the New York Democrat interpreted his unprecedented election to a second nonconsecutive term as a vote for retrenchment and a government of minimal scope. The voters, Cleveland reasoned, had signaled their support for the continuation of a "sound and stable" monetary system, civil service reform, and antitrust measures. Above all, as Cleveland saw it, the election's outcome obligated his administration to implement tariff reform. Although it was never forthrightly acknowledged, Cleveland was sold on the idea of maintaining a gold standard, which had, unofficially, been the policy of Republican and Democratic administrations since 1879, despite repeated genuflections in the direction of a bimetallic (gold and silver) standard.

Regarding the role of government, the contrast between Cleveland's party and the Populists could not have been more sharply drawn. In his inaugural address, the president deplored what he called "the unwholesome progeny of paternalism" fostered by his Republican predecessor, Benjamin Harrison. The role of government, as well as the example of history, he insisted, was clear: "Paternalism ought to be unlearned and the better lesson taught that while the people should patriotically and cheerfully support their government its functions do not include the support of the people."[2] In his view, government was obviously something quite apart and above the masses. His approach would depart from that of the Republicans. Policies and practices of long standing, such as protective tariffs, land grants, subsidies to railroads and other corporations, and favorable banking laws, would suggest that Republicans, in all candor, would be at odds with Cleveland's interpretation of the permissible limits of governmental activity. But at the same time, there likely would be considerable agreement within both major parties regarding the lines of demarcation between government and the masses. That would change.

In fact, the crash of 1893 would help legitimize a new way of looking at things. As William Allen White, by then Kansas' most prominent Republican, would later concede, the nation had entered "the shadows of a great twilight." In 1890, when the Farmers' Alliance and the People's party were building a head of steam in Kansas and elsewhere, White was fresh out of the University of Kansas and newly employed as the editor of the *Eldorado Republican,* owned by the prominent Murdock family. It was there that White began to hone his Populist-baiting skills that would bring him into national prominence as editor of his own paper in 1896. Looking back on those years, White could be amazingly candid at times, as in this passage from his much-quoted autobiography, wherein he recalled an overflow crowd of farmers gathered at his county's courthouse:

> I had a low opinion of the Farmers' Alliance credo, and a still lower opinion of the leaders of the movement. So my editorials in the Republican were biased by the fact that I wanted to please Mr. Murdock. He was my little tin god at the time. Yet I was satisfied . . . that the whole Alliance movement was demagogic rabble-rousing, with no basis in sound economics. How intellectually snobbish I was about "sound economics"! . . . I took . . . absolutely no account of the tremendous fact staring me in the face, that the short shimmering day of mass borrowing which had built a civilization in the West and the South, from Appomattox to the nineties, was done! . . . Sound economics should have warned me that another day had dawned. . . . The day of the great boom of the seventies and eighties . . . which had seen the play of free, competitive industrial capital—that day was at its sunset. Those rumps of seedy farmers sticking out of the Courthouse window in Eldorado, Butler County, Kansas, as the Farmers' Alliance county convention met, cast the shadows of a great twilight. In another three years came the night—the collapse, and the depression of '93. But I was a young fool. I sat at night in the office of the Eldorado Republican, writing reactionary editorials about Sound Economics which I had learned from Francis Walker's college textbook, just one of ten thousand other fools across the land who thought that classic economics could be fitted into the social and political upheaval that was closing a brilliant era in our national history.[3]

Except for his advocacy of protective tariffs, the "sound economics" White defended in his "reactionary editorials," written for that small-town Republican newspaper in Kansas, was not all that different from the brand of economics championed by the nation's leading Democrat from Buffalo, New York—President Grover Cleveland. It was a similarity that White likely would not care to acknowledge, even with the passage of time.

The financial "correction" leading to the panic—the coming of the "night" in White's metaphor—began in an obvious way with the 1890 failure of the London banking house of Baring Brothers. Shock waves then began to reverberate on American shores as European capitalists pulled back from what had been regarded as a prime investment opportunity. Lowered production quotas, cuts in wages, and reductions in workforces soon followed. Then, just a few weeks after

Cleveland took office, on 3 May, the stock market collapsed, triggered by the failure of one of the nation's larger corporations—the National Cordage Company. Banks then began calling in outstanding loans, and a number of prominent railroads and other corporations began to go into receivership. In the following six months alone, "8,000 businesses and 360 banks" closed their doors, and farmers saw their already depressed prices plunge further. Thousands upon thousands of workers were soon discharged, and just as many saw their wages slashed. As never before in the nation's history, unemployment figures skyrocketed. In that first winter of 1893–1894, estimates placed the unemployed somewhere between 2 million and 3 million, and the worst was yet to come. According to one careful study, approximately 4.5 million individuals understood hard times intimately. Others, certainly a large portion of the country's 63 million residents, encountered drastic wage cuts or entered the ranks of the poorly paid underemployed. At best, society condoned only self-help and the less-than-adequate system of private charity to assist those in dire need. The American credo was still, unofficially at least, "everyone for himself, and let the devil take the hindmost."

As historian Roger Grant noted in his refreshing study of the 1890s depression, to this day, the scope of "human misfortune and suffering [has] not been truly appreciated." It would be the last great depression the nation would endure in the new urban-industrial age in which the moral and political imperatives championed by the "leave-it-alone-liquidationists" of that day would win out over those who took up the cause of those unfortunate individuals at the bottom of the ladder who were made to suffer most for the sake of a "free market." But that was not accomplished without raising the specter of the roof caving in on the American society.[4]

Investors became anxious and pessimistic, and that tiny minority of Americans and foreigners owning stock and other valuable instruments of commerce began selling and redeeming their holdings for gold. Soon, the U.S. Treasury confronted what was perceived as a crisis. Gold began to flow out of the Treasury in exchange for silver coins, paper currency, and those special treasury notes that had been issued to buy silver under the terms of the Sherman Silver Purchase Act of 1890. At the time, $100 million in gold—based more on custom than logic—was considered to be the magic minimum the Treasury needed in its vaults to redeem the nation's currency. Devout gold-standard advocates—"goldbugs," in contemporary lingo—were convinced that the Silver Purchase Act was the primary culprit and that it had to go. Cleveland was in accord with that view, and before taking office, he had even attempted through private channels to get Congress to repeal the measure. In the meantime, the reserve continued to shrink. On the day he took the oath, it was less than $1 million above the symbolic $100 million mark. By the end of April, it had fallen below that level. Rumors of impending disaster mounted, and investors and business leaders commenced to put themselves into a frame of mind that would lead to the full-scale panic that began on 3 May.

At the end of June, after vacillating briefly, President Cleveland sent out a call for Congress to meet in special session beginning on August 7. In his official message, he contended that the situation confronting the nation was "principally chargeable to Congressional legislation touching the purchase and coinage of silver by the General Government." The solution was clear and at hand: all that was required was for Congress to repeal the Sherman Silver Purchase Act. In the words of historian Hal Williams, "Always sure of himself, Cleveland had staked everything on a single measure, a winning strategy if it succeeded, a devastating one if it did not."[5]

DISHONESTY OR STUPIDITY?

Although those who favored a less deflationary and more flexible monetary system were convinced that Cleveland had cowardly sold out to the eastern "money power," the president did not lack personal courage. Proof of that was his decision that summer to undergo surgery for mouth cancer, which resulted in the removal of much of his upper left jaw and palate, and to keep it secret while he recuperated at his Buzzards Bay, Massachusetts, retreat to avoid further public alarm. It was his wisdom that was suspect. Prior to the vote on repeal, late in September, he wrote this to the pro-silver governor of Georgia: "I want a currency that is stable and safe in the hands of our people. I will not knowingly be implicated in a condition that will make me in the least degree answerable to any laborer or farmer in the United States for a shrinkage in the purchasing power of the dollar." This particular comment drew a blunt response from historian Ray Ginger: "The position, if not dishonest, was stupid." After all, wrote Ginger, "the total stock of money in the United States had suffered a prolonged decline in 1892–1893. Prices of farm products had collapsed. The value of money based on gold, so far from being 'stable and safe,' had risen steadily. Other things than money have purchasing power, or exchange value, which comes to the same thing; and the farmer who sought to pay his debts had watched the purchasing power of his cotton go down and down."[6] Ginger could have added that before the total stock of money began its precipitous decline in 1892, the circulating medium available to the masses had remained virtually fixed at a level reached by the close of the Civil War, and in the interval, the United States had gone from the third or fourth position among industrialized nations to being number one without a close rival. All the same, the president would have his repeal, regardless of the consequences. He immediately mobilized the power and patronage at his disposal to accomplish that objective; in the process, the nation's chief executive, now the Lord High Protector of the Gold Standard (the famous Yellow Brick Road of a well-known children's book), touched off one of the most interesting and creative debates ever in the Congress of the United States.

Like nothing else at the time, the issue of gold versus silver was loaded with potential for dividing, polarizing, and realigning political configurations. That potential was perhaps foreseen in some offhand remarks William Peffer made in the Senate more than a year before Cleveland called his special session. Throughout his tenure, Peffer never backed away from or ceased advocating the whole Populist monetary package, making these comments all the more significant. Speaking parenthetically in the course of a long speech championing the Populist idea of a system of modern finance, he stated: "I am not authorized to speak for anyone except myself in what I am now about to say. It is my deliberate opinion that if the voters of the country who favor free silver coinage and who regard it as a vital matter would unite in a campaign to secure that result they would surely be successful. They could easily acquire a House of Representatives whose members would have the courage of their convictions; they could easily secure a Senate whose members would not forget the honorable record of this body on the silver question when it was first presented in 1890, and they could secure the election of a President who would not threaten a veto in advance of Congressional action." That certainly reads like a recipe for the political crusade that was born out of the outrage sparked by Cleveland's special session, which then culminated in the epochal 1896 "battle of the [monetary] standards." Peffer also made this prediction: "If success cannot be obtained on the single issue of silver coinage in connection with Government paper money to supply the need of a plentiful currency, other needed reforms are hopelessly lost."[7]

Like everyone else, the Kansas Populist could not have foreseen the election of a Democratic president who would become an even more determined defender of the gold standard than his Republican predecessor. Nor could he have predicted the collapse of the stock market, the onset of a national depression soon thereafter, and the consequences therefrom, but otherwise, Peffer's comments were quite prophetic indeed.

AN EXTRAORDINARY SESSION

From the moment Congress opened, debate was intense and at times heated. Much of the discussion centered on Cleveland's contention that the Silver Purchase Act (the Sherman Act for short, named for its sponsor, Senator John Sherman of Ohio) was responsible for the depression. Prominent Republicans, Democrats, and Populists found themselves in the same camp battling the president. Senator Henry Teller from Colorado, a lifelong Republican who would eventually break with his party over the issue, let it be known at the opening, "It is the height of folly to say . . . this is a panic caused by distrust of the currency."[8] In the House, Richard "Silver Dick" Bland, a Missouri Democrat, predicted that if his party followed Cleveland, it would "be trampled . . . into the dust of condemnation now and in the future."[9] The major parties were obviously split along sectional lines. This was reflected in the comments of California Republican

William Bowers in the House. Like so many Republicans from the West—where support for the coinage of silver with gold, preferably in accord with the old ratio of sixteen to one, was not a partisan issue—Bowers denied that repeal would in any way assist in overcoming hard times; on the contrary, he said, it would intensify the "distress." What would he do? "I would set the thousands of idle hands at work." How? By appropriations for public buildings in the various states. Added Bowers, "I would start those public buildings and I would double their number; I would commence internal improvements all along the line, and I would guarantee [to] the American laborer [that] . . . the American merchant will take the . . . promise to pay in legal money of the United States for all the material and all the labor that will be required. Then we will have some money to relieve the situation, and what we owe we shall owe to our own people and not to foreigners."

Bowers's position was essentially the same as that advocated by the Populists, which was unusual among Democrats and apparently the only such case among the Republicans. He acknowledged as much by this remark:

> I want to say a word to my Republican friends who have done me the honor to listen to me today. I am quite deaf, but my one ear has not failed to catch certain remarks that have been made in relation to the company that I am keeping in this matter. [Laughter.] As to that, I simply wish to say that I am the judge of my own Republicanism. I was born into the party; my first vote was cast for John C. Fremont in 1856, and I always expect to be a Republican, but the only way for the Republican party and the Democratic party to continue to meet here . . . and not to be supplanted by other parties, is to do right, and deal with the people of this country fairly."

Bowers closed by saying, "It ill becomes any Republican or any member of my party who at this juncture has joined the gold squad led by Grover Cleveland in this fight . . . to criticize my attitude."[10]

Joseph Rawlins, a Democratic delegate from the Territory of Utah, a well-educated lawyer and former professor, struck to the core of the issue. After ridiculing the notion that the Sherman Act was in any way responsible for the national and international depression, Rawlins stated: "It is indeed difficult to conceive how any rational being can ascribe to it [the Sherman Act] such potency for evil. . . . No rational man does believe any such thing. An ulterior end has been in view of enhancing the value of fixed charges and long loans amounting to more than fifty billions concentrated into the hands of a few." As he saw it, it smacked of scapegoating in the worst way. In fact, it reminded him "of the old days of ignorance and superstition, when some calamity had happened, in looking about for the cause a harmless hag was likely to be discovered. Immediately all the misfortunes of the people would be ascribed to her witchcraft, and she would be dragged forth, with manifestations of fiendish delight, to be publicly burned. So with the Sherman Act."

Rawlins's insight into the practicality of a "universal gold monometallism," which he astutely recognized as at the base of the matter, was equally profound. It was, he said, "an effort to cover the financial bed with a golden blanket which is not big enough." It was a "utopian" and "idle" notion, "an iridescent dream of fatuity and folly, resulting from ignorance." Concluded the Utah professor, "The real cause of the widespread depression" could be "found in the fact that, during the past twenty years the quantity or supply of primary money has not kept pace with the increase of population, of business production, and the growth of commerce."[11]

Many thought that Jerry Simpson's speech of 18 August was one of the best he had ever delivered. For sure, it demonstrated that the Kansan was by no means taken in by the issue. To his mind, it was far from being a panacea. The nation's problems, leading to the crisis of the nineties, were much more deeply rooted, as he made clear in the quote that heads this chapter. As he saw it, the gold monometallists were the modern-day equivalent of those charlatans of medicine in days gone by. He asked, "What do the Napoleons of finance stand up here and prescribe for the patient at this time? Why, just the same as your quack doctors used to do not very many years ago. When the patient got sick one of these doctors would come in . . . and bleed him." What were the good financial doctors currently prescribing? "That we take one-half the blood from the patient's body. No, my friend, what you want to do is not only to restore the blood that has already been lost, but give the patient more, give him something to strengthen his system, give him more blood."[12]

The new Populist senator from Nebraska, William Allen, certainly agreed with the former professor. Allen received his introduction to politics at the top during this special session, and he wasted no time involving himself in the fray. Early on, in one of the many opportunities he took to question his fellow senators, Allen asserted: "We have been told that the Sherman Act . . . has produced the panic. . . . I do not suppose there is a boy in this nation fifteen years of age, who has studied this question, who honestly and sincerely believes that."[13] Allen's opportunity to speak came in early October, and before it was over, in the last round of his effort, the Nebraskan consumed fifteen consecutive hours with running monologue and dialogue on the subject. His speech stood for a number of years as a record for the length of time one individual had held the floor in Congress, and it was not a fluffy filibuster. The Nebraska senator touched on virtually every conceivable aspect of the financial question in making his case against repeal and fielded questions from all quarters with impressive expertise and the savoir faire of a Senate veteran. At one point he said, "The Sherman Act has nothing to do in the slightest degree with the evil that confronts us." Later, in his formal speech, Allen systemically raised and then exploded, one after the other, what he called the fallacies of the money question. Among these were "the fallacy of intrinsic value," "the fallacy of the double standard," "the overproduction fallacy," "the favorable balance of trade fallacy," and another that contended that there was "no such thing as a contraction of the volume of money by going upon what is called the single gold standard." Regarding the last fallacy, Allen remarked:

> It is a little singular that when you come to the discussion of this gold question Senators should say that a contraction of the volume of money has no effect upon the price of property or labor, and just the moment you speak of enlarging the volume of money, making it greater, they begin to fear the effect of what they call the inflation of money. Inflation will affect prices, so they say and so we know, but they tell us that contraction, which is the other extreme, will not affect them.
>
> Mr. President, if it is true that inflation will affect prices of property and labor, then it is equally true that the other extreme, which is contraction, will affect the prices of property and labor and shrink the prices of those things. . . . This country is suffering to-day by reason of a contracted volume of money. The lockouts, the strikes, the difficulties that we hear of going on throughout this country are due, in my judgment, in a large measure to a contracted and constantly shrinking volume of money.[14]

Regarding the frequently used argument that the introduction of alternative devices for exchange had reduced the quantity of circulating money needed, Allen commented that those who make that argument do "not seem to take into account the fact that among the common people of this country . . . there is not actually today in circulation $15 per capita." The fact is "the great quantity of money of this country of which Senators speak so frequently and refer to as increasing the volume is to be found in the form of reserves, in banks and organizations of that kind, and is as useless to the masses of this country as though it were at the bottom of the ocean."[15]

Joseph Hendrix, a Democrat and a banker associated with a New York branch of the national banking system, was one of Cleveland's more articulate supporters in the House. In the course of a speech by Joseph Hutcheson, a Democrat from Texas, Hendrix was told by Hutcheson that the people were "starving for money." Hendrix then asked, "About what is the size of the appetite?" After some banter regarding its size in New York as compared with the rest of the country, the Texan said this: "I am glad the gentleman from New York asked me that question. New York comes and tells this country that she is in a panic, but I wish to tell the gentleman that my constituents have been in the same kind of panic for the last two years—moneyless—and have had to stand it."[16]

Even a few archconservative Republicans from the West, such as Senator Edward Wolcott from Colorado, could not buy the feeble arguments being made in support of Cleveland's push for repeal. At one point Wolcott said, "I have yet to hear a single intelligent man state on his conscience that he believes the Sherman Act has wrought the injury under which the country now suffers."[17] With such alignments increasingly being revealed as the debate continued day after day, it did not take a genius to forecast the likelihood of a standoff down the line organized around the issue of a gold standard versus a bimetallic standard.

Among the Republican speeches opposing Cleveland's defense of the gold standard, none was more significant and less heralded than that of the only black

American serving in Congress, George Washington Murray from South Carolina, who served two terms from 1893 to 1897. Several weeks into the debate he delivered a powerful speech on behalf of silver and against the gold standard. After identifying himself as a member of the "toiling and producing millions," Murray stated:

> In two respects I represent the largest constituency of any member of this House, a district of two hundred and seventy thousand, and a race of nearly eight million. [Applause.] Speaking for them I do not believe . . . the great evils with which they are afflicted are owing to the operations of the so-called Sherman law. They had been hurtfully feeling the mailed hand of the unrighteous financial policy of their country long before the silver-purchasing bill of 1890 became a law. They believe and know that the primary cause of the rueful disease which has been making paupers of them and their children for more than a dozen years lies deeper than the recent superficial, and in some respects, designing unrest in money circles.

Later, Murray made this telling observation:

> It seems that because a comparatively few bankers and large business concerns are failing, the metropolitan press having stirred and alarmed the nation, this Congress was speedily and gravely called into extraordinary session to furnish means of relief. Yet when we who have a patient and long-suffering constituency, which has been on a bended knee for years begging for aid, enter objections to aiding gentlemen representing banking and moneyed constituencies, unless some measure is coupled with theirs to give relief to ours as well, notice intimations in a portion of the metropolitan press, which disclose a design to charge us with disloyalty, recreancy, and negligence.

Then Murray put his own party on notice by saying:

> I appeal to the grand old party, which has always stood for what is greatest and best in freedom and progress, which has labored for the freedom of my race and has been loud in its protestations against its oppressors, to reflect before consigning us to the gold standard. . . . The only difference between the physical and financial masters is that our personality was the property of the former, while our labor and productions are the slave of the latter. The one was among us, the other at a distance. The former fed and clothed us, because we represented so much property; the latter cares little for our welfare, because their interest is our personal and real property.

Murray went on to say that he spoke not only for the South but also for the hundreds of thousands throughout the nation who were without work. Perhaps with the many thousands of destitute blacks in the nation's capital vividly on his mind, Murray said, as "the lone spokesman for my race, I hear voices which you do not hear, I see faces which you can not see." As regards the battle being waged, he made this observation: "The very employment of bankers, usurers, and speculators gives them an insight into the workings of financial institutions, which supplies them with offensive and defensive weapons, used and ready for use at all times, when their interests demand protection, while that of all other classes is such that they have little opportunity to learn anything of their operations, except their baneful effects upon their lives and property."

The South Carolinian closed his speech by saying, "The system of finance that produces a small crop of millionaires and an abundant harvest of paupers is antagonistic to every principle of the religion of God, and to every form of republican government, and should, and ultimately will, be wiped from the face of this beautiful earth, in which the Creator decreed every individual the enjoyment of freedom and the full fruition of his labor."[18]

THE SILVER ISSUE

One of the more intriguing revelations regarding this special session and its more than 200 speeches[19] on the money question is the degree to which many Americans (as reflected in the views of their congressmen, at least) were in denial or were simply misinformed or ignorant about the monetary standard the nation had operated under for twenty years. Murray, for example, warned his party about "consigning us to the gold standard," but the nation had already been consigned to the gold standard, and principally by his party, in every way except by official proclamation. That too would come in 1900, again thanks to his party. This reluctance to face up to what had happened since 1873, by supporters and even by moderate critics, certainly contributed to the creation of an exaggerated sense of conspiracy regarding what had been accomplished over the previous twenty years. Only those who were most disenchanted with the nation's monetary system, the country's economic radicals, managed to face up to that reality, and, as they encountered this mountain of denial and misinformation, it was too easy for them to embrace the worst-case scenario regarding how it all had come to pass.

This element of ignorance and confusion has also contributed to historical obscurantism. Likewise, it has helped make the whole issue exceedingly difficult to explain and comprehend. Since this great debate about gold and silver, the preferential position of gold was abandoned, sacrificed during the Great Depression of the 1930s, and happily without the dreadful results prophesied by its partisans in the 1890s. This is not to suggest that the domestic and foreign monetary conditions during the two periods were comparable, for they were not; nor does it suggest that a triumph for the "silverites" would have ushered in the millennium. It is to say, however, that both the goldbugs and the silverites exaggerated the significance of the gold-versus-silver issue and in their debates managed to obscure the thoughts of a number of individuals—in the camp of the financiers themselves, but especially among the critics of the financiers—who viewed the monetary needs of the nation in far more realistic terms.

The issue's roots were intricately entangled in the controversial and far-reaching post–Civil War economic revolution. It ultimately involved the whole question of what money was, how its value should be determined, and what the role of government should be, if any, in determining its value and quantity. Throughout American history, there had been advocates of paper money backed merely by the credit of the government, and the Populists drew heavily on that tradition. The Civil War greenbacks were money of that kind until 1879, when the Treasury assumed responsibility for redeeming them in coin upon demand. At that point, they became, literally, "as good as gold." In the face of an ever-deepening deflationary spiral, certain economic reformers—those who were at least as concerned with the needs of debtors as with those of creditors—viewed the resumption of specie payment as unwarranted. In contrast, influential elements of the business community attuned to orthodox fiscal thinking were inclined to believe that true money was "hard money," which had intrinsic value and thus was more readily acceptable in international trade, in addition to making the United States a better credit risk.

Until 1873, the government more or less sanctioned a bimetallic standard. The mints of the United States coined both silver and gold into dollars when bullion was presented. Before the Civil War, the ratio between them had been set by law at approximately sixteen to one—that is, sixteen ounces of silver were recognized as equal in value to one ounce of gold—and the weight of a dollar in either metal was fixed accordingly. Because of its relative scarcity, silver was slightly undervalued at sixteen to one and was not being carried to the mints for coinage. In 1873, seemingly in routine fashion, Congress dropped the silver dollar from the list of coins, an action that would later be excoriated as the "Crime of '73." Apparently, only a few key governmental leaders were aware of the timeliness of this decision. It was timely because of significant trends that had already been established: From 1861 to 1873, silver output had increased; at the same time, gold production had entered a period of relative and absolute decline. Beginning in 1871, the major European financial powers, one after the other, had also abandoned silver coinage. By 1874, as a result of vanishing governmental markets and the steadily declining price of silver, it became profitable to sell silver at the legal ratio for coinage purposes. But by then, it was no longer possible.

Silver producers obviously would have profited if the government had continued to buy unlimited quantities of silver bullion for coinage purposes at the old quasi-official ratio of sixteen ounces of silver to one ounce of gold. Debt-burdened farmers and many small businessmen, especially in the capital-starved South and West, also envisaged advantages in the anticipated increase in the amount of circulating money—a prospect that was aggravated by a significant decline in per capita circulation throughout the period. As a result, from the middle 1870s to the middle 1890s, the goal of "freeing" silver assumed a prominent position on the list of reforms.

By 1890, bimetallists had won two sops—namely, the Bland-Allison Act of 1878 and the Silver Purchase Act of 1890—halfway measures that satisfied neither the silver-mining interests nor the opponents of a "tight-money" policy. The first made provision for limited purchase of domestic silver production at the going market price, and the second provided for the unlimited purchase of silver, but at the current low market price (in 1896, incidentally, one ounce of gold exchanged for about thirty-two ounces of silver). Accordingly, the slumping price of silver in a glutted world and domestic market was not stemmed, and the deflationary spiral was not reversed.

Still, the silver agitation might never have become a major issue except for a combination of circumstances set in motion by the 1892 elections. The People's party, despite an impressive showing, had generated only a small following in the manufacturing northeastern quarter of the country, even among urban laborers from whom it had hoped to win support. Nor had the party's comprehensive radical program been embraced by significant numbers of voters elsewhere. The national ticket had been most successful in the agrarian silver stronghold of the West. Fusion with one or the other of the major parties on the basis of the money question developed a powerful attraction, even though the silver issue badly distorted the true Populist position. The election of a Democratic president and Congress in 1892 ultimately intensified this move. Grover Cleveland's determined defense of the gold standard in the wake of the national depression's onset exacerbated the disenchantment and polarized voters as never before.[20]

Cleveland's stand likewise made more believable the worst-case scenario of how the nation had come to be in such an undesirable monetary situation. The centerpiece of this sinister theory involved the so-called Crime of '73. In retrospect, conspiracy theorists were convinced that the Coinage Act of 1873 had been unduly influenced by various financial interests at home and abroad, which resulted in the nation, in stealthlike fashion, being placed on a single gold standard. Usually featured in this theory was a shadowy financier by the name of Ernest Seyd, who, it was contended, had traveled to the United States at a key moment in 1873 on behalf of the Bank of England with half a million dollars in gold, supposedly supplemented later by an additional half million, in an ultimately successful campaign to get Congress to drop silver from the coinage list.[21]

By whatever means, silver's demonetization was accomplished by the Coinage Act of 1873. Without fanfare and with little notice, the United States was placed on a de facto gold standard, an act actually completed in 1875 by the passage of the Resumption of Specie Act that went into effect in 1879. A handful of the more sensationalist critics among the third-party radicals, most prominently Sarah E. V. Emery from Michigan, later claimed that Seyd and company had carried out "the biggest and best planned financial coup of the century."[22] Emery first published her version of these events in an 1887 treatise entitled *Seven Financial Conspiracies Which Have Enslaved the American People.* Her polemic quickly enjoyed great popularity among those who were thoroughly disenchanted with the monetary situation and major-party politics.[23]

Meticulous research has demonstrated that there was indeed an element of "gold-standard malice aforethought" in these actions, but it was not nearly as great or as conspiratorial as the determined opponents of a gold standard later claimed. The deflationary spiral that set in after 1873, however, by no means defused the resentment that many in the nation came to harbor. As Stanley Jones noted in his classic study, "The situation in which the debtor farmer in the West and South found himself was bad enough in itself; but when he became persuaded that his condition was the result of a foreign [and domestic] conspiracy in which Wall Street had connived at the behest of English financiers, it became unbearable."[24] This "unbearable" anger was always just beneath the surface in Cleveland's special session, which was by itself absolute proof, as foes of the gold standard saw it, of a line of nefarious financial dealings dating back to the so-called Crime of '73.

FOES OF THE GOLD STANDARD FIND A LEADER

In the House, the high point of the special session's debate came on 16 August in the course of a three-hour speech by a thirty-six-year-old congressman from Nebraska by the name of William Jennings Bryan. He was "the 'darling' of the Democratic side of the House, the prettiest man in all the bunch," according to Tom Watson's description of the man selected to make his party's case against protectionism in the previous Congress. The young lawyer unquestionably took his audience by storm. His speech was destined to be talked about on the floor of Congress for well over a year. It was this effort on his part, more than any other single factor, that won him the leadership of the silver forces that were then in the process of consolidating. The young man was brilliant and dramatic. Clearly, his was one of those rare speeches in history. He pulled it all together in an impressive fashion, said things that others only wished they had said, carefully weaving his arguments around a framework that had been fashioned over the preceding nine days in numerous speeches on both sides of the question. As Bryan's major biographer, Paolo Coletta, concluded, his speech was destined "to be the greatest made on his side of the question, and the nation's press" would acknowledge him as "the commander of the anti-Cleveland forces." For his effort, wrote Coletta, Cleveland's "gold squad" would say "he was a demagogue, a brilliant word painter who pleaded for a section and a special interest, an 'infant phenomenon' who attacked the President because of an insolence nurtured by egotism, but from Missouri to the Rockies [not to mention points further West and South] he [would be] . . . a hero who had immortalized himself and deserved the presidential nomination."[25]

"We hear much about a 'stable currency' and an 'honest dollar,' " said Bryan. "It is a significant fact that those who have spoken in favor of unconditional repeal have for the most part avoided a discussion of the effect of an appreciating standard. They take it for granted that a gold standard is not only an honest standard, but the only stable standard. I denounce that child of ignorance and avarice the gold dollar, under a universal gold standard, as the most dishonest dollar which we could employ." Based on all the "intelligent" writers he was aware of, "there is not and never has been an honest dollar. An honest dollar is a dollar absolutely stable in relation to all other things." In point of fact, "a dollar approaches honesty as its purchasing power approaches stability." That clearly was not what the country had had for quite some time. Certainly the nation's farmers knew as much. His voice thundering, Bryan then said this about his farmer constituents:

> If he should loan a Nebraska neighbor a hog weighing 100 pounds and the next spring demand in return a hog weighing 200 pounds he would be called dishonest, even though he contended that he was only demanding one hog—just the number he loaned.
>
> Society has become accustomed to some very nice distinctions. The poor man is called a socialist if he believes that the wealth of the rich should be divided among the poor, but the rich man is called a financier if he devises a plan by which the pittance of the poor can be converted to his use. [Laughter and applause.]
>
> The poor man who takes property by force is called a thief, but the creditor who can by legislation make a debtor pay a dollar twice as large as he borrowed is lauded as the friend of a sound currency. [Laughter and applause.] The man who wants the people to destroy the Government is an anarchist, but the man who wants the Government to destroy the people is a patriot. [Applause.]

In concluding, Bryan demonstrated that he was indeed keenly attuned to the epochal changes taking place in that watershed decade. As he saw it, his party had arrived at a "parting of the ways." "On the one side stand the corporate interests . . . , its moneyed institutions, its aggregations of wealth and capital: imperious, arrogant, compassionless. They demand special legislation, favors, privileges, and immunities." Pitted against these forces and pleading for help, standing on the other side, was "that unnumbered throng which gave a name to the Democratic party and for which it has assumed to speak." Which would it be? As we resolve that question, said Bryan, let us consult with the memory of the man "whose dust made sacred the soil of Monticello." Unlike scholars of our day who have only just begun to rediscover a Jefferson they never knew—he of the Scottish Enlightenment influence—Bryan had not lost touch. With whom would they identify? Bryan asked. The Jefferson he knew "was called a demagogue and his followers a mob, but [he] . . . dared to follow the best prompting of his heart. He placed man above matter, humanity above property, and, spurring the bribes of wealth and power, pleaded the cause of the common people. It was this devotion to their interests which made his party invincible while he lived and will make his name revered while history endures."

He then asked, "And what message comes to us from the Hermitage? When a crisis like the present arose and the national bank of his day sought to control the politics of the nation, God raised up an Andrew Jackson, who had the courage to grapple with that great enemy, and by overthrowing it, he made himself the idol of the people and reinstated the Democratic party in public confidence. What will the decision be to-day? The Democratic party has won the greatest success in its history [in the 1892 elections]. Standing upon this victory-crowned summit, will it turn its face to the rising or the setting sun? Will it choose . . . life or death—which? Which?"

With that close, the secretary noted "prolonged applause on the floor and in the galleries, and cries of 'Vote!' 'Vote!' "[26] That would not happen until twelve days later. The final count would be 239 for repeal and 108 against.[27] In the process, Grover Cleveland did a thorough wrecking job on his party, preparing the way for the most severe sectional split since the great struggle that had culminated in the Civil War.

The debate in the Senate assumed the full spotlight after the vote in the House, and there was some reason to believe that the administration's drive might be stopped there—by filibuster, if need be. The eastern press was overwhelmingly on the side of those seeking repeal, and editorial opinion was engaged in that cause with no holds barred. In his speech against repeal, Senator James Kyle took notice of that effort, saying that nothing was gained by references to those who opposed Cleveland's effort as "obstructionists," "cranks," and "lunatics." My "honest conviction is," said the South Dakota Populist, that the Sherman Act "has no more to do with the financial crisis than the moons of Jupiter, except as it may exist in the imagination of frightened tradesmen." Who was truly suffering from a case of lunacy? asked Kyle. The core of Kyle's explanation for the nation's plight was contained in this passage:

> The great disaster in the Argentine Republic was followed by the failure of the Baring Brothers. . . . Austria, Hungary, and Roumania have been collecting a reserve and getting to a gold basis. . . . Our castles of credit have been built with lavish expenditure on all continents. [And] . . . beyond this still, Europe ceased to buy our products. . . . But the real cause of the panic . . . is deeper and well concealed. . . . The prime cause of the universal depression, which is not confined to the United States, is the appreciation of the gold dollar and the consequent depreciation of all commodities as measured by it. Depression has not suddenly appeared like an apparition. Agriculture has felt her clammy hand for a score of years. The present hue and cry is raised because, forsooth, the capitalist has been touched.[28]

Sensible and intelligent arguments like these were to no avail. The administration was determined. No compromises and no delays were to be tolerated. Anyone opposing the president was, if at all possible, made to feel the heat. On 30 October, the vote came. By forty-two to thirty-two, with ten not voting, the repeal was accomplished. Enough gold-standard Democrats and gold-standard

Republicans combined to give Cleveland his remedy, made easier by the fence-straddlers (a number of whom were cowed conservative westerners—neither goldbugs nor silverbugs but "straddlebugs," it was said). It was a Pyrrhic victory if ever there was one.[29]

John Avery, a Republican representative from Michigan, may have captured the insanity of it all as well as anyone with these lines: "I shall vote for the repeal . . . not because I believe it to be the sole or principal cause of the . . . distress of the country, nor because I expect any considerable relief to the business of the country . . . , but because the law . . . has served its purpose, and is made the scapegoat by the Democratic party for all the evils that have followed their advent to power. Its repeal will demonstrate to them and to the country that they have loaded their sins upon the wrong goat."[30]

Just before the final vote, Senator Peffer made some brief remarks that summed up the session rather well from the Populist perspective, while at the same time foretelling the extent to which the national economic collapse and Cleveland's special session had reprogrammed the political landscape. As he saw it, "This sixty days' debate has unmasked the power which oppresses. We now see the hand that smites us. Money is king!" It was now clear to him that "a great struggle . . . approaches—it is at hand even now. His horizon is narrow, indeed, who does not see a mighty people rising."[31] The people were indeed rising, and the "battle of the standards" was taking shape. Before the fight was over, the nation would be absolutely polarized along monetary lines.

Congress thus moved to close on 3 November, with two of the Populist senators, Allen and Peffer, pleading futilely with their colleagues not to adjourn and to do something to assist the millions of destitute people throughout the country. As Peffer said, "We can lawfully put men who are out of employment to work. The Government has authority to construct public buildings, . . . to construct railways, to build ships, to bring water upon arid lands, to open waterways, to clean out harbors, to do a thousand and one different things . . . the people of the country need to have done,"[32] but only if it subscribed to the role of government championed by the Populists. Cleveland's view was that the "support of the people" was not one of the functions of the general government. Although usually not put so bluntly or candidly, Cleveland's view was accepted as the national orthodoxy. Peffer's statement that "money is king" was just another way of phrasing that waggish version of the Golden Rule, which, if not inspired by this historical episode, should have been: "Those who have the gold make the rules." Money, whether paper or silver, especially when made the equivalent of gold, was truly king.

4

Speed Bumps on the Yellow Brick Road, 1893–1895

When McKinley gets the chair, boys, / there'll be a jollification / throughout our happy nation / and contentment everywhere! / Great will be our satisfaction / when the "honest money" faction / seats McKinley in the chair!

No more ample crops of grain / that in our granaries have lain / will seek a purchaser in vain / or be at the mercy of the "bull" or "bear"; / our merchants won't be trembling / at the silverites' dissembling / when McKinley gets the chair!

When McKinley gets the chair, boys, / the magic word "protection" / will banish all dejection / and free the workingman from every care; / we will gain the world's respect / when it knows our coin's "correct" / and McKinley's in the chair!

L. Frank Baum, *Chicago Times-Herald*, 12 July 1896[1]

DEPRESSION AND TAXATION

On 4 December 1893, the second session of the Fifty-third Congress opened. Winter was fast approaching, and the depression was deepening. By then, congressmen were frequently referring to 3 million or 4 million destitute people across the land. In the upper chamber, Senators Allen and Peffer immediately resumed their effort aimed at getting Congress to do something about the situation. A few months earlier, Peffer had introduced a bill providing \$63.3 million to be dispensed to the states for relief purposes.[2] He proposed to fund the measure by using silver dollars "lying idle in the Treasury." In an accompanying speech, the Kansan used newspaper clippings from all over the country to make his case for critical need.

It had not escaped Peffer's notice that just as the previous session closed, Congress had been considering aid for the victims of a hurricane in South Carolina; clearly, the country was also within the eye of a storm and experiencing an even greater disaster—an economic cyclone. Peffer asked, "What are we going to do about this situation?" He conceded that conventional wisdom would raise all kinds of objections to "this class of legislation." The argument was heard that the "Constitution provided for nothing of the kind." His answer was: "There are great occasions . . . when nations, communities, and individuals may call to their aid powers which, under ordinary circumstances, are not known to exist." The Senate document room clerk had aided Peffer in preparing a list of individual cases in which Congress had come to the aid of destitute citizens. Even armed with such a list, Peffer knew that he would encounter strong arguments that what he proposed was beyond the scope of federal power. "Perhaps it is," said Peffer, "but if it is, let the people understand it. The time is coming . . . when for all such purposes as this state lines must be utterly abolished."[3]

In this area, Peffer and company were only one great depression and four decades ahead of their time. After seeing their more important measures ignored or ridiculed, Peffer and Allen both occasionally directed their fire at the Senate itself, especially at its perquisites, such as the extra-mileage legislation that came before the Senate in December 1893 or the resolution of inquiry introduced by Senator Allen the following month regarding the restaurant and clerks serving the Senate. By exposing and contrasting what they regarded as congressional excesses with what was going on throughout the land, they seemed intent on shaming their opponents into doing something for the destitute. In support of his Senate restaurant inquiry, for example, Allen said: "There is suffering in this country to-day. Throughout portions of our nation there is great suffering. Thousands and hundreds of thousands of poor human beings are to-day walking up and down the earth without a habitation, with scarcely clothing enough to cover their nakedness and with scarcely food enough to satisfy their hunger. Their condition is becoming intensified each day and each week." Would it not be better, he asked, to cut out the money "wasted" on various extravagances of this kind, petty though they may be, and "appropriate it in some form for the relief of the hungry and the distressed?"[4]

The debate over taxation policies in this second session was one of the more important and revealing of the 1890s. It involved the tariff as a protective device and a revenue measure and, more importantly, as an income tax. Ultimately, it would culminate in the passage of the Wilson-Gorman tariff, to which was attached a modest income tax. The latter measure was destined to be declared unconstitutional by a hyperconservative and property-conscious U.S. Supreme Court. This debate got under way in the House in January 1894. Republicans generally favored protective rates amounting to corporate subsidies, Democrats supposedly favored tariffs for revenue only, and Populists were opposed to tariffs in nearly all forms. Certainly Jerry Simpson, as he readily admitted on several occasions, was "an absolute free trader." And in the debates that month, not long before being stricken with his heart ailment, Simpson was at the top of his form in speaking out against protective tariffs enjoyed by manufacturing interests, as were a number of other Populists. Haldor Boen, the Norwegian-born Minnesota farmer, who rarely spoke for the record, prepared what was probably the best speech of his tenure in opposition to the tariff. The bottom line, said Boen, was that "the banker, the manufacturer, the common carrier, all regard the farmer as their legitimate prey, and he humbly submits. But whether he submits or not there is no redress. The whole machinery of legislation is against him; the courts are unfriendly, the executive immovable." Speaking from experience, he said that he was forced to sell his "goods in a free-trade market" and to purchase what he needed from "a protected market." Not surprisingly, he concluded, "The result is disastrous."[5]

T. J. (Thomas Jefferson) Hudson, an attorney with two college degrees who, at various stages of his life, had been a prosecuting attorney, banker, teacher, and mayor of the small southeastern Kansas town of Fredonia, followed Boen in the debate and said, among other things, that he might be persuaded to support a protective tariff when and if the nation's laws could guarantee that those who benefit from protection would be required to share the profits of production equitably with their workers and that those same workers would be entitled to a hearing before their "wages shall be cut" or they be "discharged." In his view, "Protection is the hot-house wherein is bred and force-fed the noxious weeds of monopoly, combines, trusts, stock gambling, and vicious classes, each and all of which are unrepublican, undemocratic, unjust, un-American, and a thousand times more dangerous to the liberty of our people than all the anarchists and socialists in the world."[6] Hudson went on to call for a graduated income tax, one of the key components of the Populist platform. In this speech, he laid out in detail the schedule that he regarded as best suited to the purposes for which it was designed: $4,000–$9,999 income, 1 percent tax; $10,000–$24,999, 2 percent; $25,000–$49,999, 3 percent; $50,000–$99,999, 4 percent; $100,000 and up, 5 percent.

Hudson insisted that his schedule "lays the burdens on those possessing the ability to pay, and compels those who reap the largest harvests under the sunshine of our generous institutions to give more of that harvest for the common good." He quickly added that he did not expect this piece of legislation by itself "to relieve the distress of the country." The causes were much "deeper than the tariff question." The situation was the "result of an erroneous financial policy more than any other cause. . . . The reason that the mills and factories are stopped is because of the want of consumers. You can not have a market at home or abroad unless you can find people with sufficient money to buy your products." And the "great mass of consumers, those who furnish the real market, are the wage-earners in every department of life."

What the nation needed to do, said Hudson, was "open up our silver mines, coin all the seigniorage in the Treasury, coin all the silver that can be brought to our mints, let the people . . . understand that the Government . . . proposes to furnish them plenty of money . . . with which to pay their debts, furnish employment to all idle hands, and prosperity will again dawn upon our country." Added Hudson, "Let there be no talk of issuing bonds, which only prolongs the misery and deepens the wrong. There is no necessity of our failing to fulfill our contract with our creditors while we are caring for the interests of our people. But if there were, I would compel every bondholder in Europe and in the United States, to wait a year before I would permit an orphan in all this broad land to go to bed hungry for even a single night." Hudson ended his speech at that point, with the secretary noting "great applause."[7]

William McKeighan, the Populist farmer from Nebraska, stated his party's position on taxation as succinctly as anyone in the tariff debate:

> We are in favor of taxation as nearly direct as possible, and in proportion to wealth. We are therefore . . . in favor of an income tax as the chief means of raising public revenue, and we believe . . . this tax should be so adjustable as to reach invested wealth. So far as such taxes can be substituted . . . we would abolish indirect taxation; and, therefore, we would gradually, but as speedily as possible, abolish the entire tariff. We know for certain . . . tariffs call for revenue in proportion to the necessities of each man's family, instead of in proportion to either his income or his accumulated wealth. We want to put an end to that system and to establish in taxation, as in everything else, the rule of fairness, equality, and justice.[8]

The same day that McKeighan was making his speech in the House, Senator Peffer introduced an important Populist bill in the Senate. Designed to deal with the economic crisis, it was a comprehensive and far-reaching proposal that undoubtedly would have dealt the depression a heavy blow; it would, of course, go nowhere, except to a committee to be buried.[9]

The following day, McKeighan was at it again on the House side. Interjecting himself into the case being made by the protectionists, he proceeded to let them know what he believed their position amounted to, "stripped of all its sophistry and all its hypocrisy." It was all a confidence game aimed at plundering the consumer while subjecting farmers to unfair trade practices. What have you done? asked McKeighan. "You have shut the farmers out from the markets of the world, until to-day we are feeding wheat to our hogs. You say there is an overproduction of wheat, though thousands of people in this country can not get enough of it to eat, and when . . . there are 150,000,000 of people in the Old World who never eat wheat bread. When gentlemen talk about overproduction, they will pardon me for saying . . . there is an unjust distribution, not an overproduction. There is no overproduction of any useful thing in this country, but there is an overproduction of legalized robbers, rogues, fools, and scoundrels." That line drew a mixture of "laughter and applause."[10]

As this debate continued, a wide array of arguments and observations were forthcoming. John Davis added his opposition to a protective tariff and presented his own version of a graduated tax that resembled Hudson's, except that Davis would impose a 10 percent tax on incomes between $100,000 and $500,000. William Baker delivered a speech notable primarily for the extent to which it drew on the economic thought of Abraham Lincoln as it related to the labor theory of value. And Lafayette Pence made the longest and most fact-filled speech by a

Populist in opposition to the tariff on one day and then took more time the next day to present yet another Populist version of a graduated income tax schedule, his being less steep than the others and containing a lower exemption base of $2,000.

Jerry Simpson, who was chided by Republicans for being the "leader of the Democrats in the House" because of his outspoken opposition to the tariff, managed to draw some laughter at one point by interjecting the opinion that "combines grow out of protection as naturally as toadstools out of a rotten log." Then, after days of seeing the House grant concessions of one kind or another to various manufacturing interests, he challenged the House to do something to assist farmers; he then proposed an amendment to put barbed wire on the free list. The amendment passed, and by the time it had worked its way through the Senate, one wit had suggested that whereas donkeys and elephants were important party emblems, barbed wire would be an appropriate symbol for the Populist party, since its members seemed to specialize in prickly politics and in irritating anything and everything they touched.[11]

Toward the close of this debate, Nebraska's Omer Kem delivered a speech devoted, as he said, "wholly to that part [of the bill] relating to the income tax." In it, he signaled that the Populists were going to vote for the Wilson amendment (sponsored by William Wilson, Democrat from West Virginia and chair of the House Ways and Means Committee) providing for an ungraduated income tax of 2 percent on personal incomes over $4,000. He said, "If we can get nothing better, this being such a vast improvement on the present iniquitous system, I shall give it my most hearty support."[12] This House included 215 Democrats, 125 Republicans, and 11 Populists.[13] The vote on the tariff bill came on 1 February; the yeas were 204 and the nays 140, with 8 not voting. All the Populists voted yea. In the end, the bill likely pleased very few. And an even harder fight awaited the measure in the Senate, where the Democrats' control was tenuous, with 40 Democrats, 38 Republicans, and 3 Populists seated.[14]

Soon after this vote, the House was busy discussing, debating, and passing numerous other measures. There was, however, no escaping the depression. In February, it passed a silver bullion bill mandating coinage of the seigniorage, the difference in value between the cost of bullion and the value of the minted coin. The bill passed by a vote of 168 to 129, with 56 not voting. All 11 Populists supported the measure. It would later be approved by the Senate and then vetoed by President Cleveland, who was sustained on the vote to override.

In early March, Hudson was taken to task by William Bourke Cockran, a leading New York Democrat and arguably the most powerful orator on Cleveland's "gold squad," for his remarks during the income tax debate about certain wealthy people being less than public spirited. Hudson's reply was revealing and added to his growing reputation as quite a feisty fellow:

> I . . . said that the very rich, while there were a great many notable exceptions, were selfish, autocratic, overbearing, and mean; and when I made the

> remark I had not thought that anyone would question the truthfulness of my assertion, particularly a gentleman who professes to believe in the teachings of the Savior of mankind, who said upon a notable occasion that "It is easier for a camel to pass through the eye of a needle than for a rich man to enter the kingdom of Heaven."
>
> My language was nothing like so strong as that of Jesus of Nazareth. I was not attacking the very rich; I was only stating a truism for the sake of illustrating an argument. I said in the same statement that there were many honorable and charitable gentlemen belonging to the very rich class, and for those I had only the kindest words. I am not finding fault with the rich because they are rich. I am finding fault with that system which permits men to become immensely rich at the expense of the many, thereby bringing about that selfish and autocratic condition or characteristic which has always been markedly peculiar to the very rich.

After offering up two rather notorious examples (Vanderbilt and Astor), Hudson said that, if desired, he could come up with more examples of "autocratic," "overbearing," "mean," and "tyrannical" statements made by wealthy individuals. And if his effort aimed at "relieving the common people, including the old soldiers, of the unjust burdens . . . they now bear . . . be treason," he said, "gentlemen, make the most of it. It is but continuing in the line of the doctrines taught by Thomas Jefferson and Abraham Lincoln, and if this is demagogy I am glad to stand in line with such notable demagogues."[15]

Hudson was speaking on behalf of a relief fund and veterans pensions. In the course of the speech, he suggested that congressmen join him in agreeing to donate the $240,000 Congress had appropriated to itself for extra mileage expenses for relief of the needy. It was remarks and moves of this nature that suggested to more than a few of their more conservative, hagridden opponents the aptness of barbed wire as the Populist symbol. One suspects that members of the tiny delegation would relish and embrace—albeit carefully—that particular symbol as their own—proof that they had indeed made their presence felt in the chambers.

On 8 March 1894, this House enacted what must have been one of the earliest—if not the first—environmental measures passed at the federal level, which might be taken, in retrospect, as a sign of the times. It was a bill extending an 1885 act regarding the Potomac River. One of its sections was clearly aimed at curtailing manufacturing pollution on the waterway and it passed without a single objection.[16]

The national capital also entered into the debate over the role of government in yet another way. While discussing an appropriations bill for the District of Columbia, which contained a proviso pertaining to municipal facilities, Kem used that proposal to clarify the Populist position on the role of government generally. He began by stating that he saw it as fundamental that, "so far as it is possible, . . . no corporation or combination of men shall control any of the necessities of the people." In accordance with that principle, said Kem, "I believe each municipality should control these necessities, such as local transportation of freight, humanity, or intelligence, water systems, and lighting plants, by its own municipal government. I believe in forming a monopoly of all the people to control the necessities of all the people for the sole benefit of all the people of each municipality. And in cases where the necessities are national, affecting the interests of the whole people, I believe it is the duty of the national government to take control of them in the interest of the people."

The term was not used, but deprivatization was their goal. "Congress should never again," continued Kem, "grant a charter, franchise, or subsidy to any individual or corporation through which public necessities may be controlled." Throughout the economy, he warned, "soulless corporations" are gathering in what the many have created for the benefit of the few. "It seems to me there is no better place on earth than at the seat of this government to insert an entering wedge and begin this work of reform. It must be . . . consummated throughout . . . the land, if the masses . . . are to get the relief to which they are entitled."[17] In line with Kem's thinking, several months later, this House would pass a bill creating a "national home for colored persons" in the nation's capital with all Populists voting in the affirmative.[18]

In early April, over the course of four days, Senator Peffer delivered one of his better speeches on tariff and taxation policies. It was a subject he had studied and written about for years. He proposed doing away "with all duties, except on a few articles, beginning with those that are most necessary among the people of limited resources." He also strongly endorsed a graduated income tax, and at one point indicated that he favored "a graduated tax on large landed estates." As for the unemployed, Peffer repeated his call for putting millions of people to work. In his words, "I believe that society ought to furnish them employment, and if we were not hampered and restricted by constitutional environment, I should insist that this body . . . present within thirty days to the President . . . a bill providing employment for these men and these women, all of them wherever they may be in every part of the United States." He went on to recommend putting "unemployed people to work at building a great double track freight railway from the Pacific Ocean to the Atlantic, and another from the Northern Lakes down to the Gulf. . . . I would start all the unemployed men at work and pay them good wages at the end of every week."[19]

Populist suggestions of this kind were nothing short of wild and preposterous nonsense to their most fervent opponents, the feverish visions of crackpots; that was how they were depicted in the conservative press of the urban-industrial Northeast.[20] As this was happening, anti-Populist backbones were stiffened considerably by all the troubles visited on what was advertised as "the first Populist government on earth" the previous year in the so-called Kansas legislative war and by some spectacular Populist infighting within the Sunflower State thereafter, all of which received generous coverage by the opposition press. At this stage, one Ohio congressman even suggested that no more states from the West be added to the Union until Kansas had been finally "civilized."[21] More than a few people were probably asking themselves a question that may be familiar to iconoclasts of all eras: "Senator Peffer can't say that, can he?" Or perhaps they were thinking in banana-republic terms of "taking ten or a dozen of their leaders out, standing them against a wall, and shooting them dead," as proposed by a brash young New York police commissioner by the name of Theodore Roosevelt. Apparently, there was no doubt in the New Yorker's mind that these leaders were "plotting a social revolution and the subversion of the American Republic."[22] Earlier, during the fight to repeal the Sherman Act, the devout young Republican had been so alarmed by the perceived threat posed by the opponents of a gold standard that he had even offered a public toast to his state's leading Democrat, President Grover Cleveland, as "a bulwark against all financial heresies!"[23] This particular specter was considerably enhanced by the next important event in the nation's capital, the arrival of the "Commonweal of Christ."

COXEY'S ARMY

In the middle of that terrible depression winter, a wealthy midwestern businessman by the name of Jacob S. Coxey conceived of the idea (the result of a dream, said he; the nightmare product of an unhinged mind, said his many critics) of a march on Washington, D.C.—a "petition with boots on"—to prod the national government into doing something positive on behalf of the many unemployed workers and hard-pressed farmers and businessmen throughout the country. Coxey's idea, actually an addendum to his own suggestion and to various proposals made earlier by congressional Populists and a handful of major-party politicians, was for Congress to issue non-interest-bearing bonds to finance public-works programs in order to prime the pump that was the American economy. By spring, Coxey's "commonwealers" were organized and ready to go, with the nation's press increasingly infatuated by the unprecedented procession. On Easter Sunday, the marchers set out from Coxey's hometown of Masillon, Ohio, and were soon being emulated across the West with other "armies" originating in San Francisco, Portland, Seattle, Los Angeles, and points nearby and in between. Historians of the movement identified seven major pilgrimages in addition to Coxey's original contingent, all headed to the nation's capital to seek relief from the national government.[24]

As in the case of Populism, "Coxeyism" signified what historian Carlos Schwantes called a "double-barreled assault on the fundamental beliefs of [mainstream] Americans." As he saw it, "Not only did it seek to educate them into accepting a certain amount of federal responsibility for the economic health of the nation; but the very existence of the crusade—and especially its prominence in the West—undermined the popular belief that the fertile agricultural lands of the frontier represented America's most practical form of social security and a wise alternative to governmental paternalism."[25]

Indeed, at stake in this crisis was no less than "the traditional meaning of America" itself.[26] No event better reflected the fact that the 1890s was truly the watershed decade in the rise of modern America, as preeminent historian Henry Steele Commager recognized many years ago. As the larger society was stretched to the breaking point, the two movements, each in their own way, "straddled" the "great divide" that characterized the age. Coxeyism, like Populism, had its origins in "a popular belief in the continued viability of grass-roots democracy, and from its many opponents it elicited [extreme and bitter] condemnations firmly grounded in the self-reliant, agrarian tradition of the older America." And, we might add, Coxeyites, like Populists earlier and later, drew heavy fire from the camp of the newer yet supremely self-confident urban-industrial America. Both movements gave unmistakable expression to the hope for an immediate solution to the problem of massive unemployment, and both were mass democratic movements that, in Schwantes's words, "called into question the underlying values of the new industrial society."[27] And for all that, perhaps they needed no reminder that prophets were indeed not without honor, except in their own country and their own houses.

The disrepute and scorn arising from the march were plainly evident on the floor of Congress. On 19 April, as the odyssey of the unemployed approached the capital and the press stepped up its coverage, Senator Peffer introduced a resolution calling for the creation of a select committee to meet with the group. Senator Allen also used the occasion to deliver a speech strongly supportive of the marchers and of the right of American citizens to petition their government in person. As for those who insisted that the seat of government would be dishonored by their presence, Allen stated: "The Capitol grounds . . . are very sacred, indeed, . . . but when railroad lobbyists, tax lobbyists, bank lobbyists, and all the other lobbyists who infest this city and these Capitol grounds, come here everything is thrown open to them from cellar to dome; there is no restriction upon them; but when Mr. Coxey comes marching along with his army of the commonweal to petition Congress for the redress and relief of the masses . . . , he is to be met and not permitted to enter the Capitol grounds, to say nothing of this sacred Senate chamber."[28]

Opposition to Peffer's resolution was quick in coming. The following day, Senator Joseph Hawley, a Connecticut Republican and former Civil War general, who ironically would ultimately cast his vote for Peffer's resolution, said he did not believe "that the men who are coming here . . . represent the great voice of the American people." As he saw it, "They come here to make an impression upon Congress by mere physical presence." To Allen he then addressed these lines: "I am sorry to say it, but I feel bound to say it, . . . the speech of the Senator from Nebraska was one that would have been received with tumultuous applause in a meeting of anarchists. It had in it, not requiring a microscope, but visible to the naked eye, the bacteria and bacilli of anarchy."[29]

Following the defeat of Peffer's resolution by a vote of twenty-six to seventeen, Allen put forward another one reaffirming the right of American citizens to petition their government. It was in remarks against this resolution that Edward Wolcott, a Yale- and Harvard-educated Republican senator from Colorado, made his comments about "socialism and populism and paternalism run riot."[30] Allen managed to interject that he resented the implication of remarks by several senators that he was "advocating the cause of lawless classes." Then, after the arrest of Coxey and others for trespassing and illegally parading on the White House grounds, he made himself their major advocate by introducing a resolution calling for a senatorial investigation of their arrest. On 9 May, Allen also read into the record the speech Coxey was prevented from reading on Capitol grounds. Earlier, in police court, where he, T. J. Hudson, and Lafayette Pence had gone to serve as counsel for the protesters, Allen in a long and impassioned speech made a special point of emphasizing that he did not go into court merely to argue the unconstitutional nature of the statute under which the petitioners had been arrested but to plead the case of the American people. As he saw it, "the rough hand that was laid upon Mr. Coxey was laid upon the rights of seventy millions of American citizens." It was a blow, he said, "aimed at the head of every man in this country who may see proper to raise his voice in defense of his constitutional rights; it was a blow at free speech, at the right of free constitutional assemblage, that is granted to every citizen of the United States by the Constitution of this nation." At the time, the Senate was considering tariff legislation, prompting Allen to say that, important as he regarded that issue to be, it was "a mere atom floating upon the ambient air as compared with the constitutional right of American citizens to peacefully assemble and peacefully speak their minds with reference to the public policy of the nation and to peacefully petition any branch of the government for a redress of their grievances."

Allen was followed briefly by John Sherman of Ohio, at that moment probably the upper chamber's and the nation's most influential Republican. He advised his fellow Ohioans to go back home and remind themselves that it was better they bear their "ills" than heed the advice of Populists—or, in his words, "fly to others that they know not of." Sectional polarization was much in evidence. Another senior Republican, Senator George Frisbie Hoar of Massachusetts, responding to remarks by Senator William Stewart of Nevada, equally as senior and just as vintage Republican, said the "one thing we will not do is to lay down our constitutional functions and be clamored out of our character as American legislators by any mob spirit, whether it finds its utterance from Coxey's car or from the seat of the Senator from Nevada."[31] Stewart, a silver Republican who had proclaimed himself a Populist the previous year as a result of Cleveland's move to repeal the Silver Purchase Act, had spoken out earnestly in defense of the marchers, saying that "thousands of others walked on the grass before Coxey and weren't arrested." As he saw it, making a "martyr" of the man, "however misguided he may be, is a dangerous experiment."[32]

Stewart was not the only prominent western conservative to break ranks over the issue. Obviously deeply troubled, Henry Teller, Colorado's venerable Republican senator, found himself at odds with his state's other Republican senator and with nearly all his northeastern brethren of both old parties. Speaking in favor of Allen's resolution, Teller stated that he knew it was not "fashionable for a man to stand here and speak for the lowly and distressed. I know a man loses caste in the financial circles of the country when he does so." As he saw it, the situation more than justified his stand; the country had arrived at a critical moment: "There never has been an hour in American history, even in the great panics that preceded the panic of 1893, when there has been so much poverty, so much distress, so much danger to the Republic as there has been in the last year. It is growing worse and not better, and we have not put our hands to a single thing in this Congress that in my judgment is calculated to relieve the condition. . . . The outlook is not bright for the American farmer and the American laborer, who compose nine-tenths of the American people. If we can not do anything else, if we can not help them in any other way, we can at least show some sympathy with them."[33] But despite the effort, the marchers and the destitute had to make do without a formal declaration of sympathy by Congress.

AN EMBLEM FOR POPULISTS?

At the conclusion of the Senate's discussion of how to respond to Coxey's army, Peffer introduced another resolution that has disappeared into the musty document file of time but was a significant move in the nation's political-economic evolution. The Kansas Populist proposed that the Senate create a select committee for the purpose of looking into the causes of the panic and the ensuing depression, leading to appropriate recommendations regarding "what legislation, if any," it deemed necessary to cope with the situation. Peffer reasoned that Congress and the national government were obligated to exercise power and authority not only to assist those severely impacted by economic collapse but also to consider what steps could and ought to be taken for recovery and to avoid a repetition of similar economic disasters. His proposal, though quite sensible in hindsight to all but the most extreme antistatists, was, like so much else being proposed by congressional Populists, "too early in the season" and destined to be "frost bitten," as a devout anti-Populist would later put it.[34]

Fortunately, at least for history's sake, the "frost" did not obliterate the record of this early season; it merely buried it for a time. The remaining sessions of the Fifty-third Congress were lively and arguably the most instructive of any regarding the political response to the nation's ongoing crisis. Senator Peffer's finest senatorial hour to that point may have come on 1 June, during a speech he delivered in support of an income tax. It was then that he was drawn into a colloquy with George Hoar of Massachusetts, during which the teetotaling Kansan avoided being baited into blaming the consumption of intoxicating liquors for the nation's extreme maldistribution of wealth. Abuse of alcohol, Peffer told Hoar in no uncertain terms, was not "the taproot of the evil." There was, he believed, as much or more drunkenness among the "elite of society to-day than ever before." The basic cause, he insisted, was to be found in general economic and governmental policies—particularly policies that favored the rich over the poor, such as the nation's regressive consumption taxes, which, he went on to argue, should be replaced by a graduated income tax. That same exchange prompted Peffer to voice his support for an early version of what would come to be called social security.[35]

One of the clearer statements regarding the connection between hard times and declining purchasing power had come earlier, from one of Peffer's Kansas colleagues in the House, William Baker. Asked to explain why factories were closing their doors in the Philadelphia area despite continued high profits, Baker agreed with an interjection by John Davis that supply was being curtailed to maintain profits, and added this: "By the repeal of the Sherman law placing us on a gold basis and thereby reducing one-half of the basis upon which money of this country has rested, reducing the value of the products of labor, doubling the value of tariff duties, you have thereby destroyed in a great measure the purchasing power of the people. There is one thing this House must learn before prosperity comes to our country, that is, that you [can]not destroy the power of the people to consume and expect consumption to be in a normal and healthy condition. Wealth is not produced by spontaneous growth."[36]

The following month, Baker also delivered what was probably the best speech of his tenure in the debate generated by the move to repeal the 10 percent tax on state bank notes—a move that the Populists all opposed, even though they recognized that it might provide, as Baker himself conceded, "temporary relief." In addressing this issue, Baker ranged far and wide, developing his explanation of why the country was experiencing such hard times. "We have, on the one hand, enormous accumulations of capital held by our privileged classes." And on the other hand, "the gap between the necessities of our people and their ability to supply them has widened from day to day. Their homes are passing rapidly into the hands of the capitalists. The distress in our metropolitan districts is without parallel in our history. The press is filled from day to day with news of strikes, starvation, failures, suicides, and crimes. The juggernaut of the privileged classes is crushing out the lives of the masses." Since the Civil War, said Baker, "we have adopted principles well suited to the interest of our wealthy classes."

After referring to the economic situation confronting the nation, Baker asked, how was it to be explained? On the House floor, he said, one heard a "wonderful diversity of opinion in regard to it." It was not the tariff by itself, as some had claimed. He had even heard it said on the floor that "it might be necessary to have another war to bring prosperity to the country." But he wanted it understood that "wealth is not created by the elements of destruction." In his view, the answer resided in an inadequate and inflexible monetary system and excessive taxation—

taxation of a kind that worked to destroy the purchasing power of the masses. Some, especially in the camp of the privileged few, had talked about letting nature take its course. "I have no sympathy with those who believe in the survival of the fittest," said Baker. People, through their government, had to intervene. As a "first step," he called for a defeat of the attempt to repeal the 10 percent tax on state bank notes, followed by legislation designed "to deprive the Secretary of the Treasury and the national banks of the power of further contracting the currency and issuing any more gold interest-bearing bonds." What was then needed was a national, public bank of issue, such as that advocated by the Populists in their Omaha platform.

Thorough Lincolnian that he was, Baker also asked the House: "Have we as a people ceased to believe in the Declaration of Independence? Our enactment of laws seems to point strongly in that direction." The country, he said, had arrived at the point where "we must radically change our financial legislation or the producing classes will be reduced to vassalage."[37] Baker would be one of only three Populist incumbents—and the only Kansan—to survive the severe backlash against the party of Grover Cleveland in the 1894 election.

By June, Jerry Simpson had been seriously ill and absent for three months. The Populist House leader's absence forced others to the front, as in the case of Baker. It was in this same debate that California Populist Marion Cannon prepared some notes for a speech that he apparently did not deliver but had inserted in the record. In it, Cannon advocated what he called his "scheme," but it sounded a good deal like a variation on Thomas Mendenhall's proposal first advanced in works published in 1816 and 1834 and then advocated by Edward Kellogg.[38] His cure for the depression was a combination of the subtreasury plan and a public works program designed to put "3,000,000 idle men" to work "by furnishing money at a rate of interest that would start up all idle machinery in the country." As of now, said Cannon, "the loss to the wealth of the country, by keeping these men idle, would amount to an enormous sum. Three million men, at $1 per day, say for three hundred days in a year, would amount to $900,000,000. This is enough to build three double-track railroads from the Atlantic to the Pacific, and also to build the Nicaragua Canal, and this wealth is absolutely lost for want of a financial system that would furnish money at a low rate of interest." Cannon's close, though not without merit, might raise a few questions concerning the Ventura farmer's state of mind, although the speech was obviously written for oral delivery. It read:

> Every crank in the country has a remedy for the hard times. One class says that the Government is throttled by the gold bugs and refuses to issue an unlimited amount of greenbacks for the use of the people. The silverites say the demonetization of silver is the cause. The single taxers assert that the private ownership of land is the cause. The Prohibitionists claim that the wasting of a thousand million dollars in the purchase of whisky and beer is the cause. The woman suffragists claim that the disfranchisement of the best half of the

> people is the cause. The protectionists say that the threat of the wicked Democrats to repeal the McKinley tariff is certainly the greatest cause. The Democrats say the people have been robbed for thirty years by a high protective tariff, and this is the principal cause. The socialist says that it is because the means of production and transportation are not owned and controlled by the Government. The Populists as now organized and controlled seem to have swallowed nearly all these issues with the addition of the initiative and referendum, and lately they have tried to swallow Coxey and his . . . commonweal. Now, I suppose I must take my place among these cranks, [as] . . . I have briefly submitted my plan for relief.[39]

The dire economic situation confronting the nation continued to spawn some extraordinary proposals that would immediately be judged by many as the work of cranks or eccentrics. Among them was Peffer's suggestion early in June that the government purchase the nation's coal beds. This proposal was occasioned by the Senate's work on the tax bill. Speaking in support of a move by Democratic Senator David Hill of New York to place coal on the free list, Peffer said, "The men who have control of the coal mines are either rich individual men or they are wealthy corporations and syndicates. While every coal mine in the country and every coal field . . . ought to belong to the entire people . . . , and the coal mined and paid for at fair wages . . . , so that the people can procure it cheaply at cost." He urged the Senate to get coal "out of the hands of syndicates and corporations and wealthy individuals who control large tracts of land." Taking his proposal even further, he added, "There ought not to be a mine of coal, zinc, copper, gold, or silver owned by any private individual." No doubt Peffer was boldly extrapolating these proposals from one of his party's major planks set forth in the Omaha platform, which stated categorically that "land, including all the natural sources of wealth, is the heritage of the people, and should not be monopolized for speculative purposes." No one could accuse Peffer of being one of those plentiful politicians who viewed platforms, as Finley Peter Dunn's Mr. Dooley surely must have recognized, as "something to get in on rather than to stand on and to implement." To mainstream observers, his offhand proposal was simply further evidence of Populist political insanity. Property rights were sacrosanct to most Americans—at least among those with property to defend, and for many of those folks, it was no doubt the preeminent right—and the role of government was still, first and foremost, to maintain order and protect that property.[40]

Peffer had obviously discovered the value of Senate resolutions in getting the Populist agenda out in the open.[41] The following week, he introduced a resolution calling for the creation of a "public savings bank" that would go a long way toward accommodating the main financial reform advocated by the Populists. In the speech he delivered in support of his resolution, the senator made these remarks, which go to the core of 1890s Populism:[42]

> We must . . . eventually arrive at a system of public banking. I do not care just now to use the word government, because so many people, even statesmen, learned in law and learned in politics, have an idea, at least it so appears, that the Government is some great institution like a prince, power, or potentate, wholly disconnected from the people, whereas in the theory of our Government and the spirit of our laws and of our institutions the Government is only an agent of the people to execute the people's will.
>
> So in this resolution I have used the word "public" instead of the word "Government," but eventually it will come to that; the people will do their banking through rules and regulations provided by the Congress.[43]

Here, and on numerous other occasions, Peffer was going squarely against the predominant theory that market forces should determine the course of economic development and to a great extent politics itself, a theory that was deceptively packaged as laissez-faire. In the House the day before, Joseph C. Sibley of Pennsylvania (Peffer's native state) offered one of the few direct challenges to the theory. Sibley was an impressive speaker and an unusual Democrat who had been elected in 1892 with the support of the People's and the Prohibitionist parties. He ridiculed the doctrine of laissez-faire. It was, he said, a philosophy of "every man for himself, and the devil take the hindmost." It was, consequently, "undemocratic, both in its fibre and its essence. It is anti-Christian in its teachings, inhuman in its tendencies, and barbarous in its operation. It is the principle of negation; of indifference; of heartlessness; of stagnation, social, political, moral, and religious."

One can only wonder whether Sibley had been reading Milford Howard's newly published novel *If Christ Came to Congress.* Clearly, this Pennsylvanian was much more at home in the Populist camp than he was in the Democratic party of Grover Cleveland, and he said as much. In that part of his speech wherein he announced his support of a bill to tax options and futures trading, Sibley stated: "I do not care what the name of the party may be, if it stands by the truth. If my party shall forget its name, its traditions, and if its principles should be taken up and carried by another, I follow, regardless of party name; and if there is no party standing by the principles in which I believe, then I will go back upon my farm and have a little party all to myself."[44]

At this stage, with so many signposts popping up here, there, and everywhere, it was easy to visualize a trend that might culminate in the People's party exchanging its third-party status for major-party stature, with Grover Cleveland's Democracy as the big loser. In the Senate, Cleveland's major defender and philosophical compatriot was fellow Democrat David Bennett Hill, who in 1885 had succeeded Cleveland as New York's governor. In the debate over the income tax, Hill and the three Populist senators crossed swords on several occasions. At one point in an exchange with Allen on the subject of Populism and socialism, Hill said that he would differentiate the two as follows: "The Populist party is the Socialist party. The Socialist party is the Populist party, only a little more so. . . .

They are simply in advance of your propositions." Allen denied any significant similarities between the two but pleaded his party guilty of being committed to doing all it could to straighten out the country's priorities in order to improve the lives of the masses.

Hill's attempt at a definition had been prompted by an earlier challenge from Peffer. At the same time, Peffer had conceded that Populism did indeed mean an income tax and "a good deal more than that, and if there is to be any sort of dishonor attached to it or to anything that the Populists present, either in their platform or their speeches, I am willing to shoulder it. . . . I am proud to be a Populist." The record clearly demonstrated that this remarkable Kansas Populist was all that he claimed to be. Peffer also attempted—supported only by Allen, Kyle, Watson Squire of Washington State, and Henry Teller—to substitute a graduated schedule of income taxes for the modest flat income tax of the Wilson-Gorman tariff.

That summer of 1894, James Kyle was still identifying himself as a Populist. Coming in as an independent, the South Dakotan had managed to become chair of the Committee on Labor and Education, and from there, he accomplished something of lasting significance to the credit of congressional Populism—a kind of sympathy vote for workers, such as had been denied the previous month in the case of Coxey's legion of the unemployed. Kyle won approval on 22 June for a national holiday for labor designated as the first Monday in September; four days later, the same bill passed the House without a single objection. Ironically, the credit was destined to be given to President Grover Cleveland, whose signature appeared on the bill. But if actions count for anything, the president was not a particularly good friend of labor—especially organized and politicized labor—even though he liked to think of himself as the laboring man's best friend.[45]

Combined efforts by Allen, Peffer, and Kyle on behalf of a graduated income tax also prompted David Hill to call 22 June "Populist day" in the U.S. Senate. As part of that effort, Kyle made one of his better speeches. He quoted a variety of academic economists in support of his case, including Richard Ely, the professor he called "our freshest writer on modern economics. " After citing Census Bureau figures detailing a sharp maldistribution of wealth, Kyle related directly to Hill's remarks about Populists and Socialists "demanding a new distribution of wealth." Said Kyle, "I ask, in the face of the figures I have just read, who has been responsible for the 'redistribution' of the wealth during the past thirty years? It must be laid at the door of national legislation in the two Halls of Congress." And that legislation, he implied, had been passed without the people being fully informed. "If the Populists to-day are demanding in their platforms legislation for the redistribution of the wealth . . . , it is only to be by lawful means, by the enactment of just and humane laws." He asked someone to explain to him why those who owned and controlled "three-fourths of the nation's wealth," about 10 percent of the people, should not make a significant contribution "to support the Government which makes their wealth secure?" He reminded the senators, "Revolutions have occurred with less ferment than we see in the United States to-day. Nero fiddled while Rome was burning, and the capitalistic press of the United States to-day jeer and taunt the efforts of the bond-burdened serfs on the farms and in the workshops who attempt to rise from their pitiful condition."[46]

Hill answered the following day, devoting much of his speech to an attack on Populism and a defense of corporations and millionaires. It was then that Hill referred to the previous legislative day as "Populist day" and suggested an emblem for the party. He asked, "What has [the Populist party] accomplished by its victories? . . . It has secured the important concession of barbed wire. Tremendous accomplishment! Glorious result! Barbed wire is prohibited in some of the States of this union as a nuisance and dangerous to the people. Barbed wire antagonizes everybody; its sharp points stick out on every hand; it rasps everything with which it comes in contact; it attacks everybody who runs up against it. Barbed wire is the proper emblem for the Populist party."[47] That commentary drew its share of laughter, and New York's Senator Hill proved once again that he was a formidable foe and one of the leading anti-Populists in Congress. Later that year, while retaining his Senate seat, Hill would campaign to return to New York's governorship but would, like so many other Democrats in the voter backlash of that depression year, go down to defeat.

The Populists of the Fifty-third Congress were far from through antagonizing, rasping, sticking, and attacking the "leave-it-alone liquidationists" of their day. In fact, on 10 July, Peffer created quite a stir in the Senate by offering another of his resolutions. This one was occasioned by the Pullman strike and the American Railway Union boycott initiated in support of the Pullman workers at George Pullman's plant near Chicago, which by the time of this resolution was on its way to being broken by the use of a court injunction and federal troops at the direction of President Cleveland. This five-part resolution was a fair summing up of Peffer's interpretation of Populist doctrine. The first part stated that "all public functions ought to be exercised by and through public agencies." The second declared that: "all railroads employed in interstate commerce ought to be brought into one organization under control and supervision of public officers; that charges for transportation of persons and property ought to be uniform throughout the country; that wages of employees ought to be regulated by law and paid promptly in money." The third, unique to Peffer, asserted that "all coal beds ought to be owned and worked by the States or by the Federal Government; and the wages of all persons who work in the mines ought to be provided by law and paid in money when due." The fourth stated that "all money used by the people ought to be supplied only by the Government . . . ; that the rate of interest ought to be uniform in all the States, not exceeding the net average increase of the permanent wealth of the people." The last declared that "all revenues of the Government ought to be raised by taxes on the great wealth, incomes, and real values."

With the depression and the Pullman strike foremost on his mind, Peffer attempted to justify his resolution by saying, "These things teach us . . . the brotherhood of men; they teach us the necessity of one man to another; they teach us the interdependence among people." Society, he said, had undergone great changes "within the last thirty or forty years, so that whereas a few years ago every individual, with here and there an exception, had his own little patch of ground, his own pigs and sheep and a cow and fowls, so that he had within himself and within range of his family enough supplies to bridge over a few days of idleness." Look at the great cities now, said Peffer. People "are massed together, and you will find traffic is perpendicular as well as horizontal, and . . . there is no place . . . in the street or in the yard in these great bustling cities where a citizen can raise a flower or a herb without putting it into a pot." And "when the city working man's employment is stopped he is stopped; his source of livelihood is stopped; the supplies of his family are stopped; and when large numbers of these men quit work the machinery of commerce is clogged. So the time has come for employers themselves to learn that the best way to handle these situations is by fair treatment of their men; and if they can not do that, it is time for the people in their own sovereign capacity to interfere and say, 'This thing has gone far enough; thus far and no farther.' "[48]

Not surprisingly, a number of senators reacted quite negatively to Peffer's resolution. The ultimate form of rejection came when Virginia Democrat John Daniel moved a substitute measure congratulating President Cleveland for his actions in the Pullman strike, which passed without difficulty, as did a similar measure in the House.[49]

Several days later, Allen offered a personal explanation occasioned by a newspaper story charging that the Nebraska senator had been "under the influence of intoxicating liquors and [had been] indecorous in [his] . . . conduct." Times were certainly tense, and Populism's more determined foes were considering all the means at their disposal. It would not be the last time such charges were made against congressional Populists. Allen stated that he believed that there was "an organized attempt to have misleading and untruthful reports sent out to the country about Senators and Representatives who are known as Populists, in the hope that under the lash of the press they can be restrained from doing their duty toward the country as they understand it."[50] Perhaps, as prominent Republican leader and Kansas Senator John J. Ingalls said in a widely circulated interview a few years earlier, just as the People's party was being formed in his state, in politics, as in war, "it is lawful to deceive the adversary, to hire Hessians, to purchase mercenaries, to mutilate, to destroy." In reality, said Ingalls, "the decalogue and the golden rule have no place in a political campaign."[51] Can there be any doubt that the brigade of dirty tricks of Richard Nixon's presidency was as old as the radical specter, if not older?

Deep into that hot and sultry summer, the battle over the role that government should play in the midst of a depression was fought on the floor of Congress. Early in August, Omer Kem delivered an important speech on behalf of an appropriations bill for irrigation projects. The Nebraskan stated that he had concluded that the only way to handle the task was "by nationalizing the system and placing the distribution of water under control of Federal law that shall apply throughout the entire arid region alike." He quickly added that he did not expect his suggestion to "meet the approval of a majority of this Congress, for I have long since discovered that it is built on the way-back plan, and belongs to ages that were."

Once again, Kem used the issue at hand as an opportunity to advance the following Populist objective: "national control of all matters which are not strictly local in their nature and effect, such as railway, telegraph, and telephone lines, finance, and irrigation." Great savings to the people, he insisted, could be had by this approach. "We should abolish the present system, by which corporations control these great public necessities and build up colossal fortunes for a few by robbing the many. These necessities should be controlled by one gigantic corporation, composed of the whole people." Kem went on to insist that his "people are not asking something for nothing. We simply ask that the nation shall do for us that which is so essential to our welfare, and that which is impossible for us to do in a proper manner for ourselves, and give us proper time in which to reimburse the Government for all it expends." It was not "paternal gifts" they wanted; it was fraternal assistance. He then devoted the rest of his remarks to illustrating, as Populists did on many occasions, that the country had been practicing governmental paternalism for the benefit of the favored few for years in a multitude of different ways.[52]

The previous June, John Davis had introduced a bill containing one of the bolder antidepression proposals to be suggested by a Populist. In it, the Kansan directed "the immediate enlistment of 500,000 men to be fed, clothed, paid, and provided for, the same as the regular Army; said army to be employed on works of public improvement, canals, rivers, and harbors, irrigation works, public highways, etc." It was an extraordinary proposal and clearly an important forerunner to several programs that would one day seem not so heretical to many people faced with another great depression. Davis's bill contained the prefatory comment that "the wisdom of our forefathers in the preamble of the Constitution . . . made ample provision in the phrase 'to promote the general welfare' for such enlarged governmental functions and progressive economic measures as the growing needs and the emergencies of the country might require"(Davis might also have noted that within the Constitution itself, Article I, Section 8, Clause 1, is the same proviso about providing for the general welfare).[53]

On that note, the second session ended much as it had begun, with Populists demanding action and their major-party opponents basically biding their time, promoting traditional programs, and conducting business much as if the country were not caught in the grips of its worst depression ever.

"ONE OF THE FRIENDS OF HUMAN FREEDOM"

On 5 December 1894, the third session of the Fifty-third Congress was called to order. In the interval, the November elections had resulted in the defeat of a number of Democrats and Populists, so there were many lame ducks in attendance.[54] One of the more prominent losers was Jerry Simpson, who had recovered enough from his heart ailment to return to his seat. Among the many Democrats defeated was a bright and talkative lawyer, a one-time twenty-three-year-old college president from Bowling Green, Missouri, by the name of James Beauchamp ("Champ") Clark. He was just a freshman but was destined to be returned in the next election, ultimately becoming the Speaker of the House from 1911 to 1919 and nearly beating out Woodrow Wilson for the presidential nomination of his party in 1912.[55] In the course of his remarks on 11 December, Clark digressed from the subject at hand to share a humorous story he had heard about Simpson while conversing on a train with a fellow passenger from Hutchinson, Kansas. During the conversation, Clark mentioned that he had briefly practiced law in the Sunflower State as a young man, having departed in the aftermath of the grasshopper plague of the 1870s. He quickly added that it was his understanding that the state had not been bothered by grasshoppers since that time. The Kansan replied, " 'No . . . but we have got something out there that is a d—d sight worse than grasshoppers.' 'Good Heavens!' said I, 'what is it?' 'Why,' said he, 'it is JERRY SIMPSON.' " That drew some hearty laughter from the House. Clark then said:

> Mr. Chairman, I want to say—and I might just as well talk about Jerry Simpson as anything else—I want to say that when I came into this House [in 1893] I had the newspaper idea about Jerry Simpson. Finally, he got up here and made a speech on the silver question. I listened to that speech; and I want to say now, because somebody ought to state it to the American people, . . . that during the whole of that long, able and profound debate on the silver question there was not a man in this House on either side who delivered a speech that was pitched on a higher plane of political economy and human philosophy than that of Mr. Simpson. [Applause.]
>
> They say that "an open confession is good for the soul." . . . From that day to this, instead of having the newspaper idea of Jerry Simpson that he is a rantankerous, ad captandum demagogue, I have regarded him as a philosopher, as a statesman, as one of the friends of human freedom. [Someone at that point shouted out, "Why don't you save this for his eulogy when he dies?" Clark responded, "No, sir; I am going to say it while he is living."] . . . I do not care what party he trains with; I do not care what anybody says about him; I hail him as my brother, because he loves the human race; he has fought for it here; he has rendered it conspicuous service. . . . [Applause.][56]

For once in his life, at least on the record, Jeremiah Simpson seemed to be totally at a loss for words.

This Clark interlude was one of the session's few light moments. From the outset, congressmen resumed their activities on behalf of a wide range of governmental decisions and activities. Peffer wasted no time in taking to the floor to denounce President Cleveland's bond sales aimed at replenishing the gold reserve.

Twice in 1894, in February and in December, with not much success at adding to the diminishing gold reserve, the Treasury Department sold $50 million worth of gold-based, ten-year, 5 percent bonds. Few things could have infuriated Populist congressmen more. Peffer insisted that "in the early days of the Republic," these moves by the Cleveland administration would "have subjected the perpetrators to impeachment for high crimes and misdemeanors."[57] The following month, Allen also registered his strong opposition and insisted, "We have no right to load our children with a national debt." It would be better, said Allen, that "we impair some of the sacred provisions of the Constitution under which we live as to bequeath to posterity a national debt which will make them and their children the bond slaves of the debt and money holding classes of this nation for generations to come."[58]

Earlier that same month, Senator Teller, Colorado's dissident Republican, offered an astute appraisal of what his party's many congressional victories the previous November had signified. First of all, he said,

> It was not a vote of confidence in the Republican party or its managers or its methods. It was a vote of lack of confidence in the opposing party. The Democratic party were in power and the people said, "The party in power has failed to remedy the great evil existing, and we will turn to the other," not because they believed we would do it, but because of their anger. In their distress they said, "We will punish you because you have not done it when you had an opportunity." If we had been in power and the same conditions had existed we would have gone out of power as Democratic friends have gone out of power in the other House and as they will go out of power in this body after the 4th of March.

Teller also had a word for the Populists who might think that their party would somehow benefit from the crisis. He said that he had analyzed the situation, studied the Populist program, and come to this conclusion: "I do not think that the great body of the American people will endorse the Omaha platform with its vagaries and crudities. . . . I do not believe that party is ever to be a party of power. Full of good things and full of good men, it has wasted its energies and efforts in trying to do impossible and improper things." But despite Teller's gloomy prognosis for the Populists, he issued yet another apocalyptic warning: "Let the existing conditions continue another two years and where you have one socialist now you will have a hundred; where you have one strike you will have many; where you have one anarchist you will have numerous men of that character. The American Republic is on trial, and it is a crisis more fearful . . . than the crisis that was brought on by the rebellion."[59]

Teller could hardly be accused of being among the more hidebound of his Senate colleagues, but even he seemed to be inclined more toward the belief that the crisis confronting the nation was the growing threat of radicalism—perhaps best defined here as a fundamental challenge to the right of the economic system and its managers to operate without interference— rather than the conditions that spawned the radical persuasion. That point of view emerged clearly in the debate that took place in this Congress over a move to exclude anarchists from the list of those eligible for immigration to the United States. The most fearful were even willing to exclude those who were merely advocates of philosophical anarchism. Populists in the Senate and in the House played a key role in blocking the anarchist exclusion bill in this particular Congress; its advocates would have their way in a law passed in 1903.[60]

Several weeks after Teller's comments, Allen, in the course of a discussion of a bill providing for government ownership and construction of a cable to Hawaii, managed to get some of his more conservative major-party colleagues to concede that the national government had the constitutional authority to build and operate railroads. The difference between the Populists and their opponents was conceded to be one of policy and choice, not legitimate power.[61] At the conclusion of this colloquy, Allen said, "I have nothing further to say upon this amendment than simply to thank Senators for their concession of this controverted doctrine of the Populists."[62]

At about the same time, William Harris began to make his presence felt in the House due to his special expertise derived from having worked in the West nearly thirty years earlier as a civil engineer engaged in the construction of the Union Pacific transcontinental line. At the time, the Pacific railroads were defaulting on bonds that had come due, thus the whole question of what to do about the situation was open for discussion. At the end of January, working primarily from personal experience, Harris spoke about how the American taxpayers and settlers had been fleeced in the process of building the Pacific roads. At one point, the Kansas Populist responded to a general question about governmental interference with business by saying, "I am not in favor of the intrusion of the Government upon private affairs anywhere. I think it would be a great misfortune. . . . I am in favor of the Government seeing to it that these quasi-public corporations perform duties which their charters require them to perform, fairly and honestly, to the people of this country."

Unlike Peffer, whom he would replace two years later, Harris was less inclined to utilize the solution of government ownership, but he left the door open with this comment: "I believe in strengthening the Interstate Commerce Commission. I believe in strengthening the State boards of railroad commissioners, and I believe that when everything of that sort is exhausted, and there are companies that defy the law, who spit upon the authority of this country and trample upon the rights of the people everywhere, then I would invoke the supreme remedy of Government ownership against such corporations [applause], and I would see to it that the work for which they were created was performed either directly or indirectly by the Government itself."[63] Harris's approach would one day be called "progressive" and generate a much larger following than the more radical position of Peffer and the Omaha platform he embraced so fully, which was predicated on the belief that regulation was self-defeating.

Foreign affairs also gradually began to loom larger toward the close of this Congress. On 21 January, Republican Senator Henry Cabot Lodge introduced a resolution that included a call for the annexation of Hawaii. Lodge and Maine's Republican Senator William Frye were especially eager to see that accomplished. They were joined by Kyle and Allen, although the two Populists were not in total agreement as to motivation and justification. Several days after Lodge submitted his resolution, Allen introduced one of his own calling for Hawaiian annexation. After condemning the manner in which the Hawaiian government had been overthrown in January 1893, declaring it "inexcusably unlawful," Allen said that we had "suffered the wrong to go unrepaired for such a length of time that we are estopped to deny the loyalty of the present Government." Allen made it clear that he was not speaking for his party but only for himself. The core idea that seemed to dictate his none-too-consistent course was probably embodied in this line: "these islands are highly important to American interests. They are important in our transpacific trade, and we can not in justice to our own country and people suffer them to pass under the dominion of any foreign government."[64]

James Kyle was an even more avid supporter of Hawaiian annexation. Unlike Allen, he minimized and excused American involvement in the overthrow of the island's monarchy. In this area, one is likely to find the primary explanation for why Kyle gradually drifted toward the Republican camp. His views were distinctly imperialistic in nature. Ironically, during this particular discussion, he ridiculed the position of his state's senior senator, Republican Richard Pettigrew, who had delivered an anti-imperialist speech on the subject and would thereafter become more of a Populist than a Republican on most issues.[65]

The fact that the country did indeed confront an extraordinary crisis was perhaps signaled by the quick passage of an unusual bill with an unexpected sponsor: in early February, Senator John Sherman introduced a measure to appropriate $10,000 for the "suffering poor" in the District of Columbia. The bill passed without comment.[66]

On 4 March 1895, this historic Congress came to an end after the discussion of a resolution facilitating an international monetary conference. Thus, as was noted by Colorado's Lafayette Pence, the Fifty-third Congress began and ended with a discussion of the financial question, which was destined to remain on the front burner for some time to come.

5

Metamorphosis, 1894 and Afterward

I do impeach Grover Cleveland, President of the United States, of high crimes and misdemeanors on the following grounds: 1. That he has sold or directed the sale of bonds without authority of law. 2. That he sold or aided in the sale of bonds at less than their market value. 3. That he directed the misappropriation of the proceeds of said bond sales. 4. That he directed the Secretary of Treasury to disregard the law which makes United States notes and Treasury notes redeemable in coin. 5. That he has ignored and refused to have enforced the "antitrust law." 6. That he has sent United States troops into the State of Illinois without authority of law and in violation of the Constitution. 7. That he has corrupted politics to influence legislation detrimental to the welfare of the people: Therefore Be it *resolved by the House of Representatives. That the Committee on the Judiciary be directed to ascertain whether these charges are true, and if so to report to the House such action by impeachment or otherwise as shall be proper in the premises.*

Milford Wriarson Howard,*Congressional Record,*
54th Cong., 2nd sess., 23 May 1896, 5627

By 1894, the political landscape had certainly fractured in unusual ways. This was especially evident across that variegated terrain occupied by Populists and Democrats. While significant numbers of the latter moved toward the middle of the spectrum, thoroughly alienated from the party of Grover Cleveland, many of the former found themselves increasingly pulled toward that same center to wage a concerted fight against the defenders of the gold standard. Simultaneously, other Populists grew more determined to wage their fight on behalf of the entire Omaha platform on the left, while even more Republicans and Democrats rallied around the gold-standard banner on the right side of the landscape. That year, a leading Kansas Populist, G. C. Clemens, was so concerned about these developments that he took time out from a busy legal career to write a novel aimed at convincing his associates to stay the course. One of the novel's more impressive didactic devices was the parable of the old gristmill—his metaphor for why reforms that did not reach to the heart of the matter would be a disaster.[1] He pleaded with his fellow reformers to avoid tinkering, to stay the course. There was, he passionately believed, no viable halfway approach to resolving the severe crisis that gripped the nation.

Many if not most Populists would certainly have disagreed with Clemens's contention that there was no middle ground from which to battle society's ills, as would most Americans from their day *until* the general-welfare state launched by Franklin Roosevelt's New Deal came under increasingly heavier attack from the latter-day philosophical descendants of the anti-Populists of the 1890s. This was particularly the case when they learned the hard way, as in the case of the Kansas Populists, that there was a harsh limitation on voter support to be generated by their adherence to the more radical course. The same year that Clemens published his novel aimed at convincing Populists that they needed to sustain and even broaden the party's commitment to fundamental reform, Kansas Populists spurned cooperation with the state's more conservative Democrats, conducting their one and only nonfusionist campaign.[2] Their reward, as the fatally discredited incumbents in that depression year, was a crushing defeat at the hands of their Republican opponents. Thereafter, pressures in the direction of moderating the party's platform and toward coalition politics (fusion) could not be denied. The search was under way throughout the land to identify and then to emphasize the least-common-denominator issue advocated by the disparate factions seeking reform—especially among those that had become prominent following the national economic debacle of 1893. A monetary issue increasingly filled that bill, an issue that the People's party had advocated from the beginning, but only as an aspect of a much more fundamental reform of the economic system—the "free" and "unlimited" coinage of silver and gold in accord with the old quasi-official ratio of sixteen ounces of silver to one ounce of gold.

THE FIFTY-FOURTH CONGRESS

On 2 December 1895, the political consequences of the 1890s depression were graphically on display when the first session of the Fifty-fourth Congress opened. The 1894 elections had yielded a turnaround of historic proportions: Republicans gained 117 seats, while Democrats lost 113. Thomas Reed of Maine was elected Speaker, receiving 240 votes to the 95 cast for Charles Crisp of Georgia, the former Speaker. Officially, there were 244 Republicans and 105 Democrats. Colorado Populist John Bell received the vote of his six Populist colleagues present at the opening. Bell, William Baker, and Omer Kem were the only Populists to reclaim seats; they were accompanied by three new North Carolina Populists, Harry Skinner, William Strowd, and Alonzo Shuford. Alabama's Milford Howard also claimed his seat. Charles Martin from North Carolina and Albert

Goodwyn from Alabama, both of whom were involved in contested elections, would be seated much later, bringing the total number of Populist House members for this Congress to nine. This small contingent would find it increasingly more difficult in this Republican-controlled House to gain access to the floor or to garner assignments to important committees.

It was a different story in the Senate, where Peffer, Kyle, and Allen were joined by the nation's youngest senator, Marion Butler of North Carolina. Having only a slender plurality, the Republicans were literally permitted by the Populists to organize the Senate. At one point, Senator Allen was asked by Tennessee Democratic Senator Isham Harris why his party had allowed that to happen. He answered that the Populist senators were aware that they "held the balance of power." And it was their intention, he said, "to utilize that power to the fullest extent as we go along." As regards the organizational vote, Allen indicated that the Populists were confronted with two choices: "We could . . . join our forces to the Democratic party, which we did not propose to do, or we could refuse to vote, and by our negative action . . . we could permit the Republican party to take charge of the Chamber. We saw fit to do the latter. Evil was the result either way [laughter], and we chose what we considered the lesser evil."[3]

In reality, the Populist contingent in the Senate was not quite so solid as might appear on the surface. Early in the session, James Kyle, who had been drifting away from their camp for over a year, announced that he regarded himself as an "independent all the way through" and was no longer going to be bound by the Populist "caucus." It is likely that Kyle used the threat of a vote on behalf of Republican organization, given the prospect of Democratic party control, to leverage the no-vote Republican victory in the Senate. The vote came after an attempt aimed at organizing the Senate "on silver lines" went absolutely nowhere, even though there were said to be "52 friends of silver among the senators." Apparently, William Stewart, Nevada's "servant of power," as he was aptly called by his biographer, with the support of Allen, Peffer, and Butler, was the primary architect of that maneuver.[4]

From the opening, Senator Butler was active in speaking out against the financial policies of President Cleveland. The Tarheel Populist made an early special effort to prevent any additional presidential bond sales by introducing a resolution prohibiting "the issuance of interest-bearing bonds . . . for any purpose whatever, without the authority of Congress." Not long thereafter, the young senator was put to a test of wits in an exchange involving Kyle, Allen, and one of President Cleveland's staunchest defenders, Democratic Senator David Hill of New York. At one point, Hill asked Butler what North Carolina wanted. Butler gave Hill a quick and detailed answer: "I will state that she wants a just system of taxation; she wants more money, every dollar a full legal-tender dollar standing on its own bottom, not to be redeemed in gold dollars, and enough of them to maintain the stability of prices. . . . She wants a stop put to these infamous bond issues; she is opposed to increasing taxes and piling up an interest-bearing debt in times of peace; she would rather cut down expenses than increase taxes; she would rather pay debts than to pile them up. That is what she wants. Is it not plain?" Having gotten a bit more than he bargained for in the cross fire with the young southern Populist, Hill replied: "It is very plain [laughter], and it is very plain further that North Carolina is not going to get what she wants, either from the present Congress or from any other Congress for a great many years to come."[5]

The next day, Butler delivered a major speech in support of his resolution to prohibit sales of bonds by executive fiat, an action that would ultimately be approved by the Senate. At one point he alluded to the Venezuela boundary dispute of the previous year that had seen President Cleveland momentarily boost his sagging popularity by engaging in a classic case of twisting a few kinks off the British lion's tail. Said Butler, "It is perfectly absurd to think of England going to war with this country over the few acres of bog, inhabited chiefly by crocodiles, down in Venezuela." How could anyone ignore the fact that "Great Britain makes now more money annually out of this country than the whole of the disputed territory, if not more than the whole of Venezuela, is worth." The British knew that the United States was their "most valuable colony. She does not want to fight us with arms when she has already conquered us in peace; or, rather, I should say, when she has subjugated us and laid heavy tribute upon us by an industrial warfare more deadly and relentless to our interests and prosperity than any war that has been waged with sword and musket in the history of the world." As he saw it, the phenomenal outpouring of resentment that President Cleveland was able to tap into over the boundary dispute with his none-too-diplomatic defense of the Monroe Doctrine was created primarily by "industrial warfare," "hardships," and "tribute" the British had imposed on the American people. Populists, said Butler, were inclined to believe that the president's "message was used to divert the people's attention from the industrial warfare of Great Britain and to give [that country another] . . . opportunity to make a new raid upon our industries and our Treasury."[6]

Several days later, Allen resumed his fight for a measure passed in the previous Senate but rejected in the House, providing for a government-owned and -operated oceanic cable to Hawaii. The House had substituted a measure of its own providing for a privately owned and operated cable. In advocating a government cable, Allen referred to the by then failed example of the transcontinental railways to make his case against private ownership. The Pacific roads, he insisted, should have been built and operated by the general government. When a Republican senator questioned that, Allen responded: "And run them. Why not? It is paternalism, is it? Yes, that is the only trouble. There is the great bugaboo." He went on to say that he had noted a change in attitude since he had arrived in the Senate three years earlier. Government ownership of railways "is not as bad a thing now as it used to be." There were still those who would "hold up their hands in holy horror and say, 'that is populism'; 'that is paternalism'; but you never undertake to define paternalism. You undertake to scare the country with a word." At the same time, Allen renewed his call for the annexation of Hawaii.[7]

Benjamin Ryan Tillman of South Carolina commenced his long senatorial career with this Congress. As the leader of his state's agrarian forces and its former governor, he had a formidable political force behind him. He had already earned the nickname "Pitchfork Ben," after remarking that he would use his "trusty pitchfork to tickle fat Grover's ribs"once he arrived in the Capitol.[8] The anti-Cleveland Democrat was in a number of ways indistinguishable from the Populists but was nonetheless first, last, and always a southern Democrat and fiercely proud of it. At the beginning of the session, Senator William Chandler, the senior Republican from New Hampshire, commented that he believed Tillman was utilizing arguments quite similar to those of the Populists. That prompted this immediate response: "I beg the Senator's pardon. I thought the Senator understood that I am not a Populist. If I am not a Democrat there are no Democrats here."[9] Clearly, in the eyes of opponents, Tillman and "Tillmanism" were competing with something not all altogether similar called "Pefferism" or "populism" as the label for any and all radical—especially agrarian—challenges to the prevailing urban-industrial order that had emerged but was still in the process of being legitimized during the 1890s. One suspects that in the minds of most of his conservative contemporaries, this "One-Eyed Plowboy" (Tillman had been blinded in one eye as a youth) would aptly symbolize all the worst aspects of the revolt then in progress.

Despite his southern and party connections, Tillman would also do quite well as the prototype for the Wicked Witch of the West a few years later in the minds of L. Frank Baum and his cartoonist-illustrator W. W. Denslow—or at least as part of a composite with a good bit of the Mary Elizabeth Lease caricature thrown in. As Baum wrote it, the "Wicked Witch of the West had but one eye"; she was, in fact, drawn by Denslow with a patch over her left eye. She was a woman, of course, as witches were supposed to be—by definition, "an ugly old hag"—but Denslow's two drawings of this archvillain, except for the pigtails, would certainly do justice to a manly caricature. However that may have been, from 1895 to well beyond the turn of the century, "Pitchfork Ben" Tillman would epitomize to many the worst features of agrarian radicalism. In the area of racism and one of its more prominent by-products known as race-baiting demagoguery, those fears would be amply justified. Seemingly deficient when it came to that all-important sense of human decency, Tillmanism was the southern version of a shadow movement, a counterfeit rendition of Populism that would, over time, be mistaken by some for the genuine article or be identified by slightly more sophisticated interpreters as "reactionary populism."[10]

As regards the issue of race, one of Peffer's first bills introduced in this session repeated the earlier call for the creation of "a home for aged and infirm colored people" in the nation's capital.[11] In February 1896, North Carolina Populist Harry Skinner's earliest remarks in the House were also on behalf of retaining a

$9,900 appropriation designated for a "National Association for the Relief of Destitute Colored Women and Children." Skinner called a Nebraska Republican's move to strike out the appropriation "a mistake."

A few days later, Skinner also made his first address in the debate relative to the coin redemption fund. Future possibilities were much on his mind. Both old parties, he insisted, would likely back the gold standard in the coming presidential race. If that happens, he asked, "what is to become of your silver professions?"

Skinner also employed in this speech a line of reasoning that would be put to good use, in modified form, a few months later in William Jennings Bryan's famous "Cross of Gold" speech. "If you wish," said Skinner, "divide the country into cities and farms. In that instance the cities must realize their absolute dependence upon the country. To illustrate, you can throw an impassable wall around every city in this country, and within the short space of time as ninety days bats and owls would frequent and live in marble halls where once reigned human life in the revelry of wine, pleasure, and summary happiness. Your accumulated wealth might be in the shape of marble blocks, in Government bonds, or in the much-coveted metal, gold. All these would be powerless to support and maintain human life if you had no access to the country for food and raiment, while the country would and could live, be happy and prosperous, without the assistance of the cities." Then, after conceding that the House would vote to continue the policy of using bond sales to shore up the gold reserve fund, Skinner recommended his bill to replenish the fund: a reduction of "all official salaries"at the federal level by one-third. He said that he had been assured that such action would yield approximately $100 million, the equivalent of the magic number thought to be needed in a gold reserve.[12]

Several months later, Skinner would also make the case for the Populists against a bill authorizing annual clerks for congressmen. He called the proposal a "gratuity of about $215,000 during the vacation of Congress to our clerks." It was, he said, "criminally extravagant," considering the "hard times" confronting most people. The measure passed in any case by a vote of 130 to 109, with all Populists voting nay.[13]

Alabama Populist Milford Howard followed Skinner with his maiden speech. His was a flamboyant one, as would befit the author of *If Christ Came to Congress* (1894) and *The American Plutocracy* (1895). Among other things, in opposing President Cleveland's financial policies, Howard stated that he wanted to "appeal to-day for justice for those who sow that others may reap, for those who toil in poverty, hunger, and rags that the American plutocracy may revel in wealth and luxury beyond the dreams of avarice." The nation, he said, had arrived at a critical juncture in its history, such as had been immortalized by these Shakespearean lines: " 'There is a tide in the affairs of men, which, taken at the flood, leads on to fortune; omitted, all the voyage of their life is bound in shallows and in miseries.' That tide has come in the history of this country," said Howard. "The tide of protest, of popular indignation against the unlawful encroachments of the money power. The murmurs have grown to curses, mingled with the prayers of starving women and wails of helpless children. The masses of the country are like a great, troubled, restless, heaving ocean. . . . Wake up from your long sleep and stay the swiftly onrushing tide by just and wholesome laws ere it be too late."[14]

This Congress would pass few laws that Populists would regard as "just and wholesome." Near the close of its first session, in fact, the Fifty-fourth Congress would earn the label "do-nothing," bestowed on it by dissident Republican Senator William Stewart. It was "an outrage," said the Nevadan. "Never in all history have there been such galling hard times, such discouraging conditions, so much despair and want and misery among the masses of the laboring people, and particularly among agriculturalists."[15]

Instead of working to provide relief, this Congress was destined to spend much of its time debating whether to intervene on behalf of the Cubans struggling to end Spanish colonial rule and whether to impose immigration restrictions, issues that will be treated later separately. In the meantime, however, this Congress also provided an interesting and revealing record regarding the thought and program of Populism at the congressional level and, in the process, about the state of American politics generally.

"UNWARRANTED AND INVIDIOUS DISTINCTIONS"

What exactly made one a Populist? No doubt a variety of factors came into play. Among them, none was stronger than the belief that people were, in the final analysis, of equal worth. Senator Allen articulated that thought at various times more clearly than others. He especially deplored elitism and notions of hierarchy grounded on position and wealth, and he never failed to take issue with those who implied otherwise. In February 1896, he said: "I am a democrat, not a Democrat in the sense of belonging to the Democratic party . . . but I am a democrat in the broader and more comprehensive and catholic sense of the term. I believe every human being who walks upon the face of this earth, male or female, who discharges his or her duties conscientiously, reverently, in the fear and sight of God, in the station in which he or she may be placed, is the equal politically, naturally, and socially of every man or woman." He sensed a pronounced tendency in his time toward hierarchy and elitism, which was contrary, he thought, to the best traditions of American democracy, a trend toward "making unwarranted and invidious distinctions among men and women."[16] On another occasion he said, " I have thus far in my humble life and in my humble station supposed that there is no natural difference between individuals, and that whatever distinction exists between them is in consequence possibly of their own conduct or their own environment."[17]

No doubt such attitudes shaped Allen's position regarding capital punishment, as might have been the case with other Populists. Early in 1896, Congress had before it a bill reducing the number of crimes for which the penalty could be imposed. Populists in both houses supported the measure. Allen stated for the record, "If I had it within my power, I would abolish capital punishment; I do not believe in it."[18]

Perhaps because of his belief in the idea of a "common humanity"—people being fundamentally of equal worth—and because of his confidence in his own considerable abilities (strengthened, no doubt, by his large physical stature), Allen was not one to back away from a clash of ideas or wills. An interesting example of this occurred in an exchange with Iowa's Senator John Gear, a Republican businessman and former governor of Iowa, as well as assistant secretary of the treasury under President Benjamin Harrison. Gear told Allen that when the Nebraskan had voted for James Weaver of Iowa for president in 1892, he had voted "in favor of confiscating all the railway property and public property, the telegraphs, and everything of that kind and issuing irredeemable paper money for them." Allen immediately took exception and was told by Gear that he could "dispute with James B. Weaver himself." Allen's response was: "No, I will not dispute with James B. Weaver himself; I dispute with the Senator from Iowa. He is in this Chamber. I am his equal here, and anywhere else, for that matter. He can not stand here and utter falsehoods of that kind against one of the greatest and most illustrious citizens of the United States because he happens to be a Populist and go unwhipped of the rebuke his language justly and necessarily deserves." Senator Hoar asked that Allen's words be "taken down." Allen shot back, "I call the Senator from Massachusetts to order and demand that his words be taken down." Allen was quickly allowed to proceed in order. He then spoke at length in defense of Weaver and the Populist call for government ownership of railroads and telegraphs. His answer to the charge of confiscation was that Populists intended "to purchase them, paying a fair equivalent," in order to "operate them in the interest of the people at large."[19]

Having experienced what they considered an abuse of executive power by President Cleveland on behalf of financial interests, Populists were not at all sympathetic to moves aimed at enhancing executive power. The proposal for an item veto, for instance, received no support from their quarter. Senator Butler, as a matter of fact, introduced a joint resolution proposing an amendment to the Constitution reducing the percentage of votes needed to override a presidential veto to a majority on second consideration. Butler called the two-thirds vote rule a "relic of monarchy" and "a dangerous power," making the president "almost an autocrat."[20]

On 9 April 1896, in making his case for a government-owned postal telegraph system, Senator Butler also denounced the extensive use of child labor by the Western Union Telegraph Company. He argued that monopoly control made it possible for the corporation to work "its operators from nine to sixteen hours a day," paying "them only about $40 per month on an average."[21] This reference by Butler to the practice of child labor must have been one of the earliest statements of concern about a practice that would, in subsequent years, increasingly draw the attention of social justice reformers.

The Senate prided itself on a degree of comity not always present in the House. But in the tense atmosphere of the crisis of the nineties, there were revealing lapses. One of these involved David Hill and Ben Tillman, who represented opposite sides of the Democratic coin. Hill alluded to the fact that on naval appropriations, Tillman was traveling in the company of Populists. Tillman responded, "Well, I think I was in very good company. I certainly feel I was in better company than I am with some Democrats who go around on this side labeled 'Democrats,' and are nothing but Republicans in disguise." That drew laughter from the chamber, and Tillman then told Hill, "You represent the 'people.' Yes, you represent the bondholders, the bankers of New York, and nobody else on this floor." After some banter regarding the possibility of "bloodshed," Tillman told Hill that his people "were desperate." Hill conceded that that was "very evident." Tillman responded, "Yes, and before we starve we will make somebody else desperate, my friend. I have been in the West. Do not consider that this is [merely a case of] a fire eater from South Carolina, who has lost his head. I know whereof I speak. There is to-day more hatred and anger in the hearts of the people west of the Mississippi for New York and Wall Street and the bondholding, bloodsucking East than ever they had for the South."

Tillman went on to say, "If silver coinage were instituted by Congress I dare say there would be a rush and an effort made by the Shylocks to foreclose their mortgages and reap the fruits of their roguery before the country could get on its legs again. They are swallowing us by degrees now." Frankly, he said, "I prefer to go inside the whale all at once, like Jonah did, than be slowly swallowed with the accompaniment of crocodile tears."

The Democratic party of Cleveland and Hill was certainly not Tillman's cup of tea. He mused, "As to where I will go I do not know. I can not go to Populism, for Populism is simply an explosion of wrath and anger on the part of disgusted Democrats and disgusted Republicans at the rottenness and corruption and cowardice and treachery of both parties." The Populists, he added, "tried too much and simply splattered themselves on the wall."[22]

A few days later, Senator Hill spoke in opposition to Senator Peffer's call for an investigation into the Cleveland administration's bond deals. His principal argument was that the proposal was without merit. "It is the Populist sentiment which is being encouraged—a sentiment which is clamoring against capital, whether capital is acquired properly or improperly. It is an effort to antagonize men of wealth; it is an effort to denounce men who have accumulated property or men who have obtained public position."[23] The next day, Hill added the charge that "vile flings" were being made against the Jews. Tillman had used the word "Jews" at least once for the record, speaking in support of an investigation. In response to Hill, Tillman said this: "I have no disposition to make any vile or contemptible fling at Rothschild & co. because it is said they are Jews."[24]

Congressional opposition to Cleveland's bond policies came, with rare exception, from Populists and Democrats from the West and South. In the House on 9 May 1896, John Corliss, a Michigan Republican, added his voice to the growing chorus. " 'To enjoy a good reputation,'" said Corliss, "give publicly and steal privately!" As he saw it, "the bond holders of Wall Street, under the present administration, have been using this principle and proclaiming themselves philanthropists while robbing the Treasury of our nation."[25]

Perhaps Corliss's speech planted an idea in Milford Howard's mind; a few days later, the Alabama Populist rose to "a question of privilege" and asked the clerk to read the impeachment inquiry resolution that heads this chapter. As soon as his indictment of President Cleveland was read into the record, Nelson Dingley quickly raised the question of consideration, and Howard's question of privilege was overruled.[26]

Howard had also gained the attention of the House the previous week on a point of personal privilege. On that occasion, it was to refute stories that had been picked up by several newspapers charging him with drunkenness on the floor of the House several months earlier. Howard apparently had been seriously ill on that occasion and had been assisted from the House and was absent for some time thereafter. He read a portion of a version of the story printed in the *St. Louis Republic* and said, "I brand this a lie and slander. I was lying at death's door, and for a month I was unable to leave my bed; and only the day before yesterday was I able to come here and resume my duties." He added, "I am here to say, further, that no member of the People's Party has ever been seen on this floor under the influence of whisky, and you can publish that to the world." With these two episodes behind him, Howard's statements for the record in this session apparently ended.[27]

On 3 June 1896, David Hill introduced to the Senate a proposed constitutional amendment giving the president a line-item veto. Senator Butler, who in April had attempted to initiate an amendment limiting the president's veto power, reacted immediately by saying that the proposal was "a most natural one to be offered by a Senator who opposed the anti-bond bill which passed yesterday afternoon. It is a most natural one to be offered by a Senator who believes that the revenue power of this Government should be taken from Congress and placed in the hands of one man—the Executive. In addition to the power which the President already has to accept or reject a measure on its general merits, he proposes to give him the power to strike out and insert—that is, to legislate in detail."[28]

From the Populist perspective, executive power wielded heavy-handedly on behalf of financial and propertied interests was not the only menace to a people's government; they were also quite disturbed by a number of decisions handed down by a conservative Supreme Court in 1895, and this led to moves on their part to undo the damage. Early in the Congress, Butler had introduced a joint resolution proposing an amendment to the constitution legalizing the income tax, and in June 1896 he talked about the need "to call a constitutional convention through the State legislatures to protect the people . . . against the aggressions of the courts." Senator Allen likewise proposed a constitutional amendment designed to lessen the power of the judiciary; his proposal would require a unanimous vote of the Supreme Court to overturn acts of Congress.[29]

PUBLIC OWNERSHIP VERSUS PRIVATIZATION

One student of Populism at the congressional level assured us years ago that Populists rarely had anything to say about government ownership of the railroads as advocated in their party's platform of 1892.[30] Apparently, that conclusion was more of an academic hunch than anything else. If the Populists were going to back away from this aspect of their program, surely it would have been the case with this Congress in the years 1895–1897, following the party's severe drubbing in the 1894 election, the rise of the issue of gold versus silver, and the shift in Populist representation from the West to the South. The moderating effect of the 1896 fusion effort in support of William Jennings Bryan was noticeable, but there was no significant and lasting retreat from principles.

Commentary by William Allen regarding the two principal institutions of his era's feeble regulatory state is as good a place as any to begin this examination of Populist positions vis-à-vis the relationship between the state and the economy. Early in February, Allen rose in the Senate "for the purpose of saying (and I do not know whether it is wise for me to say it or not from a personal standpoint, but I will take the chance anyway) that two of the most gigantic and useless institutions in this country that are constantly absorbing the public funds for their support are the Civil Service and Interstate Commerce Commissions." As for the Interstate Commerce Commission, "no man can be appointed unless his opinion is known in advance" to be "consistent with the interests of the railroads." Besides, he said, "what jurisdiction" do they have? "What power have they? They have the power to draw their salaries, and that is about the extent of it." As for the Civil Service Commission, "Whenever a . . . Commissioner develops the slightest amount of backbone or independence and believes that the law should be carried out in its letter and spirit and acts slightly independent of the ruling power, that moment he hears a voice from the White House telling him there is a vacancy in the Civil Service Commission."[31]

A few days later, Allen was listening to Senator Richard F. Pettigrew speak regarding a resolution before the Senate relating to foreclosure on the Kansas Pacific Railroad. The South Dakota Republican seemed to be entertaining the notion of government ownership. Allen asked him if that were the case; Pettigrew answered, "I can see no possible objection to the Government owning the road and operating it." Allen replied, "I then beg to call the Senator's attention to the fact that that is paternalism and Populism, according to the Republican definition of those two words." Pettigrew made no comment regarding that. He merely said that he saw government ownership and operation of the roads as the best way to reestablish "competition between individuals and between cities and towns." It would help bring "fair and equal opportunity" to "all the people and all the towns along the line."[32]

In April 1896, Senator Butler won Senate approval for a $50,000 test program of rural free mail delivery. It was the beginning of his effort on behalf of a program that would yield positive results for him and for rural residents across the nation. Several days later, Butler also delivered a speech on behalf of his bill creating a postal telegraph and telephone system. This address was a major statement of Populism that has been lost for a century in that musty document file of time mentioned earlier. In the speech, Butler referred to a series of articles written by Frank Parsons and published in *Arena* magazine from January through April 1896; Parsons was a young academic economist and a Populist. Butler quoted the professor in support of his contention that "the Federal Government is a constitutional agent of the people for the transmission of intelligence." The senator also referred to Henry Clay's pre–Civil War objection to turning the telegraph system over to private ownership. And he quoted Supreme Court Justice Henry B. Brown and a judge of the North Carolina Supreme Court in support of his proposition.

This speech is a major example of why the roots of the right-wing political phenomenon visible since the 1930s and occasionally identified as "populism" are located in the anti-Populist camp of the 1890s rather than that of the Populists. Referring to a comment by Postmaster General Wilson in the January 1896 *Arena* reflecting a mode of thought that would be called "privatization" a century later, Butler stated:

> According to his idea, we should allow private monopolies to run the asylums, because certainly it can be done by private individuals if they can find some way to make a profit out of it; we should abolish our public-school systems, and let them be run by monopolies; we should abolish our jails and courts, because can not each man protect himself after some kind of a brute fashion? A man can protect his personal liberty without the help of the courts or police officers as well as he can protect himself against the telegraph monopoly or any other monopoly, and better, too. On the same reasoning it would be just as sound to say that the jails and the courts should be left to private management.

Butler would have none of that, of course; nor would his Populist colleagues. They would, however, heartily second his statement, for the views he expressed were deeply rooted in the American past.

> I hold that the correct theory is that the Government is simply an agent of the people to do for all the people what can be better done by a public agent than by each private individual in his own behalf. I challenge contradiction of that statement as being the correct theory of a republican form of government. Those businesses which affect society in general . . . should not be intrusted to individual management . . . , but should be performed by the agent

> of all the people, for the benefit of all the people alike. That agent is the Government, and if this be not correct, then you need no Government.
>
> Corporations want dividends; the people want a good service at low rates. Therefore no monopoly per se should ever be placed in the hands of a private corporation; but should in every case be used as a Government function for the public good. They [the founders] considered monopoly the greatest menace to liberty and the deadliest foe to free institutions. They took the position that any business that affected all or a great portion of the people under circumstances where there could be no successful competition by men of small means was a Government function, and should be owned and operated by the Government at cost for the benefit of all the people."[33]

Butler went on to insist that had it not been for the "wisdom" and "foresight" of "the nation's founders we would to-day be cursed by a tremendous mail monopoly which would be daily absorbing the substance of the people on the one hand and building up another class of haughty and oppressive millionaires on the other . . . , who would probably be styled 'postal kings.' " If the mail were controlled by private interests, said Butler, "over one-half of the citizens of America would be even without the facilities of a post-office. Half of [that number] . . . would have to ride ten miles at least to mail a letter, and then pay five or ten times as much as they pay now."[34]

Several weeks later, Senator Peffer again added his voice to the call for government enterprise. On this occasion, the Senate was considering an amendment that would deny the government the authority to manufacture its own stamps. Peffer opposed the measure, saying that he thought "the Government ought to do all of the Government's work that it can do." This would include, he added, "ships" and other equipment for the military. Connecticut Republican Joseph Hawley interrupted to ask, "Including the construction of railroads?" Peffer answered, "And to build railroads." Shortly thereafter, Senator Hawley returned to the topic and made an observation that was not easily dismissed: "It is proposed that the Government shall take charge not only of the railways, but of all the great savings-bank interests as well." Hawley suggested that if the proposal were given some serious thought, it would be seen "what an enormous machine the Government would come to be—how practically the power over everything that enters into our daily life would be centered in the Government, and in some cases at the very demand of the people who are all the while denouncing Government as corrupt, denouncing the Senate and the House of Representatives, the President, and everybody else as unfit to conduct business."[35]

Hawley's remarks led to something not witnessed previously: Peffer offered up a questionable interpretation of his party's stand on the railroads. "There is nothing in our political creed," he said, "so far as I am aware . . . that has ever looked toward the taking possession of the present railway systems . . . and bringing the entire transportation business . . . immediately under Government control—nothing of that kind." No doubt the operative word in this comment was "immediately," and in retrospect, he may have wished that he had included the phrase "without just compensation." But the Omaha platform included no such qualifications, and Hawley would later point out as much by quoting from the document. In the meantime, Peffer went on to make this important statement: "We do believe that the Government . . . should control by Government agencies; that all public functions ought to be exercised by public agencies in one way or another. That is the fundamental principle and doctrine of the party to which I have the honor to belong; but we do not propose to go about and make a holocaust of this business; we do not propose to tear everything down, as anarchists would. . . . We are builders . . . ; we are not destroyers. In some respects, perhaps, we might be called iconoclasts, because we are breakers of images, but they are party images. We are not dangerous at all."[36] Contained within this statement one finds support for the proposition, highlighted in the introduction, that the differences between Peffer and William Harris, who would be elected to Peffer's seat less than a year later, were not quite as great in 1896 as might be supposed.

With the prospect of the Democrats and Populists getting together to bring back a bimetallic standard—i.e., "free silver"—gold-standard supporters began to emphasize how truly different the Populists were from the silverites. The tactic, as in Peffer's case, produced some interesting but nonetheless disingenuous Populist arguments. Several weeks after Peffer's exchange with Hawley, William Allen announced that Senator David Hill had said that "there was an offer here on the part of Populists, or upon my part, to abandon in favor of free silver everything that was in the Populist platform. That is not true," insisted Allen. The Nebraskan then made this statement: "There are a great many gentlemen in this Chamber and outside of it who have been giving out in interviews and letters and speeches their views of Populists and Populism. A great many of these gentlemen have spoken of the socialistic . . . and paternalistic features of . . . Populism. I challenge any Senator in this Chamber, or any man outside of it . . . to point out in any authentic document issued by the Populist party a solitary thing that is paternalistic or socialistic in its faith."[37]

Several weeks later, James Kyle, once again identifying himself as a Populist, was drawn into a discussion of a bill aimed at providing for municipal ownership of the District's gas plant, which resulted in his candid attempt to clarify exactly where the Populists stood on the subject of public ownership.

> I grant . . . that municipal ownership is in the line of socialism; but the Republican party, the Democratic party, the Populist party, and all good citizens are in favor of a modified form of paternalism and socialism. Populism is not socialism. The adoption of a modified system of socialism such as we have under consideration does not brand us as socialists. Our insane asylums are socialistic. Our system of public schools . . . is socialistic. Our standing armies, our system of post-offices—all these are socialistic. Socialism, in the

> modified sense of the word, as applied to the great American enterprises, means that the American people can better do these things than they can be done by private corporations. In that sense the Republican and Democratic parties are socialistic in kind, as well as the Populist party. We differ only in degree. The Republican party is a little more socialistic than the Democratic party [of Grover Cleveland or the Bourbon wing], which believes that all things should be done by the States or by individuals as far as possible.

To support his case, Kyle then quoted from letters written by James S. Cowden and Daniel DeLeon, Socialist leaders, saying afterward, "Mr. President, this . . . is not Populism. It has nothing in common with Populism. In my judgment, and in the judgment of all who may listen to the reading of these declarations, it means the destruction of private enterprise, and the people of the United States are not ready for such an innovation. But . . . municipal ownership of gas, electric-light, and water works and street railways is not socialism to the extent of destroying individualism. It is merely the application of business sense and business methods to these great public functions and enterprises for the purpose of serving the people economically and well along these lines."[38]

The next week, William Allen reacted to remarks by Senator Lucien Baker, Republican of Kansas, who had repeated the old charge that the Populists were "in favor of an irredeemable paper currency." To offer his version of what Populism was all about, Allen read the Omaha platform into the record, providing a running commentary on the document. One revealing observation related to a printing error in the document apparently has gone unnoticed by historians. He said that the preamble's statement, "They propose to sacrifice our homes, lives, and children on the alter of mammon," should have read "wives" instead of "lives." When he came to the section on the subtreasury plan, he stated, "Let me say right here that this is the only weak point that Democrats or Republicans could ever find in the Populist platform." He went on to claim (incorrectly, unless he meant to say during his tenure, which may have been his intent) that the plan had "never been advocated in either branch of Congress." He said that the Alliance, which had brought the plan forward in 1889, had in its national meeting the previous January dropped the proposal; thus it was "no longer a part of the doctrine of the party." The Alliance, of course, was not competent to drop the plan for the party; that could be accomplished only by a second nominating convention of the People's party yet to be held. When asked by a senator how Populists proposed to get $50 per capita into circulation without the subtreasury plan, instead of merely quoting the platform, Allen answered essentially by saying, the same way it is now. "It may be paid out in construction of public works." The bottom line was, said Allen, that "the Populist party wants gold and silver, and a paper currency redeemable as it is now, . . . increased by healthy and safe degrees to $50 per capita."[39]

No doubt Allen and others were trimming their sails in Congress as they approached the 1896 election. On 29 May 1896, however, Allen spoke at the annual banquet of the Massachusetts Populists. In this address, the Nebraskan embraced the whole Populist program, including government ownership and management of the railroad, telephone, and telegraph networks. In his close, Allen attempted a definition of his party's mission that may well have come close to the core of the movement: "New and undefined as it may be, but rugged, mighty, and powerful, there has arisen a party whose teachings to some may sound strange. Its foundation rests on the cause of labor and the brotherhood of man, and it seeks to solve questions other parties have failed to solve—how to prevent unjust accumulation of wealth in the hands of the few; how to resist the encroachment of capital and of greed upon the rights of the masses, under the names of trusts and corporations; how to find and remove the causes that have led to discontent and stifled the cry of hunger in a land of plenty."[40]

The issue of government ownership carried over into the postelection session of the Fifty-fourth Congress. Republicans had drafted a Pacific Railway funding measure aimed at rescuing the Union Pacific and Kansas Pacific without resorting to government ownership and operation of the bankrupt lines. In debate accompanying the measure, John Bell, Populist speaker, spoke out forthrightly on behalf of state-managed railroads and against the bailout. Republican leader William Hepburn at one point directed these remarks to Bell: "[I] ask the gentleman from Colorado, does he believe that this is the entering wedge? Does he not believe that it will be followed on and on and on, no matter at what expense, until every mile of railway in the United States is under the control and operation of the . . . Government? Look at every platform, repeated over and over again as the years go by. If there is any one thing above all others that somewhat whimsical Populist party is addicted to it is to this proposition of railway ownership by the Government." This particular measure was defeated in the House by a vote of 168 to 103 (84 not voting), with all the Populists voting no. The Fifty-fifth Congress would inherit the problem of what to do about the nation's failed transcontinental lines. All this suggests that if the Populists were the least bit reluctant to advocate government ownership, particularly of the railroads, it seems as though someone neglected to inform their opponents of that posture.[41]

IMMIGRATION RESTRICTION

At the urging of the Knights of Labor, the Populists attached to their 1892 platform several resolutions, one of them a call for restriction on what was described as "undesirable immigration," a restriction aimed at stopping the flood of "pauper and criminal classes of the world," who were said to be taking the jobs of American workers. Although the demand on the Populist side originated in this economic concern, it was difficult, if not impossible, to separate the many elements that factored into one's position on the subject. The voices of those who were opposed to an open-door policy for antiradical and ethnocultural reasons easily blended with the voices of those who were primarily concerned about strengthening the hand of organized labor and improving the bargaining power and the lives of wage earners. By 1896, in fact, the two groups advocating immigration restriction voted together, but for dissimilar reasons, thereby passing through Congress a restrictive bill that would be vetoed by President Cleveland just before he left office. It would be nearly twenty years before a similar vote in Congress could be mustered for a restrictive measure.

Historians have been somewhat mystified by what took place: in 1896, when the influx of so-called new immigrants—primarily of southern and eastern European extraction—was a relatively small trickle, a majority was in favor of restriction; yet after the turn of the century, when these numbers skyrocketed and the number of new immigrants was disproportionately high, a vote for restriction was hard to come by. The answer lies in the peculiar 1890s concatenation of conservative, liberal, and radical support for restriction. After 1900, the call for restriction on economic and pro-labor grounds (especially of radical-agrarian origins) was much abated. The call for restriction on racist and ethnic grounds grew and became even more strident and was for that reason less influential until the second and third decades of the twentieth century. At that point, this old-stock, nativist movement managed to work its will on the national government, with immigration quotas heavily weighted in favor of what had by then become an ethnic (or white nationalist) movement on the part of a white, Anglo-Saxon, Protestant majority that frequently labeled itself "100 percent American."[42]

The major sponsor of immigration restriction during the 1890s and for years thereafter was Senator Henry Cabot Lodge. His bill prescribing a literacy test was embodied in the measure that was passed by Congress in 1896. In the fight for restriction, the Massachusetts Republican's arguments were inclusive, but his reasons seemed to be ethnocultural and antiradical at their core. Early in March 1896, the nation's only historian in Congress with a Harvard University Ph.D. opened his fight for restriction with a major speech that spelled out his reasoning rather fully. He conceded that the literacy test (the ability to read forty words in any language) would discriminate in favor of the old-stock, "English-speaking" newcomers, a desirable circumstance, he believed, that would serve as a corrective for the tendency of the new immigrants— "Italians, Russians, Poles, Hungarians, Greeks, and Asiatics"—to "remain for the most part in congested masses in our great cities," where, said Lodge, "they furnish . . . a large proportion of the population of the slums." The committee had proved, he said, that "illiteracy runs parallel with the slum population, with criminals, paupers, and juvenile delinquents of foreign birth and parentage." They also "bring the least money to the country and come most quickly upon private and public charity for support." The greatest danger, however, was contained in the threat they posed to the "mental and moral qualities [of] . . . our race." Changes would occur in "the quality of our race and citizenship through the wholesale infusion of races whose traditions and inheritances, whose thoughts and whose beliefs are wholly alien to ours and with whom we have never assimilated or even been associated in the past." It was now time to act, said Lodge. "The danger has begun. It is small as yet, comparatively speaking, but it is large enough to warn us to act while there is yet time and while it can be done easily and efficiently."[43] Apparently, everyone understood exactly what Lodge meant by his reference to "our race."

In this debate, the Populists did not voice their sentiments, for whatever reasons, but they did support with their votes the move to impose restrictions on immigration, as their party convention had pledged them to do. No doubt some of them bought into the same fears that drove Senator Lodge and others. It was an issue that had garnered considerable support by 1896, with both major parties including a plank in their national platforms calling for restrictions on "foreign pauper labor." Populist silence in the House may have been due, in part, to their not being granted floor time. During the critical debate on the issue, Omer Kem had refused to go along with unanimous consent requests to protest the lack of floor time granted to his side. That was not the situation in the Senate, thus their silence in the debate, coupled with their vote in support of restriction, might suggest that they had mixed feelings regarding the measure, one way or the other, but were fulfilling the party's pledge nonetheless. Even without Populist comment on the record, however, the debate was quite revealing regarding one of the more significant issues confronted by the Fifty-fourth Congress.

In the Senate, Charles Gibson, Democrat from Maryland, took sharp and particular exception to Lodge's call for a literacy test. He said that the measure was "undemocratic, unrepublican, un-American, and has no health in it. It is barbaric and cruel; in its operation it will separate families and divide those among them who may be able to read and write from those who can not." Furthermore, the "uneducated laborer, whose strong muscles and willingness to work we are in need of, will be driven back and, while the communist and socialist, and loud-mouthed and filthy anarchists who labor with their tongues, demagogues, *et id omne genus*, because they are able to read, will be allowed to come in—evil fellows who work not themselves, but who foment discord and discontent among working men, who, if left to themselves, would be good citizens." Despite his obvious antiradicalism, Gibson went on in this long speech to take issue with Lodge's claim that "race deterioration" would occur without his proposed restriction. As he saw it, "the ultimate perfection of the human race depends upon recognition of the right of every man to be treated as a man, whether he be Jew or Gentile, literate or illiterate. Character is largely the result of environment." Gibson also said that he detected "hostility to the Catholic Church" in the measure and referred to the support for the measure provided by the decidedly anti-Catholic and nativist American Protective Association.[44]

Samuel McCall, a Republican from Massachusetts, conceded in his remarks that the bill was "principally prepared" by the Immigration Restriction League headquartered in Boston, with John Fiske and Prescott Hall, both prominent Anglo-Saxon nativists, among its principal officers. McCall spoke for the measure, saying, among other things: "To say that because we are a nation of immigrants . . . we should place no restriction on immigration, is a good deal like saying that because Rome was founded by bandits it should therefore forever have been an asylum for the criminals of every nation. We are to do all those things which are necessary to preserve our liberties and our civilization. Even if we are, as might be inferred from some of the broad principles laid down here, a great charitable organization, an international soup kitchen, for the benefit, primarily, of the rest of the world, we should yet do what is necessary to keep our charity shop running to the best advantage and not adopt such utterly loose and unbusinesslike methods as would speedily make us the objects and not the dispensers of charity." That segment drew applause from the House. McCall then proceeded to explain why the literacy test was needed: "The figures show that the races that are so well suited to our institutions and civilization have been in the last twenty-five years becoming less and less factors in our immigration, while other nations, those races which are not suited to our civilization, which are so radically different from us in education, habits of life, and institutions of government, are taking their place." The burden on the nation's public school system was too great. The literacy test would admit Anglo-Saxons and exclude those from "Mediterranean ports" and other areas. At the same time, it would help alleviate the problem of the urban "slums."

Shortly thereafter, Kentucky Democratic Representative John Hendrick, an opponent of restriction, gave the whole business quite a different spin—in his view, rubbing Republican noses into a mess of their own making. Toward the end, Hendrick stated, "If the pampered kings of protected monopolies had not gone to foreign countries and imported labor, 'scum' if you please, . . . there would be no such complaints as are now going on. You gentlemen upon the other side are the ones who have fostered classes in this country. You have nurtured the men who have brought this objectionable immigration upon us, if we have such, and now you ought to stand up like men and reap what you have sown and not try to cut off the development of the whole country, simply because there are a few cities overcrowded with unworthy immigrants brought here by your tariff barons. If they are criminals, enforce the laws against them . . . but in God's name, where a man seeks to better his condition by coming to a new country and taking a new start in the race of human progress, do not cut him off and say that he shall not enjoy the same rights and the same privileges that you have enjoyed." It was noted that this passage drew "loud applause" from the House.[45]

Democrats were the major opponents of the literacy-test approach to immigration restriction in the House and in the Senate. In December 1896, the bill cleared the upper chamber by a vote of 52 to 10, with 27 not voting. Allen, Butler, Kyle, and Peffer all voted yea. The House debate concluded with a vote of 131 in favor and 117 opposed, with 107 not voting. Shuford, Martin, and Goodwyn were among the latter group. Baker, Kem, Bell, Howard, Skinner, and Strowd all recorded affirmative votes. President Cleveland then vetoed the final measure, giving as his principal reason his belief that the literacy test would allow the "agitators and enemies of governmental control" to enter and would shut out the wrong parties. "Violence and disorder do not originate with illiterate laborers," said Cleveland. "They are rather the victims of the educated agitator." Besides, he added, the measure represented "a radical departure from our national policy relating to immigration. . . . Heretofore we have welcomed all who came to us from other lands, except those whose moral or physical condition or history threatened danger to national welfare and safety." Consistent with what had gone on in his administration following the economic collapse, Cleveland was unmoved by the arguments of those who pointed to the nation's huge unemployment problem as reason enough to put limits on immigration, saying that the situation would eventually resolve itself once the economy was back on its feet.[46]

Ultimately, the House managed, by a vote of 193 to 37, with 123 not voting, to override Cleveland's veto, with all the Populists in attendance voting yes. The veto was, in effect, sustained by the vote of the Senate. Thus ended for the Fifty-fourth Congress the growing debate over the nation's open-gate policy.[47]

CUBA LIBRE

For a generation, rebellion on the part of the Cuban masses against their colonial overlords had blown hot and cold. After 1893, the worsening economic situation internationally and especially within the United States and Cuba added to circumstances that had long been intolerable, provoking dissident Cubans once again into open rebellion.[48] By 1895, the struggle had become so widespread and so brutal, in addition to being sensationalized by the American press, that it could no longer be kept out of the political arena.[49] By December 1895, the Senate turned to the situation. Henry Cabot Lodge and William Allen early on introduced separate resolutions calling for recognition of the Cuban revolutionaries. The two senators represented distinct elements in a growing interventionist block. Both were jingoistic regarding Cuba and in agreement that Spain's hold over the Caribbean colony needed to be ended. In a short speech defending his call for recognition of the rebel government, Allen said that he believed "it to be the true . . . doctrine of our country that wherever a people show themselves desirous of establishing a republican form of government upon any territory adjacent to us they should receive our encouragement and support." Allen went on to make it clear that on this issue he spoke only for himself and not for his party. To those who would object to helping the Cubans because "they are not our race or tongue," he said that that should not matter. "It ought to be sufficient for us that they belong to a race of people who are striving for liberty."[50]

In contrast to his approach to the Venezuelan boundary dispute, occurring at about the same time, President Cleveland was cautious regarding Cuba. Thus the issue of whether to force the situation by urging the administration to take steps toward recognizing the Cuban insurgents divided the Senate Committee on Foreign Relations. The majority was reluctant. Thus in late February 1896, Senator J. Donald Cameron, a Pennsylvania Republican, presented a resolution on behalf of the increasingly impatient minority on the committee. It stated, "Resolved, That the President is hereby requested to interpose his friendly offices with the Spanish Government for the recognition of the independence of Cuba." Cameron laid out most of the arguments that could or would be raised about intervention. "Our immediate pecuniary interests in the island are very great," said Cameron, and those interests "are being destroyed. Free Cuba would mean a great market to the United States; it would mean an opportunity for American capital, invited there by signal exemptions; it would mean an opportunity for the development of that splendid island." He went on to talk about what could be done but had not been done by the Spanish to develop Cuba. He then turned his attention to strategic concerns. "The great island lies there across the Gulf of Mexico. She commands the Gulf, she commands the channel through which all our coastwise traffic between the Gulf and our Northern and Eastern States passes. She lies right athwart the line which leads to the Nicaragua Canal. Cuba in our hands or in friendly hands, in the hands of its own people, attached to us by ties of interest and gratitude," would be "a bulwark to the . . . safety . . . and . . . peace of the United States." We "should never suffer Cuba to pass from the hands of Spain to any other European power." As for Spain, its rule over the island had all but formally ended. "Spain may ruin the island. She can never hold it or govern it again." Finally, Cameron turned from economic and strategic concerns to what he called "a higher ground than either of those, and that is the broad ground of a common humanity."[51]

Historian Richard Hofstadter asserted in one of his most influential books, "Populists distinguished between wars for humanity and wars of conquest. The first of these they considered legitimate, but naturally they had difficulty in discriminating between the two." Although they did make this distinction, they most certainly did not have a problem differentiating one from the other. Those who had the most difficulty—either intentionally or because of a value commitment that automatically equated the extension of the American economic system with the extension of democracy—were represented by the group that Hofstadter labeled the "imperialistic elite," a group well defined by two of its most prominent leaders: Henry Cabot Lodge and Theodore Roosevelt.[52] People within that circle were indeed quick and effective in drawing on the cause of humanity to justify other, more materialistic ends. [53]

By late February, the House also began to get into the act. At that point, Robert Hitt, an Illinois Republican, introduced a concurrent resolution that stopped just short of calling for recognition of Cuban independence but hinted at that as the ultimate course, given the continuation of hostilities. At the same time, Allen rose in the Senate to plead his case for stronger action regarding hostilities in Cuba. He made these revealing remarks:

> I am not radical in anything, not even in my Populism. I believe that it is but policy to consult conservatism and to act conservatively. But there comes a time in the history of nations when the national heart as well as the national judgment is appealed to. By our situation upon this hemisphere, by our stand at the head of republics upon the face of the earth, we owe a duty to those who are in close proximity to us to see at least that they shall receive humane and just treatment at the hands of their rulers. . . . If need be, I would muster every man in the United States and every war vessel necessary to the accomplishment of the task, and I would erect on the ashes and ruins of Spain's control of that island a Republic modeled after the institutions of our own.

Allen also noted that it had been said that the course he advocated would likely "involve us in war." He was prepared to accept that possibility, believing that the cause more than justified that probable outcome.[54] Allen's resolution was defeated, but he had the support of seventeen colleagues, most of them from the western states. Soon thereafter, the Senate passed the Cameron resolution by a lopsided majority. The House version, urging greater action by the administration, passed by a vote of 262 to 27, with 76 not voting.[55]

In the debate over Cuba, some unusual positions emerged on the question of race. Senator Eugene Hale, a Maine Republican, was one of the more outspoken opponents of support for the Cuban revolutionaries, denouncing them as "guerrillas" and "savages." Alabama Senator John Morgan, a Democrat, picked up on Hale's arguments to say: "The plea of the Cubans for liberty is answered by the assertion that negroes are fighting those fierce yet sacred battles," and that one of their leaders is a "mulatto," that they are "poor dejected outcasts without the right to human benevolence." Morgan then made a point of emphasizing, "Those men of the North mistake me when they assume that I could have any prejudice toward the negro race that would cause me to deny to them [the Cubans?] good government, safety in life and property, and every personal liberty that I enjoy in our free Republic." He followed this judicious comment, however, with this peculiar observation, apparently without sensing even the slightest contradiction: "I do not believe, any more than Congress or the people of the District of Columbia believe, that the negro race is a useful or necessary factor in the government of a great Republic. We place the Indian tribes and the Chinese on even a lower scale in political government, while we give them the full measure of liberty. But the negro has the same right as the white man to escape from the tyrannical despotism of Spain and to have a fair opportunity to enjoy the true and full value of independence."[56]

Senator Horace Chilton of Texas was a good example of a white southerner who seemed to be genuinely alarmed by the prospect of the racial mixing that might be encouraged by establishing closer ties to Cuba. The nation's Civil War and Reconstruction history also loomed large in his thinking. "For more than a half century," said Chilton, "the negro question formed the groundwork of difference between the North and South, until it finally culminated in red-handed war.

And when the main question was settled . . . the problem seemed to have lost none of its complexity." Let us "ponder long before we set in motion a train of events which may bring another puzzle of mixed races to confound us." As he saw it, "it is not part of wise statesmanship to settle questions before their time." First, deal with "the disorders of our financial system," devise "a fair plan of taxation," and see to it that "the power of unlawful combination [is] disciplined, our population enhanced, our vast undeveloped territory well settled, [then] it will be time enough to search out new fields for the beneficent application of American principles."[57]

Ultimately, Congress agreed on a concurrent resolution reported from a conference committee in early April. That, in turn, brought on another round of debate. In the House, Charles Boutelle made one of the more telling speeches on the side of those opposed to intervention. The Maine Republican told his colleagues: "We can not right all the wrongs in the world if we try; and if we make the attempt we abandon the mission which is given to us of working out the destinies of a free people whose example of self-government, of self-control, of the creation of liberty and prosperity within their own domain, will do more for liberty in every land than all the foreign embroilments we could enter upon in generation after generation." After a brief interruption for applause, he resumed by saying, "It is not our duty to be the Don Quixote of the earth; and if it were, we are not capable of performing the function." He then turned his attention to the economic situation and the inability of Congress even to agree on a measure "to obtain revenue or to borrow money with which to pay our debts. Yet we are absolutely aching to waltz out into the international arena and 'lick' all other nations of the world." He was at that point interrupted by "laughter and applause."

Boutelle then brought up an even more serious subject—equal rights for black Americans. "We have that great race of people—I do not know of how many souls it consists, eight or ten millions of colored people, I believe—concerning whom it [has been said on this floor] . . . that over a vast expanse of our own country there are these millions of people who are still denied some of the most sacred rights guaranteed to the people of this country in the Declaration of Independence. With this condition confronting us, it is strange, indeed, for us to insist that the first duty resting on us is to dash across the Gulf of Mexico and establish and maintain the independence and freedom of the insurgents . . . of Cuba."[58]

Boutelle simply could not understand such a policy. That by no means deterred Harry Skinner, who followed with one of the more flamboyant flag-waving appeals to be heard on Cuban independence. The tenor of the speech was contained in what he called his prefatory remarks, wherein the North Carolina Populist called attention to the American flag displayed in the chamber and melodramatically referred to a number of famous battles from the Revolutionary War period and later. "I tell you, Mr. Speaker, the Cubans look upon this flag to-day as the emblem of liberty, as we look upon the cross as the emblem of Christianity; . . . I take that flag as the counterpart of the cross, as the emblem of liberty. I would place it over Cuba, and it ought to be made a State of this Union."[59]

Frederick Gillett, a Massachusetts Republican, spoke the next day and delivered a speech that, compared with Skinner's and a number of others, was replete with common sense and realism. He began by noting his sympathy with the cause of the Cubans. "I do not see how an American citizen . . . can feel otherwise toward an American colony struggling against a European power, though I do not admit that the Cuban insurgents are of the same stuff as were our Revolutionary ancestors." In addition, he conceded that "self-interest" of the United States "calls for the absolute independence of Cuba, for Cuba free and independent would present an opening to our market and our industries and for the investments of capital and a reciprocal trade greatly to our advantage." Yet the resolutions pointed to the wrong course, because they would likely "embroil us in war with Spain." The nation did not need that kind of action. "However we might think that we do it from love of humanity, certainly the other nations of the world would say we did it for greed of Cuban territory, and it seems to me it is wise for the United States, if it is going to wage war as a champion of humanity, to do it in a cause where we can not be accused of using humanity as a mere cloak of ambition." Later, Gillett said, "if the basis of our action is ambition we ought to make it known. . . . I think hypocrisy is a vastly worse vice than ambition or greed of territory."[60]

Henry Gray Turner, a Georgia Democrat, delivered remarks replete with references and examples of how unsuited he—and others who thought as he did—believed people of color to be when it came to self-government, while at the same time singing the exaggerated praises of "Anglo-Saxons." Good government was a "great and glorious endowment" bestowed by the creator on whites, as the Georgian saw it. Latins and Africans were simply incapable of self-government. The "African race" in particular, he insisted, "has never yet manifested that genius for liberty and good government and free institutions." As for him, he wanted nothing to do with any mission to "set [the Cubans] . . . free from Spain. I, for one . . . have had enough of Reconstruction."[61]

Lemuel Quigg, Republican from New York, felt compelled to respond directly to those who believed that inaction was really a neutral option, saying that it was the "duty" of the United States to end the war, primarily for economic reasons. A "do-nothing" posture was not what it was cracked up to be: "We can not do nothing. We are not on earth to do nothing. And by doing nothing what they mean is to do something that is very bad indeed. By doing nothing they mean that we shall take the part of Spain as against this struggling colony. . . . By doing nothing they mean that we shall take the part of despotism as against liberty."[62]

Not all southern Democrats were as closed-minded as Henry Gray Turner on the question of race. Charles Buck of Louisiana used his time to respond directly to Turner, a fellow southerner he obviously admired. He said, "No one realizes or feels more comprehensively than I do the magnificence of Anglo-Saxon civilization. But the Anglo-Saxon people are not the only [human beings] . . . of this world whose hearts are inspired by the instincts of freedom. . . . The instincts of liberty belong to the human heart, as a portion of its divine being and its immortal aspirations."[63]

William Baker also stepped to the front to engage in debate. "On this question," said Baker, "there is a law as broad as humanity, as deep as human affection." For him, it was a matter of the humane preference put to the test. "How far we should go in extending our sympathy and aid to people struggling as the Cubans now are I know not. Possibly I am too radical in my views on this question. But I say this, that in adopting these resolutions we take a step which I have no doubt future generations will approve. More than that, I believe that the cause of humanity . . . will take new vigor; the cause of education and of civil and religious liberty will receive an impetus that will help forward the progress and elevation of the human family." Baker's speech was said to have ended with "prolonged applause" from the House and galleries, a first for the only survivor from the original Kansas Populist delegation that had burst on the scene nearly six years earlier.[64]

Thadeus Mahon, a Republican and former railroad president from Pennsylvania, was recognized to counter the effective speech by Charles Boutelle against the resolutions. Mahon pitted the Maine Republican against himself by quoting some of his remarks made in the Fifty-third Congress in support of the Harrison administration's move to annex the Hawaiian Islands. It was said that he was ready then to involve "our Government in a war if necessary for the purpose of giving these Hawaiian people their freedom." Mahon added, "The passage of these resolutions is not a declaration of war. As a great nation we have a perfect right to give to Cubans belligerent rights. If Spain sees fit to declare war, she must take the responsibility and consequences. The conflict will be short and decisive. Cuba will belong to the United States and Spain will have learned a lesson she will not forget. One more victory will be won over despotism and inhumanity."[65]

The debate ended on 6 April, with the opponents of the resolutions mustering only twenty-seven votes. The outgoing Cleveland administration and the incoming McKinley administration would continue for almost a year longer trying to resist the call for more precipitant action.[66] In the meantime, the nation experienced one of the most important presidential elections in its history.

6

Denouement: Populist Meltdown, 1896–1897

No truer words were ever uttered than [these] . . . by the great and patriotic Lincoln . . . : "Labor is above capital. It is prior to and independent of capital, for capital could not exist were it not first created by labor." But we are endeavoring to protect and build up capital, losing sight of labor, hoping that when capital prospers, when the millionaires grow fat on the labor of the masses, [and] . . . have piled up a few more millions into their already bursting coffers, that some good spirit will prompt them to unclasp their greedy, Shylock hands and allow some of their prosperity to drop down on the common herd below. We have reversed the natural order . . . and placed capital above labor. Labor sits at the gate of Dives, gaunt and hungry, clothed in sackcloth and ashes, licking its sores, watching for the crumbs to fall from Shylock's table, which the dogs refuse to eat.

You may protect the manufacturer all you please, but unless you give us proper financial legislation, destroy the trusts and monopolies, and curb the arrogant power of the railroads, the day is not far distant when the looms in your cotton mills will be silent, and the cotton of the world will be manufactured in China and Japan, and your factories and furnaces will become the dwelling places of bats and unclean birds. [Applause.]

Milford Wriarson Howard, *Congressional Record,*
55th Cong., 1st sess., 23 March 1897

In 1894, William Jennings Bryan decided not to run for a third congressional term and thus spared himself a likely defeat, as was the lot of most western Democrats. Instead, he aspired to be a senator and had his name put on the Nebraska ballot as a candidate for the U.S. Senate. At the time, the vote was nothing more than a popularity contest (the direct election amendment was not ratified until 1913). Republicans then regained control of the Nebraska legislature, as they did throughout the West, thus assuring the election of one of their own. Having already established himself in the special session of 1893 as one of the outstanding orators in the country and one of the major leaders of the silver forces, Bryan set to work in earnest on behalf of the silver cause, speaking throughout the nation, slowly but surely building a formidable grassroots political organization in support of silver and for his own presidential candidacy.[1]

At the beginning of 1896, Bryan was in touch with leading Populists pleading the case of those who were convinced that it was essential that all factions opposed to a gold standard unite behind a single candidate. According to one of his biographers, he even "suggested that the Populists hold their national nominating convention after the Republicans and Democrats,"[2] the idea being that if the old parties embraced the gold standard, as anticipated, the People's party would then garner the support of numerous disenchanted silver supporters across the land. The Populist national committee was already thinking along those lines. In June, at their St. Louis convention, the Republicans followed the script well by nominating William McKinley of Ohio on a platform that essentially confirmed the party's ties to a quasi-official gold standard. The following month, the Democrats gathered in Chicago. Bryan's candidacy continued to gain momentum going into the convention. Then, just as he had done in Congress less than three years earlier, the Nebraskan unveiled a carefully crafted and spectacular speech during the opening that "parlayed" his "splendid baritone voice, engaging smile, and magnetic personality" into a presidential nomination. But of course he could not have done it without Grover Cleveland's help—that is, without the president's stubborn defense of the gold standard and his dogged refusal to utilize his office, positively, over the previous three years to counter the nation's worst depression.

The secret of Bryan's appeal seems to have been embodied in his assertion in this speech that his party believed in legislating "to make the masses prosperous." It was an approach to economic recovery that Bryan called the "Democratic idea." It was, however, not the settled policy of his party. Indeed, one could argue that it owed more to the Republicans of Lincoln's day than it did to contemporary Democrats. Since its creation, the People's party had most clearly advanced the idea of government that Bryan so warmly embraced in 1896. The fact that he endorsed and championed this "bottom-up" or "percolate-up" approach to promoting economic health and prosperity, as opposed to the "trickle-down" version (better known in the 1980s as "supply-side economics"), explains the Nebraskan's primary significance in the history of American politics. Not until Franklin D. Roosevelt's New Deal would this approach achieve legitimacy, but by then, ironically, the agrarian, small-town world that Bryanites and Populists hoped to save had changed beyond recognition, and the nation seemed to be incapable of choosing between the two approaches, opting instead for generous helpings of both (especially "trickle-down," by virtue of military spending, appropriately and variously labeled "perverse," "reverse," or "military" Keynesianism), long past the time when circumstances made such programs defensible.[3]

Bryan's nomination seriously complicated Populist politics. What was the party to do? What sensible choices did it have? Populists nearly everywhere—

outside the South especially, where Democrats were frequently allies and not enemies—were now vulnerable to the logic that there must be only one silver candidate in the campaign, lest the reform vote be split and the success of their gold-standard foes assured. It was not all that clear at the time, but Bryan may well have saved his dear old Democratic party from being consigned to the status of a third party; for sure, the transformation of the People's party into a major party was dependent on the continued domination of Bryan's party by conservative gold-standard advocates of the industrial northeastern quarter of the nation. By aligning Democrats with the cause of silver and reform, Bryan certainly set in motion a process contributing to the fade-out of Populism—a kind of meltdown, the creator of Oz would likely have called it.

But could the Populists support the Nebraska Democrat and still maintain their identity and viability? To extreme antifusionists, who existed everywhere but were most numerous in the South, where Democrats were passionately and not without good cause hated, the answer was a resounding no. Another, larger contingent of antifusionists had doubts but recognized that the party had little choice. To the fusionists par excellence and to those Populists who had by 1896 conceded everything to the silver issue, the question mattered not at all.

Several Populist leaders in advance of the convention suggested that the best solution would be to endorse Bryan without naming a ticket of their own. That course confronted two potential and mighty obstacles: the determination of extreme antifusionists to carry on no matter what; and Bryan's running mate, Arthur Sewall of Maine, a national banker and railway director, who was unacceptable to all genuine Populists. Confronted with these realities, the delegates at St. Louis in July, after considerable maneuvering, no small amount of skullduggery, and considerable turmoil ("fighting like cats in a backyard" was one Republican editor's graphic description), first nominated Tom Watson for vice president and then Bryan for president. The hope was that an agreement could be made later to replace Sewall with Watson on both tickets. It has also been suggested that Watson—a strong antifusionist—was put forward in the hope of scuttling the fusion effort.[4] Senator Allen, as chairman of the convention and as Bryan's friend and avid supporter, played a major role in arranging the solution finally agreed on at the convention; it satisfied virtually no one, created all kinds of special problems, and, worst of all, was ultimately associated with a losing cause. Thus the Nebraska senator became the object of considerable hostility on the part of more determined antifusionists—especially among Texas and Georgia Populists.[5]

Probably because of the fixation on the Bryan-McKinley campaign, the platform that came from this convention has been totally ignored in earlier histories.[6] Not surprisingly, it reflected the changes that had occurred within the nation and party since 1892, but it was nonetheless a remarkable document and should not have been overlooked. The specific preamble of the Omaha platform was gone, but the sentiments expressed in this St. Louis platform retained much of its flavor. It declared: "We realize that, while we have political independence, our financial and industrial independence is yet to be attained by restoring to our country the Constitutional control and exercise of the functions necessary to a people's government, which functions have been basely surrendered by our public servants to corporate monopolies."

The three main planks of Omaha headed the platform and were basically unchanged, except that the subtreasury system was omitted as a means of implementing a reformed banking and monetary system. As before, government ownership of the railroad and telegraph systems (telephones were omitted) was included. This convention's platform also departed from the Omaha document by incorporating within its core, rather than specifically excluding them, several other favored reforms, including the referendum, military pensions, economy in public salaries, and direct election of president, vice president, and U.S. senators.

Several new and quite extraordinary planks were added. Delegates endorsed the idea, consistently advanced by Populist congressmen, that "in times of great industrial depression, idle labor should be employed on public works as far as practicable." Even more remarkable was the plank dealing with voting rights, given the nation's regressive course in that area: "Believing that the elective franchise and an untrammeled ballot are essential to a government of, for, and by the people, the People's party condemns the wholesale system of disfranchisement adopted in some States as unrepublican and undemocratic, and we declare it to be the duty of the several State legislatures to take such action as will secure a full, free and fair ballot and an honest count." (The use of the words "unrepublican" and "undemocratic" by themselves suggest a significant evolution in terminology and in political thought.) The last segment made it clear that the entire platform represented what the party aimed to accomplish, yet it conceded that the "financial question"—that is, bimetallism and defeat of the gold standard—was the "pressing issue" and welcomed the opportunity of joining with others in the campaign in support of that measure.[7]

Despite an unprecedented and prodigious effort by Bryan and his many devoted followers, the end result spelled defeat for the "Great Commoner." The losers could console themselves by noting that their ticket had done well, considering the enormous amount of money available to the Republicans. To put campaign financing in perspective, two extremely wealthy benefactors—Standard Oil and J. P. Morgan—had contributed more to the McKinley campaign ($500,000, to be precise) than Bryan had managed to raise from all sources. As they explained the defeat, Bryanites naturally tended to overemphasize the role played by money, intimidation, and corruption. They could also point to the fact that Bryan's losing popular vote constituted a total higher than that of any previous presidential candidate, winners included, and that he had carried the electoral votes of twenty-two states, encompassing the entire South and much of the West. Yet McKinley's victory margin—over half a million popular and ninety-five electoral votes—was a decisive one for the Republicans.[8]

At the state and local levels and in the size of the congressional delegation, however, all was not so bleak. This new Congress would not meet until called into special session by President McKinley in March 1897, but the election had produced the largest Populist delegation ever, numbering six senators and twenty-five representatives. In the meantime, the second, lame-duck session of the Fifty-fourth Congress had yet to meet beginning on 7 December, and if there was ever justification for a constitutional amendment putting an end to such an anachronism, this session was it (that would not be done, of course, until ratification of the Twentieth Amendment in 1933).

"A PASSIONATE CRUSADE OF DISHONOR" OR A MISSED OPPORTUNITY?

Although it would not be determined until late in January 1897, the second session of the Fifty-fourth Congress was destined to be Senator Peffer's last. The Kansas Populist had announced several months before the election that he would be willing to serve a second term if the legislature desired. He continued to champion Populist principles in the Senate as vigorously as he had throughout his term, one week into the session introducing a joint resolution providing for the appointment of a national monetary commission. Early in January, he also spoke in support of a bill for free homesteads on federal land in Oklahoma Territory.[9]

Several days later, Allen added his support for this measure, asking the rhetorical question: "What can make our institutions more secure, what can make American society more permanent and more enduring, than giving every man and woman and child an opportunity to own and occupy a portion of the soil that they [can] . . . truthfully say is their home? You can not make good citizens of tramps. You can not make good . . . citizens of men who [are without] . . . homes." To those who would say that it was better that they "pay" for the land, that "no one should get something for nothing," Allen pointed to the nation's practice of "subsidizing railways and steamship companies and giving public money to improve rivers and harbors" as a precedent, and added that if those measures are "wise . . . , it is infinitely more wise, as it is more just, to give to those who are struggling to establish a home."[10]

Appropriately enough, Peffer's last words for the record were uttered on behalf of a House bill providing for a nonpartisan commission to collate information regarding the condition of business, labor, and agriculture and to recommend, if need be, legislation to cope with the problems created by the depression. It was a variation on an effort he had called for nearly three years earlier. Its passage marked perhaps a small degree of progress within Congress regarding such matters and was, in its own unheralded and unintended fashion, a kind of tribute to Populism's first U.S. senator.[11]

Senator Allen also managed to enliven the session a bit by taking issue on the floor with some remarks made by George Hoar in Boston several weeks after

McKinley's defeat of Bryan. Hoar had said, "It is certainly a sad thing to think that States like Kansas and Nebraska, children of New England, that have great farming populations, where we expect to find—if we find them anywhere—sobriety, integrity, steadiness, conservatism, the great communities where churches abound and where the schools are the best in the world, should have lent themselves to this crazy attempt at revolution and this passionate crusade of dishonor." Allen asked, "What was the 'crazy attempt at revolution and passionate crusade of dishonor' of which the Senator of Massachusetts spoke? Nothing . . . more than that a majority of the people of Nebraska, believing that silver is money of the Constitution."[12] But of course the battle between the advocates of silver and gold ran much deeper than the mere use of the two metals as money.

William Allen White, author of the 1896 campaign's most famous editorial, knew as much and sized up the election as well as anyone, hitting on its larger meaning in the process. "The fight came squarely," said White. "Mr. Bryan arrayed class against class. He appealed to the misery of the poor; he indexed [highlighted] the luxurious appointments of the rich. He attempted to draw to his side all of those on the debit side of the ledger." McKinley and his gold-standard supporters among Republicans and Democrats, in contrast, "fought out their fight on the principle of individual responsibility for individual failure or success." Their position was that of "laissez faire" or "hands off." McKinley's people "stood squarely for 'vested rights.' They said, in effect, you can not cut off the rich man's wealth without curtailing the poor man's income." Free silver was just a "dummy issue," wrote White. "The issue went deeper. It permeated the political structure of the nation." If Bryan and his Populist allies had won nationally, it would have signified "a resolution—a resolution to a mild yet dangerous form of socialism." White was convinced that the issue had been "settled" for his "generation."[13]

The young Kansas Republican was certainly on target with respect to that crucial election, especially if the challenge was seen as Populism rather than Bryanism. But who can say whether Bryan's election would have made an important difference? As president, how bold might the Nebraskan have been? Would he have moved even more clearly to the Left? It seems plausible that he would have made it at least as far as, or even further than, Woodrow Wilson's administration nearly twenty years later. We can also be fairly confident that Bryan and his Populist allies would have been much less inclined to take the imperialistic road in the aftermath of the Spanish-American War, nor would they have been so inclined to accommodate the corporate merger movement as occurred after President McKinley and the Republicans assumed control in 1897. From that perspective, one can easily visualize quite a different course for American history in the twentieth century.

However that may have been, Bryan's defeat was a heavy blow to the cause of reform. Even though Populist congressional numbers were significantly increased, it was plain to everyone that a grand opportunity to alter America's course had been lost. In fact, the Fifty-fifth Congress, with its three sessions from March

1897 to March 1899, was for all practical purposes the last act in the history of congressional Populism, even though the two succeeding congresses were not without special significance, in spite of their greatly diminished Populist numbers. During this time, fusion politics was constantly at issue, as party leaders attempted to steer in a direction that they hoped would sustain their cause. Ultimately, there appeared to be no viable course open to the party, and with the aid of hindsight, one might argue that its fate had indeed been sealed by the takeover of the Democratic party by William Jennings Bryan and the anti-gold-standard wing at Chicago in 1896. If so, the best the Populists could hope for was to utilize whatever political clout they could muster on behalf of principles that nearly all conceded were far more important than the party itself. The issue of whether it was better to try to advance that goal by going it alone or by cooperating with willing and reform-minded Democrats and Republicans was a highly contentious one that troubled Populist politics greatly, at all levels, throughout the fade-out period.

Following the devastating defeat in the presidential contest, Senator Butler, as party chairman, circulated a letter to the national committee soliciting advice regarding the party's future course, saying that he believed the party might be best served by placing the demand for a government-owned railway system at the top of its agenda. The response was immediate from all over the country, pointing in just about every direction on the political compass. One response from J. H. ("Cyclone") Davis of Texas included an open letter that Davis had recently published on the same subject. He cautioned that the party "must not drift towards socialism, [because] there is," he wrote, "a distinct line of demarcation between Populism and Socialism. The state ownership of muncipal, state, and county [facilities], highways, such as railroads, telegraphs, etc., is no more Socialism than operation of the public school system." This observation was commonly agreed on, but Davis's next piece of advice touched on an area fraught with disagreement. He advised Butler,"add protection to our platform and our party is safe in the future."[14] Several southern Populist congressmen, among them Milford Howard and Albert Goodwyn from Alabama, and Harry Skinner from North Carolina, perhaps because of their closer affiliation with Republicans in their states, were indeed flirting with a protective tariff. However, opposition to this bedrock Republican measure had been and would remain the position of western Populists .

In April, Kali S. Williard, a member of the national committee from Ogden, Utah, responded to the Butler letter by writing an obviously hurried but nonetheless revealing message, exposing a different kind of problem, also growing at the time:

> I do not agree with . . . your plan of action. The feeling of the "middle of the road" Populists is too strong to be buried & as you suggest—line up with you & the other fusionists—the plan of fusion made our party the butt & ridicule of everyone & our position must be defined before any work can be done—as for your plan of making government ownership of railroads the main

> plank in our platform—[it] is folly. The R.R. corporations were no more aggressive than . . . other corporation monopolies. Why single out one alone? Make our fight on . . . government ownership of all means of distribution[,] communication & transportation—& we will have the good will of all reformers. . . . You must know as I know the silver question is only a catch.[15]

Another committee member from Utah, James Hogan, provided an even grimmer report: "Senator, I am of the opinion that the People's Party has had too much fusion and as a natural result it has reached its climax." He closed by writing: "I am . . . insane enough to believe that collectivism or Socialism is the only cure for existing ills. I shall henceforth ally myself with the party which has the complete overthrow of the present wage system as its ultimate object. I am through with middle class movements."[16] All of which seems to prove once again that nothing fails like failure.

MCKINLEY'S SPECIAL SESSION

Cleavages in reform ranks were apparent from the opening of the Fifty-fifth Congress. Shortly after his inauguration, President McKinley summoned the new body into special session to raise import taxes, made necessary, it was claimed, by the budget deficit carried over from the Cleveland administration and compounded by the Supreme Court's invalidation of the income tax enacted in 1894. The House assembled on that date, and the victorious Republicans elected Thomas Bracket Reed of Maine Speaker with 200 votes, against 114 received by Democrat Joseph Bailey of Texas and 21 received by John Bell from the Populists. Jerry Simpson returned to this Congress, and he nominated John Bell as Speaker. As had been the case after his absence in the Fifty-third Congress following his heart ailment, however, Simpson would be the de facto Populist leader; his particular skills and stature within the party were just too great for him to be kept on the sidelines.

The seating arrangements in this House also required some special juggling: Republicans claimed the entire 179-seat section to the "west of the main aisle," with twenty-four Republicans spilling over onto the opposite side, where they were joined by twenty-one Populists and ten Silverites to form a cordon not so sanitaire between the Republicans and Democrats, which was promptly dubbed "the Cherokee Strip" by Jerry Simpson.[17]

The session naturally made the protective tariff the center of attention once again. John Bell led off for the Populists in the debate, telling his listeners that his party had not taken a "decided stand" on the issue heretofore because "it never has believed that the tariff was in fact the seat of our difficulties." He concluded, however, by conceding that it was futile "to protest against the passage of this bill [the Dingley tariff] as your cherished remedy; but we predict that until you legislate some for the consumer and laborer . . . the masses will continue to go into bankruptcy, and the army of the unemployed will continue its tramp in search of work. . . . This bill will make the rich richer and the poor poorer. . . . The scramble for private interests in this bill has blotted out the lines between public duty and selfish private interests." By its passage, he predicted, "the great aggregations of capital at the centers of population will be made complete masters of the interior of the country and of the wage earners."[18] This was a rather dire set of consequences for a program that was said not to be at "the seat of our difficulties."

William Laury Greene, by turns a teacher, lawyer, and judge, was one of the more impressive newcomers among the Populists (but his career was destined to be cut short when he died soon after his reelection to a second term in 1898).[19] The Nebraska representative followed Bell with an impressive first speech. He began by taking issue with what others had said regarding the causes of the nation's economic woes. Regarding President McKinley's message to Congress, he said, "If that document had been written by a Democrat or a Populist . . . four years ago, they would have said he was a calamity howler. At last our President has become a calamity howler. He has pointed out to us the dire distress, the poverty, and the misery of our people." Unfortunately, President McKinley and his allies misrepresented the origins of the situation quite badly. "How is it," asked Greene, "that gentlemen so early forget the facts of history?" Let us not kid ourselves into thinking all was well "before Grover the First" or "Grover the Second." The country's problems, he insisted, were much more deeply rooted than the advocates of a protective tariff would have the nation believe.

Speaking as a westerner, Greene then said: "We love New England. We love the East. But we want to see such laws enacted that the people of the East and the people of the West and people of the North and the people of the South will all be protected in their rights and enjoy the fruits of their labor. We want that, and that is all we want. [Applause.]" Why not provide "the only honest protection there is?" asked Greene. "I want the laborer protected. I want him honestly protected in New England and in New York; I want him protected on the great plains; I want him protected in the great mines; I want him protected on the farm, in the workshop, on land and sea, wherever he may be. I want this great Government to reach out its strong arm and say we will give equal rights to all and special privileges to none. That is all we ask." And with that Greene's speech ended with quite a round of applause.[20]

The next day, Milford Howard stood in the well to deliver what was perhaps his most provocative speech. At one point, the Alabama Populist drew a round of "prolonged applause" with these revealing lines: "When 3,000,000 black slaves were pleading for freedom, Wendell Phillips and William Lloyd Garrison were told their agitation would disturb business; but, fearlessly and undaunted, they raised their voices in protest against the foul blot on our civilization until the slaves were freed. To-day there are more than 20,000,000 white slaves in this country, and when we dare plead for them we are told that we are anarchists—that we will disturb business."

Howard's words, as revealed in the excerpt from the same speech that heads this chapter, were strongly weighted on the side of labor and against capital in the tradition of Abraham Lincoln (for a white southerner who had grown to manhood amidst the culture of the lost cause that was in itself a noteworthy occurrence), but he also announced his intention of voting in favor of the Republican tariff measure under consideration. At the same time, he said that he wanted it understood that he was not "so foolish as to believe that we can make the people rich and prosperous by taxing them, but . . . I believe in the broad, patriotic principle of protection to American industry and American labor." It was not, as some believed, "a panacea . . . but . . . it, in some measure, protects American labor against the pauper labor of other countries."[21]

The next day, Curtis Castle, the physician from Merced, California, made his maiden speech. It turned out to be a major statement in the annals of congressional Populism, the purest example of the old radicalism that historians are fond of calling "neorepublicanism"— a persausion that loomed large in the origins of the Alliance and the People's party. Castle began by arguing that the title of the bill being debated was "wholly misleading." He conceded that it would "increase revenues" but emphatically denied the claim that "it will encourage" American industries. "The proper title for this monstrosity," he said, "would be, 'a bill to foster trusts and to pauperize and peonize the agricultural laborers of the United States.'" The whole scheme, as far as he was concerned, resembled the forms of government against which Americans had successfully rebelled more than a century earlier. He explained:

> The foundation of monarchical government rests upon privilege, and their laws emanate from the idea of class inequality. The very essence and spirit of monarchies is that the laboring classes are by nature and divine law inferior to the nonlaboring class. Hence their whole legal system is so constructed as to rob the producer for the benefit of the nonproducer. . . . On the other hand, privilege has no part or place in a republic. Republics are founded upon the divine truth of human equality and brotherhood. The essence of republicanism is found in the language of that noblest of Americans, Thomas Jefferson, when he penned those immortal words, "All men are created equal." The objects of a republican government are to secure to all men exact and equal protection under the laws. There can be no such thing as privilege in a republic. There can be no class distinctions before the law.

Castle went on to note that the Declaration of Independence and the Constitution had pointed the way to that kind of society. Nevertheless, "after a century of national life, and in the high noon of our national glory, we are confronted by a band of commercial pirates, who demand that we . . . [turn back] the hands upon the dial of progress. . . . In short, we are asked to give up the essence of republicanism and accept as the rule of our national conduct the essence of monarchy, namely, privilege."

Later in this remarkable restatement of the old radicalism, Castle closed with this powerful and revealing statement: "In behalf of the men who toil beneath the burning sun to produce the great staples which sustain life, and without which we could not live, I protest against the passage of this monstrous iniquity. Nero fiddled while Rome burned, but we have no record to show that the Roman citizens danced. While the American government totters to its fall, we behold the gruesome spectacle of the Republican party enacting legislation whose only result will be to hasten the ultimate destruction of the Republic. With the destruction of the independent agriculturalist, the last prop of the Republic will have fallen, and we will have no further occasion to advocate the equality of all men before the law."[22]

There was not the slightest hint in Castle's speech that the people he represented would benefit from a protective tariff. That was also the position of Idaho Populist James Gunn, the former editor of the *Boise Sentinel,* who delivered a much less spectacular speech the following day, directing his attention primarily to describing the depressed condition of the "mountainous regions" and especially the situation confronting silver miners. Anyone, he said, "who thinks he can revive them with a tariff is more fitted for a seat in an insane asylum than in this House."[23]

Jerry Simpson followed Gunn and spoke for fifteen minutes, proving rather quickly that he was the "same old Jerry" and that his two-year absence had in no way lessened his speaking ability or his opposition to protective tariffs. Simpson devoted most of his time to arguing against the contention, prominently on display, that the Republican tariff was in the interest of both the laboring man and the farmer. He especially resented the argument that farmers were not laborers. "If the farmer's interests as a laborer are not greater than they are in any other direction," said Simpson, "I do not know anything of the farmer or farming. If there are any people in this country who rise earlier . . . , work earlier and work later than the farmer—and the wife and children of the farmer—I have not yet discovered them."[24]

If pushed on the point, one suspects that Simpson would have readily conceded that the farmer was also a businessman. This aspect of the farmer's dual personality was more plainly in evidence later that same day in the course of Harry Skinner's remarks before the House. Sounding more like a "New South" booster than a down-and-out Populist farmer, Skinner announced himself as "a Populist, and hence a protectionist. Not in a narrow or sectional sense," he quickly added, "but in the broad sense that all sections and all interests should be protected." On the tariff question, said Skinner, my party "occupies the proper position. It believes in equitable protection, the protection of the masses as against the classes, and the protection of all legitimate industries, but no protection to trusts."

After making reference to a fairly extensive system of manufacturing in his state of North Carolina, Skinner chided southern Democrats for not doing more over the last twenty-five years to secure protection for the South's manufacturing interests. Had they done so, he argued, "in lieu of an impoverished and perishing South we would be the richest and most prosperous country that the sun in its diurnal course falls upon."

Skinner also extolled the South's workforce, particularly its black workers, recalling especially the "faithful" role of the slaves during the Civil War. "An attack from the rear, a thousand torches in the hands of these slaves at any time would have demoralized Lee's army," he noted. It did not happen. "History can furnish no parallel for such conduct and faith under such circumstances. I shall remember them by trying to secure for them more constant employment at better wages, more education, and an improvement intellectually, morally, and financially." Enterprisers take notice, Skinner seemed to be saying. "We have the best labor, white and colored, in the world. We have no lockouts, no strikes, no anarchy or communism, and manufacturing of all kinds has become more profitable at the South than elsewhere." If people of the South would merely embrace the protective principle, "we would soon have the advantage of the North and East in having the raw material at hand; transportation, a big item, would be saved, and in two decades we would supplant the North and East and become the manufacturing section of the country." It would happen; he guaranteed it. "Capital is selfish, and it will take advantage of the net savings wrought by placing the plants beside the fields."

Later, Skinner opened the door a bit wider on that hidden room containing his thoughts on the question of race. He alluded to himself as "the junior son of a large slaveholder." As such, "I think I am capable of being entirely fair to the colored man. I thank heaven . . . the shackles of slavery have been stricken from the limbs of the colored man. This was a blessing to the South in disguise."

What did Skinner think the role of people of color should be in this new industrialized South? "The colored vote can never and should never control the South. I believe in securing for the colored man better education and opportunities, and I believe that their ballots should be honestly counted; but the man or party that encourages them to believe they should control is an enemy to the race [white, black, human?] and the country." Skinner's position on the race question, with the possible exception of black enfranchisement (given the fact that the move to disfranchise adult males of color was already under way in the South), was indistinguishable from that of his region's so-called New South Democrats. But at the same time, one cannot help but wonder what his position would have been if the votes of North Carolina blacks opened the door to the kind of "control" he feared, or even to a degree of participation in government commensurate with the number of blacks in the population. Frankly, given that scenario, it seems most likely that an honest ballot count would no longer be among those paternalistic compensations for faithful service that this particular North Carolina Populist would "try to secure" for people of color.

As for the tariff bill under discussion, Skinner made it clear that he regarded it as inadequate to the task of restoring prosperity to the masses. Most importantly, it would do nothing to improve the economic health of the "agriculturalist," who, he insisted, must first prosper "before he can sustain the merchant, the lawyer, the doctor, or the manufacturer."[25]

In the course of this debate, Missouri's "Champ" Clark, who also resumed his tenure with this Congress, managed to enhance his reputation for wit by interjecting a comment occasioned by the inclusion of ashes on the tariff-free list. Said Clark, "When I read that item in the bill, I thought it was to encourage farmers in the production of ashes [laughter]; but lo and behold, it is to help the Republican soap makers fry more grease out of the American people! [Laughter and applause on the Democratic side.] My Republican friends, let me give you a suggestion. . . . While you are putting ashes on the free list, put sack cloth there also [laughter], for you will need it when the people find out the iniquities of this bill."[26]

Representative George Henry White, a Republican lawyer from North Carolina elected as a result of the split in the Democratic camp brought on by the Populist revolt, also struck a blow for witticism in this debate, in his case by ridiculing the Democrats' boast of being the champions of free trade. On entering this Congress, White laid claim to the distinction, previously held in the Fifty-third and Fifth-fourth Congresses by George Washington Murray of South Carolina, of being the only person of African descent serving there (interestingly, he would be the last black elected from the South until Andrew Young's election in 1972). In his speech, White said that he was not at all impressed by the Democrats' position on trade. "Why, they have from time to time [even] advocated 'free whisky' . . . ; and in the last campaign their shibboleth was 'free silver.' In fact," added White, "the Southern element of the Democratic party has advocated 'free' everything except free ballots and free negroes." That remark was said to have drawn considerable "laughter and applause on the Republican side and in the galleries." White went on to say that he spoke "as the sole representative on this floor of 9,000,000 of the population of these United States, 90 per cent of whom are laborers," whom he insisted were "protected" under the bill being debated.[27]

The House vote came on the last day of March, and to no one's surprise, the measure passed by a nearly perfect party-line vote of 205 to 122. No Populists supported the final bill (apparently Milford Howard was absent or did not register his vote); only Jerry Simpson, Edwin Ridgely, and Mason Peters, all Kansans, along with Charles Barlow and Curtis Castle of California, voted against it; the others simply voted present.[28]

Senate discussion of the tariff was much more subdued. At one point, Senator Allen, in a noteworthy manner, attempted to discredit protective tariffs per se. He indicated that his reading of constitutional law convinced him that it was "well settled that the power to impose taxes, duties, imposts, and excises is limited by the purpose which is expressed in the same paragraph; that is to the payment of the debts and to provide for the common defense and the general welfare of the United States." Taxes not mandated for those "purposes" were "unconstitutional" and amounted to "confiscation of the property of one citizen for the benefit of another." Said Allen, "The purpose of taxation must be a public purpose; it must have some reference to discharging the debts of the nation or providing for the common defense or the general welfare." He conceded, however, that the meaning of the phrase "general welfare" and what that enabled the general government to do by way of programs and taxes were matters of considerable disagreement. The general-welfare clause, he said, had led "many" to claim that "it was within the power of Government to impose taxes, to encourage, sustain, and promote all things, however remotely connected with the Government, that in any manner contributed to the upbuilding and enlightenment of society." In the context at issue here, at least, Allen was not prepared to embrace that view; yet he was convinced that a tax imposed for protective purposes, in a time of peace, was a violation of the Constitution and a species of special favoritism contrary to the general welfare.[29]

Allen was much more easily and deeply moved by the continuing struggle of the Cubans to win their independence. Early in April, during the debate over his resolution calling for a stay of execution by Spain of a Cuban rebel leader, he crossed swords once again with Senator Hoar, in an exchange that became rather personal. Allen responded to remarks by Hoar by saying: "Oh, I wish I had the power to send American soldiers upon the Island of Cuba and to put the Navy in Cuban waters, I would grind to millions of infinitesimal pieces the harsh, brutal Spaniard unless he relaxed his grasp upon the people. . . . Yet, because I say this in true Western style, and not with the conservatism of Massachusetts and Massachusetts statesmen, . . . I am, in the judgment of the Senator from Massachusetts, guided by an inflamed and heated imagination; my language is intemperate." Retaliating in kind, Allen added that he sometimes was inclined to believe that Senator Hoar was "mistaken in his mission in this Chamber, and he forgets that the mantle of an intellectual giant may occasionally, through the intervention of two or three generations, descend to an intellectual pigmy."[30]

In early May, Senator Kyle occupied the floor briefly to deny press reports that he had gone over completely to the Republicans. He said that he occupied "the same position" he had "always occupied." He was an "independent," a member of no caucus, and "free to vote on all questions" as he pleased.[31]

The following month, Senator Butler occupied the floor to speak forcefully on behalf of the income tax amendment he had introduced earlier. At the same time, he strongly endorsed public ownership of the railroads. Referring to a bill to legalize pools pending in the Senate, Butler said that he thought "it best for all the railroad lines . . . to be operated as one system, provided that system is operated as a public function at cost for the public good. . . . Public ownership and not pooling is the remedy. The railroad corporations want a legalized trust for their own profit and power, not for the welfare of the public."[32]

A few weeks later, Allen argued in favor of the government taking control of a number of troubled, bond-assisted railroads in order to "squeeze out all the water" in railway stocks. He calculated that $6 billion of the $11 billion at which the railroads were capitalized was "absolute water."[33] "The very rates fixed by the Government upon its lines,"said Allen, "would force every competing road to come to the terms of the Government." As he saw it, the only argument that could be made against the proposition was "prompted by greed." Where was it written, he asked, that "a few corporations must have an opportunity to fleece the people at their will?" The nation now had "an opportunity to test the doctrine of Government ownership. . . . We have constructed canals and locks and own them, charging toll. We are talking of constructing the Nicaragua Canal, 168 miles long, and owning and operating it, putting probably $300,000,000 into it before we get through, and charging tolls."[34]

Senator Peffer's replacement, William Harris, devoted much of his time as a member of the Committee on Pacific Railroads to drafting a bill providing for the takeover of the bankrupt Union Pacific. In mid-July, a bill to that effect was reported from the committee by Harris.[35] Allen immediately became its primary defender and advocate. Once again, as he pursued that course, he found himself engaged in a colloquy with Iowa's Republican Senator John Gear and, in the process, made one of the more persuasive arguments on behalf of this fundamental Populist proposal. At one point, Allen said, "I bring the Senator back to the proposition that the solution of the railroad problem in this country is Government ownership. He denies it. I wish to call his attention to the fact that the great governments of the world are rapidly passing to government ownership of railroads." A bit later he asked,

> Why are they doing that? Because a railway is a great natural monopoly. It is a thing in which all the people are interested—like the sun light, and the air, and the water. A railroad is a necessity to a community. All the people are interested in the question of transportation. All are interested in the transmission of news by telegraph. . . . Now, here is an opportunity. Here is a property the Government of the United States built. There is not a stockholder in the Union Pacific Railroad Company who, practically speaking, put a dollar into it. It was a gift by the Government. Why not take possession of this road and reduce it to Government ownership and operate it in the interest of the people who paid for it?

Butler then interrupted Allen to say that if the Union Pacific were owned and operated by the government as the people's agent, so to speak, it would force other railroads "to reduce their fares and rates to a reasonable and honest basis. The Southern Pacific would be afraid of the competition if the Government would operate the Central Pacific and the Union Pacific as a through line. So would the Northern Pacific and every other railroad." Butler went on to tell Gear that here was "a chance to test what you charge, that the roads can not be operated practically by the Government, and you are afraid of the test, and run from it. This would make a fair [and] practical test and would kill Government ownership forever if it did not prove successful. We are ready to make the test, and you are afraid of it." Gear's response was: "I have no doubt the Senator from North Carolina is ready to test anything."

Allen then regained the floor and provided an extensive list of countries that had, in whole or in part, government-owned and -operated railroads—or had at least reserved to themselves that option at some point in the future. After that he alluded to the record to show that the states of Illinois, Indiana, Pennsylvania, Massachusetts, Michigan, and "several" others had constructed and/or owned railroads. Georgia, he reported, still owned one. Then, Butler once again interrupted Allen to say, "North Carolina has constructed two railroads, extending from the Atlantic Ocean up to the mountains, and is now operating one of them, and the other is leased, both paying a profit."

Later, Senator John Thurston, Allen's Republican counterpart from Nebraska and at one time an attorney for the Union Pacific Railroad, asked a question that may have been on the minds of more conservative reformers; it may also have appealed to those whose aim was to retain private ownership of the system. Why would it not be better, he asked, merely to"fix rates on all interstate railroads" rather than resorting to government ownership and operation? Allen replied: "Simply because Congress will not do it." It was impossible; there were too many railroad senators and representatives in the capital. Without "a radical change in the Government," he added, "not a person in this Chamber, not even one of these little pages, will ever live to see the day when the Congress will pass a maximum freight rate [bill]."[36] One can only wonder what Allen thought the chances were of Congress mandating a government-owned and -operated system; but in this situation, Allen, Butler, and Harris were, after all, concerned primarily with the more doable proposal of taking over one bankrupt national line to provide a single, alternative transcontinental railroad to serve as a yardstick and competitive spur for all the other privately owned lines.[37]

On the House side two months into the special session, Speaker Reed still had not appointed the standing committees, apparently aimed at expediting passage of a protective tariff. No doubt these tactics helped secure Reed's title of "Czar," earned as Speaker of the "billion dollar" Fifty-first Congress of 1889-1891. Jerry Simpson continually tried to get the Speaker to complete the organization. Early in April, he referred to the Speaker's tactics as "a case of political 'soonerism' unequaled in the annals of legislation in this country."

During this period, the House adjourned frequently and simply waited on measures pending before the Senate. Finally, in late July, committee assignments were handed down. Simpson's appointment to Agriculture and Bell's to Appropriations were among the more important assignments; Skinner's to Ventilation and Acoustics and also to Buildings and Grounds was among the least important.[38]

In May, the House had before it a joint resolution authorizing the expenditure of $50,000 from the Treasury to assist Americans in Cuba who were said to be in need. Simpson used this measure to make a point about destitute people closer to home. Said Simpson, "Ordinarily I am very ready to vote for propositions of this kind for charitable purposes. I voted to send relief to the sufferers along the Mississippi. But, Mr. Speaker, that was at home. We have many thousands of people on the verge of starvation in this country, and it seems to me we ought first to address ourselves to their needs." He went on to quote from the newspaper regarding suffering in Philadelphia. "Charity," he said, "ought to begin there." As for

Cuba, "whenever the great 'property interests,' as you are pleased to call them, give consent that the belligerent rights of struggling Cuba shall be recognized, then the Republican party will fall in line . . . and not before."[39]

In early June, Simpson found himself involved in an exchange with Richard Bartholdt, a German-born Republican journalist from Missouri, with Simpson uncharacteristically coming across a bit gruff and with just a hint of anti-Semitism in his remarks. Bartholdt asked, "When the gentleman employs the term 'we'—pluralis majestatis—does he mean that it shall be applied to the Populists, to the Democrats, or to the combined forces on that side?" Simpson replied, "I mean it to be applied to every man who opposes the Republican party, the enemy of mankind. [Laughter and applause on the Democratic side.] I will ask whether the language which the gentleman from Missouri addressed me is Hebrew or 'United States'?" Bartholdt, who may well have been Jewish, answered: "I am aware that the gentleman has not had a classical education." To which Simpson replied, "The gentleman from Missouri has the advantage of me, because he knows enough to call things by two different names. I only know enough to call them by one name; but I generally get there."[40]

The following month, another, more humorous affair involving Simpson cast some light on the Kansan's well-known spelling problems, as well as on the much less excusable tactics of his opponents. It all began with Simpson's comment: "Mr. Speaker, yesterday, by the kind indulgence of the Chair, I rose to correct the RECORD. It seems now the correction needs correcting. The correction which I desired to make yesterday was that where I had used the word 'brutal,' designating the majority of the House as a 'brutal majority,' the word 'frugal' appeared, and I wanted the word 'brutal' substituted. To-day my correction appears with the word 'prudent' instead of the word 'brutal.' [Laughter.] I want to correct that error." After still more jostling, several Republicans suggested that Simpson spell the word he wanted used. He quickly extricated himself from that trap, with a round of laughter to complement his mental dexterity. Said Simpson, "I am not going to start a spelling school here for the benefit of the Republican party."[41]

The art of spelling may not have been part of the Populist curriculum, but Simpson and his compatriots had certainly started a school in political economy from the day they entered Congress; and as the first session of the Fifty-fifth Congress ended, that school was barely past midterm. Quite a number of lessons remained.

7

"Come Out on the Side of Eternal Justice and Human Liberty," 1897–1898

> *Yesterday I was discussing [with a leading Democrat]... a needed reform that can never be gotten except by the exercise of the power and authority of the General Government.... He turned and said: "I admit that we need such a reform, but Thomas Jefferson said that the best government was the government that governed the least. Therefore I am in favor of the Government simply collecting taxes and policing the country, and stopping there, leaving everything else to private enterprise.". . .*
>
> *I . . . protest, as a Democrat of the Jeffersonian school, against such statements as representing Democratic principles, I rise to state that there has been nothing perverted, distorted, and twisted so badly during the last one hundred years in this country as what is known as Jeffersonian Democracy. While Jefferson used about that language, yet when it is quoted as a statement from Jefferson to prohibit having the Government do what is necessary to be done to promote the happiness and general welfare of the people of this country, they are libeling Thomas Jefferson. . . .*
>
> *The Democracy of . . . Jefferson stood for the Government doing whatever was necessary to protect the life, liberty, and property of the people and promote the general welfare and preserve to ourselves and our posterity all the inalienable rights of man.*
>
> Marion Butler, *Congressional Record,* 55th Cong., 2nd sess., 3 February 1898

The first session of the Fifty-fifth Congress ended the same day that Jerry Simpson attempted to get back on the record what he believed was the most descriptive adjective for the Republican majority. By the time the second session convened five months later, the fortunes of the People's party were clearly in precipitous decline. Perhaps a comment from an Illinois Populist to Marion Butler late that year told the story: "We are making no converts. . . . Our brothers are fighting each other, our papers are half dead, the other half dying, and old and true workers are going back into the old parties. Something unusual, something heroic, must be done to rally the forces and renew the battle."[1] That extraordinary event was soon to happen, but it would work against rather than for the Populist cause. That something was the Spanish-American War, aided and abetted, we should note, by the slow but steady economic recovery that had finally set in after four long years of national depression.

It was indeed ironic that it would be the Cuban cause and a war with Spain that would work in this way, because no element in Congress was more eager to take action against Spanish colonial misrule than the Populist delegation. That desire even intensified in this Congress, because Republican leaders were doing everything they could to shut down debate on the floor. One can only speculate about how different the course of events might have been had Bryan won the presidency.

At the opening of the Senate, William Allen wasted no time introducing—for the seventh or eighth time, actually—another resolution calling on the executive branch to "acknowledge by appropriate act the political independence of Cuba." Speaking on behalf of his resolution, he asserted that inaction by President McKinley was the product of a "cold and heartless commercialism that freezes the blood of patriotism in his veins and that is willing to sacrifice human rights, the honor of women, and the lives of children, if need be, [so] that the course of business may not be checked or that the channels of trade be not obstructed."[2]

In the House on 5 January 1898, William Greene used the opportunity afforded by a discussion of a bill to strengthen the Civil Service Commission to say that he favored aid to the Cubans but was convinced that "the best aid we can send them is a resolution of this House recognizing their independence. But the capitalists say that will bring on a war with Spain." That mattered not, said Greene, because "human life and liberty are of more value than all the stocks and bonds on earth. . . . If, by protecting suffering humanity and lending our influence to liberate a suffering people from the hand of tyranny, war should be forced upon us, at the first sound of *Yankee Doodle* a million bayonets would shimmer and shine under a Northern sun and at the first strain of *Dixie* a million sabers would leap from their scabbards in the South, and as one unconquerable army under the Stars and Stripes we would take care of the issue."[3]

Several weeks later, Curtis Castle managed to have his say on the matter. At the opening, the California Populist had introduced a resolution calling for the recognition of the belligerent rights of the Cubans. Castle had doubts about whether the country any "longer [even had] a government of the people" when the "people's representatives" were denied the opportunity to debate the issue of Cuban belligerency. There was no question in his mind that a small financial circle controlled the situation. "Rothschild and his American agents, Belmont, Morgan, & Co., hold $200,000,000 in Spanish bonds. Should Cuba achieve her independence, the market value of these bonds would depreciate; hence, Rothschild favors Spain and will until he perceives that Cuban independence is inevitable. Then, provided he can persuade Cuba to issue bonds for his benefit, he will permit the United States Government to interfere. Rothschild controls Morgan, Morgan controls Hanna, and Hanna controls McKinley, the Supreme Court, the Senate, and the House of Representatives. Hanna is America and America is Hanna."[4]

Call it outrageous hyperbole—the manifestation, if you will, of the "paranoid style" in American politics—but quite a number of congressmen (and who knows how many Americans) were as convinced as Castle that Marcus Alonzo Hanna, who had directed McKinley's successful run for the presidency the previous year and who was Ohio's replacement for John Sherman in the Senate, was the evil genius behind the McKinley administration's policy of inaction regarding the Cuban fight for independence. The day following Castle's remarks, for example, the irrepressible Champ Clark used the opportunity of a discussion over an appropriations bill to plead for the recognition of Cuba's independence. "If Spain does not bring the war to a speedy conclusion," said the Missouri Democrat, "the United States ought to expel her from the Western Hemisphere." American foreign policy in the future should make it clear that "we intend, at all hazards and whatever cost, to thoroughly dominate the western world." That line drew applause, as did Clark's discussion of what he called the "evils of McHannaism."

Clark's concluding advice for the Republican majority was: "Lay aside the weight that is holding you down, assert your rights, and *come out on the side of eternal justice and human liberty*. . . . We Democrats and Populists stand here ready and anxious to remove from America her great reproach. We on this side will contribute 155 votes to the good cause. If only 24 righteous men can be found in this Republican Sodom—if only 24 Republicans will break their heavy yoke . . . and join us in this noble work, before the sun sets this day we will send glad tidings ringing round the world that Cuba is free! Free thank God, by the act of the American Congress!"[5]

Jeremiah Botkin, a Methodist minister and former chaplain of the Kansas senate, made his first speech a passionate plea for Cuban independence. The other Jeremiah in the Kansas delegation (better known as Jerry), sensing the boost that militarism was bound to receive from a war no matter how righteous, was the least jingoistic of all the Populists. During this debate, Simpson said that he was "not lying awake at night over the condition of Cuba." For some time, he had taken a position "somewhat between the two great political parties" on the issue. He was not at all surprised that the Cleveland and McKinley administrations were like "two peas in a pod" on the issue of Cuban independence; both, he contended, were beholden to the same "bond-holding interests." As in the case of Castle, Simpson was convinced that nothing would happen until the bondholders had secured their huge investment— $400 million, in Simpson's estimate. Once again, Simpson picked up on the argument, repeatedly made, that the Cubans were starving, saying, "If people are starving in Cuba, they are starving and suffering in this country also." Why not "display American statesmanship in regard to the enactment of laws which will give our own people a better Government and better condition, instead of devoting so much time to the Island of Cuba."[6]

On 15 February 1898, the explosion that sank the American battleship *Maine* in Havana Harbor gave the whole issue a very different complexion, as all parties prepared themselves for what seemed inevitable. In the meantime, Congress concerned itself with other important issues that have been all but ignored due to the rush of events toward war.

IMMIGRATION

Immigration restriction was back on the front burner as the second session began, and this time the Populists joined the debate, questioning the approach advocated by Senator Lodge and the Immigration Restriction League. Senator Allen announced several weeks into the session that he was "satisfied" that his vote for the Lodge immigration bill in the previous Congress had been an "error" on his part that likely would not have happened had he subjected the measure to "closer inspection." The legislation he wanted would end the evasion of laws against "the importation of contract laborers." He urged the senators to reject the bill reported by the Committee on Immigration as both insufficient and too restrictive. They should remind themselves that the nation had been an "asylum of the oppressed of all nations and that here, under the aegis of our flag, all who love liberty and are willing to abjure allegiance to the king or potentate of whom they were subjects shall in the course of time become citizens and receive our protection." Later in the speech, however, Allen acknowledged his agreement with those who insisted that "ethnic conditions should enter into the question," announcing that he "would cheerfully vote to exclude any of the various tribes of Mongols as alien in sympathy and whose presence here would impair, if not endanger, the nation. But for the man or woman who belongs to the Caucasian race, wherever he or she may have been born, who looks to this country for aid and protection, and who in turn is willing to give to it of his or her strength of body and mind a full measure of service for its preservation and perpetuity, I would open the gates until the millions of acres of our land now lying idle are occupied, brought into cultivation, and made to yield to the commerce of the world their boundless wealth."[7]

Two days later, George Turner, the newly elected Populist senator from the state of Washington, delivered his first speech in this immigration restriction debate. It was unquestionably a noteworthy effort. Unlike Allen's, Turner's was free of racist overtones, decidedly liberal, and deeply insightful regarding the conditions that had produced so much resentment toward immigrants. As he saw it, "The essential factors in the problem of immigration . . . are those of health and virtue. Given these and any man or woman is desirable as a resident, and may in the course of time become a useful and valuable citizen." He then said, "The springs of Christian charity and humane benevolence in this country, so copious in the past, have not suddenly dried up and ceased to flow. The people of this country will not approve such a policy. For myself, I would as soon refuse food and drink to the hungry and thirsty as to push away from our shores the poor, struggling unfortunate who seeks for himself and his children the boon of freedom and enlightenment at our hands." In his judgment, "Such a course is not in accord with the policy of this country, with the spirit of the people, with the genius of our institutions, or with the history and the traditions of our Republic." He said that he could vote for "an educational qualification for those admitted to citizenship. . . . But I will never vote to deny to any man the protection of our laws and the benefits of our free institutions on the score of learning; such is not statesmanship." He had what he thought was "a better remedy." Why not "put the people of the country to work. Give us a wise and a just economic system which will insure labor its fair reward, not only in the factory but on the farm. Do that and the engorged population of our great centers will soon be remedied, and those centers will reach a normal and a healthy condition." Apparently, scapegoating poor, illiterate immigrants was not the answer. "It is much better," he added, "that we should endeavor to remedy the disease rather than attempt to combat the symptoms."

Turner then proceeded to elaborate on his understanding of why the country was experiencing such hard times. As he saw it, the sad fact was that for years, "legislation has been too much in the interest of moneyed corporations and aggregations of capital and not sufficiently in the interest of the people." This "indiscriminate legislation in the interest of capital" had led to the abandonment of public functions to private interests and the proliferation of monopolistic corporations run by the philosophical descendants of the "robber barons of the Middle Ages," men who were foremost concerned with enriching themselves.

This Spokane attorney, only forty-six years old at the time but the beneficiary of a rich background of political experiences that began in Reconstruction Alabama, closed his speech with a strong plea for an open door by saying, "It has been our policy from the inauguration of the Government to invite immigration; it has been our proud boast that none were turned away from our shores who were worthy and deserving."[8] And if George Turner had his way, that was precisely how it would remain.

In contrast, the remarks of Indiana Republican Senator Charles Fairbanks, who would serve as Theodore Roosevelt's vice president from 1905 to 1909, went to the heart of the concerns of those on the antiradical and nativist side of the debate. Fairbanks called attention to the significant shift that had occurred in the national origins of immigrants since 1880—a shift from "western and northern" Europeans (the so-called old-stock immigrants) to those from the "eastern and southern parts of Europe" (the so-called new-stock immigrants). The figures he cited showed an increase from 8.5 to 51.7 percent in the proportion of the latter and a decline from 64.5 to 36.7 percent in the proportion of the former. His concern, of course, was in checking the flow of the new and restoring, if possible, the old ratio favoring the old-stock immigrants—a thoroughly nativist position. His preference, in fact, was to admit "only those able to read and write." He also noted that the bill did not but should have included "anarchists" and "ultrasocialists" who otherwise would not be excluded by a literacy test. This latter restriction, as previously noted, would be enacted in 1903 after congressional Populism had become a faint memory.[9]

Democratic Senator Donelson Caffery of Louisiana was one of the most outspoken opponents of the Lodge-Fairbanks brand of restriction. "This bill," said Caffery, "is but the feeble echo of the nativism that was rampant in 'Know Nothing' times. The same clamor was raised against the Irish and the German as is now raised against the Italian." He asked, would "the proponents of this bill . . . say an illiterate Jew, of the race of Him who has founded a moral and a religious kingdom greater than this Republic . . . , is an undesirable immigrant?"[10]

Caffery moved to liberalize the Lodge bill in significant ways; his amendment was defeated by a vote of thirty-six to twenty-nine. Three of the six Populist senators, Allen, Henry Heitfeld of Idaho, and James Kyle, supported the Caffery amendment. George Turner had been granted a leave of absence; Butler was paired with another senator. Only William Harris voted against Caffery. The final vote on Lodge's bill for this session came on 17 January, and it passed once again by a vote of forty-five to twenty-eight. Allen and Heitfeld voted no; Harris and Kyle voted yes. Turner and Butler were both paired on the final vote.[11]

This bill never came up for debate in the House and was essentially a dead issue for the remainder of the time Populists were involved at the congressional level. On 20 January, during the debate over Cuba, however, Jerry Simpson raised the specter of a flood of Cuban immigrants to strengthen his argument against moving too quickly to intervene on the island. In addition to "the expense and the horrors of a war," said Simpson, "we would admit to citizenship and to naturalization the inhabitants . . . and thereby gain a large number of very undesirable citizens as a part of our population." Several days later, without explanation but obviously after having second thoughts on the matter, Simpson put himself on record as being in favor of a much more liberal approach to the general question of immigration. "I believe . . . that the gates should be thrown wide open, so that any man on the face of God's earth who desires to improve his condition and better his fortunes shall be permitted to make his home here in this land."[12] Simpson's comment was roundly applauded, and the whole issue was soon lost sight of in the activity brought on by the Spanish-American War and its imperial aftermath. As previously indicated, the effort of the literacy-test restrictionists would finally be successful in 1917. In 1924, with the National Origins Act, which took effect five years later, the quota system they had advocated, based on the percentages of various ethnic elements represented in the population as of 1890, coupled with outright exclusion of Asian immigrants, would also become the law of the land.[13]

GOVERNMENT RAILWAYS

The Populist agitation on behalf of government railroads was probably not without some positive results. Late in 1897, the McKinley administration received the full amount owed to the American public by the bankrupt Union Pacific, and it appeared that the Kansas Pacific Railroad would likely pay the full amount it owed. The specter of government ownership may well have helped set the wheels in motion. That by no means checked the effort by Populists on behalf of that part of their program. Senator George Turner, in the same impressive speech opposing a restrictionist immigration policy noted earlier, also made one of the more forceful commentaries on the abuse of power by railroad corporations and the need for public ownership. To illustrate what he meant by "indiscriminate legislation in the interest of capital" at the expense of the people, Turner said that the nation had "imperceptively parted with a governmental function of the most important character, and vested it in hands where it will be and can only be used for private and selfish purposes." How could such a thing have happened? Turner seemed to be saying. "One of the most important functions of government in all times and ages and among all peoples has been the right to build up, own, and control the highways of the country. Our public men have parted with that function to the railroads, and the railroad corporations to-day tax at will seventy million people for the privilege of using the public highways. That that power should be used selfishly and exactingly, overbearingly and cruelly, to the people of this country was only what might have been expected. . . . No individual ever yet exercised a governmental power granted to him for private gain wisely and well, and he never will." Turner then said, "The robber barons of the Middle Ages were not more ruthless in their forays upon the unwary traveler passing along the roads beneath their castles than these railroad barons of to-day are in their forays upon the general public. Their rule in the West has been to reach down into the pockets of the farmers as deep as they could and take therefrom every dollar and every penny left over and above the cost of production."[14]

This long-forgotten Washington Populist may well have been the primary inspiration for the robber-baron metaphor that historian Matthew Josephson later made such a fixture of history. For sure, he was a strong advocate of government ownership or reform of the nation's railroad system. A year later, speaking in support of a bill authorizing government construction of a Nicaraguan canal, Turner also argued: "The completion of the waterway across the Isthmus . . . will release them [the people of the Pacific coast] at once from the octopus grip of the transcontinental railroads, and only those who have suffered from the exactions of those gigantic monopolies can appreciate the extent to which they deaden the energy, paralyze the industry, and crush the independence of a free and an independent people." He went on to say that he was not "unmindful of the great benefits conferred by the transcontinental railroads on the Pacific Coast." But enough was enough.[15]

That same January, in the House, Arkansas Democrat John Sebastian Little, later governor of his state, delivered one of the more revealing speeches of the 1890s in support of a bill he had introduced aimed at ensuring fair practices and rates by the railroads by means of a strengthened Interstate Commerce Commission. Little's approach clearly foreshadowed that of the so-called progressive reformers who were only just beginning to build momentum in isolated pockets across the nation. As he delivered this speech, Jerry Simpson was in his seat interjecting questions and making observations as only he could. Simpson and the Populists represented one side of the debate at odds with Little's approach. At the outset, Little said that he was "not unmindful of the fact that on the one hand this bill will be attacked by many of the railway companies as inquisitorial and destructive of property rights, and that on the other hand socialists will condemn it as a mere palliative, which will fail to bring about the desired reform." He was convinced, however, that his middle-ground approach was the correct one. "The theory of abandoning all governmental regulation of transportation and leaving it to self-regulation is utterly indefensible." It would, he said, "result . . . in the control of the Government by the transportation companies and their natural allies, the trusts and syndicates; while the change from private to national ownership of the railways not only involves a radical change of our industrial conditions, but a like change of our present system of civil government."

Little went on to oppose governmental ownership for a variety of reasons, chief among them the notion that it would not stop with the railroads, and the entire fabric of the American government and society would be altered in a "revolutionary" fashion. What was involved, he said, was "the eternal and irrepressible struggle between collectivism and individualism, which is as old as the hills and which has been going on since the dawn of civilization, and which will continue until the human race has run its course."[16]

Jerry Simpson and William Greene both asked Little whether he agreed that the time had arrived for government ownership. In effect, he said no, but he conceded that the time might soon come if the Republicans remained in control. He then identified three approaches for dealing with the railroads, each with its share of advocates: Pooling, with certain legal restrictions applied, was one. Government ownership and management was another. The third, and the one he favored, called for regulation under a commission with the power to fix rates and to prevent abuses. The regulatory approach would increasingly gain support among those who were opposed to the idea of government doing nothing at all or doing too much.

By February 1898, it was conceded that Senator Harris's effort regarding the defaulting Union Pacific had actually played an important role in saving the federal government about $25 million. Harris was still working at the time toward saving another $6.7 million in the case of the Kansas Pacific. At the same time, Allen may well have been running interference for Harris on the Senate floor by letting it be known that the way to avoid losing what was owed was for the federal government to "acquire the railroad and operate it." He also took to the floor to answer the arguments of those who were vehemently opposed to government ownership, led by Republican Senator John Spooner of Wisconsin. In so doing, Allen argued that, by all means, if the Kansas Pacific did not pay the millions it owed, government ownership was the logical recourse.[17]

Populists continued to speak out in favor of public ownership at every opportunity. In the discussion occasioned by the appropriations bill for the Post

Office, for example, Jeremiah Botkin said that "when we come fully to understand that this Government is for the people instead of the corporations, we shall build and own our postal cars." In that way, said Botkin, "we shall . . . save $30,000,000 a year now paid in transportation [of the mails]. With such economy, the Government could easily establish a system of free rural mail delivery, so long the dream of millions of our best citizens."[18]

That same month, Allen made a move, supported by only his fellow Populists, to amend a Senate bill pertaining to Alaska so that the federal government could, if it were deemed necessary, exercise an option to "purchase or to take by proceedings of condemnation any railroad that may be constructed" in the area under consideration. On several other occasions that month, Allen was active in support of government ownership. In one exchange on the floor, he stated: "I believe in the Government ownership of railroads. The time is here, or at least is rapidly coming, when the railroads will own the Government or the Government will own the railroads." In this particular case, interestingly enough, he was speaking to oppose a move to purchase a branch line that he and others believed would be ruined by alternative lines.[19]

In the House that March, John Bell let it be known that he favored government ownership only as a last resort. He wanted the railroads controlled, however. "You must either control the railroads or the people will own them." In the course of this debate, it was said that the railroads had engaged in "open and palpable frauds" of the government in carrying the nation's mail.

Populists objected especially to the subsidies paid to the railroads. Harry Skinner, for example, said that they were an "unwarranted and a needless subsidy." At the same time, Skinner called for government ownership of the roads.[20]

The debate over railroad subsidies even produced a rare example of two Populists at odds with each other on the floor. Simpson endorsed a $25,000 appropriation to fund a fast-train mail delivery service affecting Kansas and the Southwest. A short time later, California's Charles Barlow said: "Mr. Chairman, I regret that my friend from Kansas did not spend twenty-four hours in mending his fences. [Great laughter.] For a man, a member of my party, to rise in this House and advocate a subsidy to a railroad corporation, he can never justify himself. [Laughter and applause.] . . . We stand opposed to subsidies to railroad corporations and all other corporations. There is not a man in this House who has advocated this question but has acknowledged it to be a subsidy. I hope this appropriation will be stricken out in the name of common decency. [Laughter and applause.]" John Kelley, the South Dakota Populist, followed Barlow and added his voice in opposition to the appropriation. At the same time, Kelley spoke in favor of government-owned railroads as the only proper solution to the problem of there "being great natural monopolies."[21]

But was that not paternalism and a flagrant violation of the wisdom of the illustrious fathers of the Republic? The Populists were repeatedly confronted with arguments to that effect, especially by conservative southern Democrats. On this matter of paternalism, Representative William Adamson, a Georgia Democrat, made a point that perhaps could only be made by someone not in the camp of either the Populists or their more determined opponents. Speaking during the debate over the Indian appropriations bill, Adamson said that he had long noted how "the protectionists and the mongers of money" were so quick to denounce others seeking particular kinds of governmental assistance. These people have been especially adept, said Adamson, at charging "our Populist brethren with infringing on their domain and making some paternalistic demands. But the Populists are mere amateurs in the practice of paternalism, their efforts in that line having been utterly insignificant in comparison with the shameless abandon with which the manufacturers and financial speculators have demanded and used the powers and privileges of this Government."[22] As in the case of Adamson, southern Democrats were especially critical of what they called "Daddy government."

However, none addressed the question of the proper role of government more brilliantly than did another southerner, Marion Butler. He made some impromptu remarks in the Senate early in February 1898, a portion of which begins this chapter. After insisting that the Constitution (see its Preamble and also Article I, Section 8, Clause 1) amply empowered Congress to "provide" for the "general welfare, he said that those who would turn public functions over to "private individuals" were "perverting"Jeffersonian doctrine for their own selfish ends. "There is not," said Butler, "a monopoly, there is not a trust, there is not a combine in creation but what will be satisfied for this Government to adopt the doctrine that the Government will leave everything to private enterprise and management and do nothing but collect taxes and police the country. That is the most favorable condition of things that any Government can establish—to let trusts, combines, and monopolies run rampant and run your country."[23]

That same day in early February, Jerry Simpson addressed some of the same issues in the House and, in the process, found himself involved in an exchange with Benjamin Howell, a Republican congressman from New Jersey, the state known by then as "the home of the trusts." It was a topic that was receiving more and more attention as the corporate world entered into an unprecedented cycle of mergers beginning in 1897 with the advent of the McKinley administration. Simpson told the New Jerseyite, "the very foundation of trusts and combines have been laid by Republican legislation in New Jersey as well as throughout the country. It is the very spirit of that modern Republicanism for which the gentleman and his party stand; and if he is candid he will admit . . . that without the support of trusts and combines there would be no more use for the Republican party as a political institution than for a refrigerator at the North Pole." At that moment, another Republican, Samuel Smith of Michigan, asked Simpson if he had introduced a bill aimed at taming the trusts. Simpson replied by asking what he could possibly do in a "Congress where the Speaker is the whole thing [laughter] and himself a part and an eminent representative of the party that has become the defender of the trusts? I might as well file a bill down here in the Potomac River as to put it before any committees of this House."

In this commentary, Simpson insisted that the trusts were the result of "deep" flaws in the country's economic system. "It lies, in my opinion, in the great fundamental blunder of the age—the private monopoly of . . . natural opportunities. . . . We have crowded our statute books with laws for the protection of property, and have failed to recognize the necessity for the protection of man's right of life, liberty, and the pursuit of happiness."

There are, said Simpson, "two species of wealth produced by man's activity. We term them individual property and the property of the community. . . . The one arises directly from the labor of the individual. The other arises directly from the activity of the people composing a community or state. And the right of each individual is just as inalienable in the one as in the other, subject to the necessary regulations to protect all others in their equal rights."[24]

This discussion of the role of government and how far it should go in curtailing the power wielded by corporate monopolies or trusts was only just beginning to heat up when the *Maine* blew up in the harbor off Havana. From that moment on, as Tom Watson would later say, "the blare of the bugle drowned the voice of the Reformer."[25] In all candor, Watson should have added that more than a few of those bugles were blown by the reformers themselves.

AMERICA'S "SPLENDID LITTLE WAR"

It was on the evening of 15 February 1898 that the *Maine* exploded, claiming the lives of 260 military personnel, only 119 fewer than the total number of Americans destined to die in the battles of the brief Caribbean war that was to follow.[26] Two months would pass, however, before President McKinley would agree to the use of military force; in the interval, the clamor for action grew to irresistible proportions. Concern mounted steadily that Congress might act on its own to declare war. Some of McKinley's advisers apparently began to have visions of the commander in chief being "run over and his party with him" in the stampede. Under the circumstances, McKinley's sensible call for patience and suspended judgment pending an investigation was to no avail. Coming on the heels of the building clamor for action to free Cuba that had begun nearly three years earlier, the destruction of the battleship was the proverbial final straw. Whether an accident or a treacherous deed, to many, it mattered not. The popular slogan "Remember the *Maine* and to Hell with Spain!" mirrored well the attitude of the vast majority of Americans.

War fever was nowhere higher in Congress than among the Populists and Democrats, although there was a faction within McKinley's party—the "imperialist elite," historian Richard Hofstadter aptly called them—that was just as supportive of intervention. Shortly after the disaster, William Allen introduced a resolution calling for an inquiry to be conducted by the Senate's Committee on Naval Affairs.[27] He and others of the anti-imperialist persuasion, longtime advocates of bold initiatives regarding the Cuban struggle for independence, were convinced that it was primarily "commercialism" that accounted for the inaction of McKinley and the Republican congressional leaders. A combination of "cowardice" and "investments," they believed, was dictating the course of the reluctant warriors at the helm.[28]

While President McKinley pressed for and won some concessions from Spain, the debate continued. Early in March, the president requested from Congress a $50 million emergency military appropriation to be used at his discretion for military preparedness. The bill raced through the House in two days, approved by a vote of 313 to 0, with 44 not voting; the measure passed in the Senate the following day, 9 March, without debate, by a vote of 76 to 0, with 13 senators absent. The discussion in the House, although limited, included some revealing commentary. At one point, North Carolina's George White, the lone black congressman, offered an amendment aimed at the inclusion of a colored artillery regiment among those being created. In his plea for support, which was eventually ruled out of order, White reminded the House, "The last amendments to the Constitution guarantee to us all the rights of American citizenship. . . . That we are capable and worthy of any place in our Army was evidenced in the recent rebellion by the enlistment and patriotic action of thousands of negroes in the infantry, cavalry, and artillery service of the United States Army. No one familiar with the facts will dare say that the negro did not do his whole duty to perpetuate the nation and maintain the honor of the flag in our late war." He also reminded the House of the record of the loyal slaves in the South. When the master and son went forth to battle to perpetuate our bonds, we protected, revered, and held intact the honor of the wife and daughter who remained at home, and history fails to record a single instance where that trust was betrayed." He pointed out how far blacks had come, beginning "with nothing, but by dint of hard work, strict economy, and the exercise of a little common sense we have acquired over $400,000,000 worth of property."

White then acknowledged the assistance his people had received at the hands of a "long line of patriots who so nobly espoused our cause." However, he regretted "to say that the nation has not at all times given us that protection to which our loyalty has entitled us. This is painfully evidenced by the almost daily outrages chronicled, showing lynchings, murders, assassinations, and even cremations of our people all over the Southland; and when we protest against this inhuman conduct toward us, we are quietly told that our redress is relegated to the several States . . . and that the nation has no power to interfere in the premises."

White's closing remarks were said to have drawn "long and prolonged applause." This came as a result of his assurance that "regardless of the faults of this grand Union of ours, we love her still, and if the nation should find it necessary to resort to arms and our present strained relations with Spain should develop into a war, I pledge you that the black phalanx is ready to be mustered in, one-half million strong." All his people wanted for their loyalty and service to the nation was to be accorded "at this late day all the rights of American citizenship enjoyed by you. An even chance in the race of life is all that we ask; and then if we can not reach the goal, let the devil take the hindmost one!"[29]

The next day, just prior to the vote on the emergency appropriation, John Bell made a speech whose tone was well represented by its opening line: "Mr. Speaker, it seems to me at this time there are no Republicans, there are no Democrats, there are no Populists, but we are all American citizens." Although "not in favor of war," Bell assured the House, "we will all stand as one man behind the President, and we will uphold him at every point in this crisis now or hereafter. I hope and believe that there will not be a dissenting voice in this House or a dissenting voice in the country."[30]

Following Bell came John Fitzgerald (the grandfather of a famous family of Democrats from Massachusetts and the namesake of one who would become president, John Fitzgerald Kennedy) with a similar appeal. Said he, "I never was prouder of my American citizenship than I am to-day. The story of the proceedings of this session will be heralded from one end of the world to the other." It will teach everyone that "while we may differ in our opinions as to general policies . . . , when the time of danger comes we cease to be Democrats, Republicans, or Populists—only Americans."[31]

As previously indicated, although John Bell was the official Populist leader or speaker, Jerry Simpson was the unofficial voice of the party in the House. On this issue, Simpson was in a category all by himself. While all the others succumbed to the beat of war drums, Simpson maintained a consistent and principled posture. He had, of course, a long record of opposition to all forms of militarism. In early April, speaking during the debate over naval appropriations, he registered his opposition to building a large naval force "for aggressive purposes," as he put it. "I am a man of peace," said Simpson. "I believe firmly in the possibility of securing among civilized nations an agreement that will make unnecessary the maintenance of expensive armies and navies. I know of nothing more absurd than the rivalry of the nations in the matter of building unwieldy ships of war and in the construction of guns to pierce them." He conceded, bowing to the crisis precipitated by the sinking of the *Maine,* "that until this world has progressed further from barbarism we must continue this waste of our substance, not merely for our protection, but to aid those who lack our power and are hindered in their progress by more powerful though less civilized nations."[32]

At about the same time, William Allen rose in the Senate and defiantly described himself as "the jingo of jingoes," the one senator who, along with Florida's Wilkinson Call, had compiled a long record of support for Cuban independence. Unlike Senator Lodge, another early opponent of Spanish control over Cuba whom he did not mention, Allen wanted it understood that his support for the Cuban cause was clear in its intent and without strings attached. "We have no greed for Spanish territory nor for Spanish gold," said Allen. "Our policy is that of a contented, domestic people. We do not want Cuba. We do not even desire to be her guardian. But we are determined she shall be free and that for all time we will be rid of the close proximity of a nation whose chief occupation is the shedding of innocent blood."[33]

On 5 April, George Turner may have registered a better claim to being "the jingo of jingoes." The Washington Populist conceded that he cared not how the *Maine* was destroyed. Ultimately, no matter what the verdict, "the hand that planted the mine was the hand of Spain." As he saw it, "four hundred years of living hell" inflicted on the people of that island was more than enough justification for the nation to simply leap to the conclusion "that our citizens have been brutally and treacherously murdered by that nation . . . under circumstances of atrocity and cruelty and perfidy and treachery that are unparalleled in the history of the world." He added that he would "vote for anything which will give us an opportunity to drive that infamous nation from this hemisphere and to cleanse and purify the [otherwise] pure air of this continent."[34] It seems likely that Turner's views (he would have a lot of company among his contemporaries, of course) would not have changed even if he had been aware, based on subsequent disclosures, that the ship most likely was not destroyed by a mine at all but by an internal explosion, an accident of some kind. The fact that the ship was later floated, examined by the American military, and then towed out of the harbor to be sunk again in a deeper stretch of ocean seems to be silent but strong testimony that matters were not quite what nearly everyone immediately assumed them to be.

In spite of the headlong rush to get ready for war, Bell and Simpson both spoke against a measure before the House providing for an increase in the regular army from 25,000 to 104,000. Bell said that he much preferred using the National Guard units. As he saw it, the 25,000 base was enough in peace or war. "Militarism" and "military despotism" were seen as inevitable byproducts of reliance on a professional force. Simpson seconded Bell's concern and added a few serious thoughts of his own. "The tendency of all republics," said Simpson, "is toward imperialism, and as time goes on, as a republican form of government drifts toward a strong centralized power, then the demand comes for a large standing army." It appeared to him that the nation had "traveled along that road so far now that it begins to be necessary, as an adjunct to the tendency toward imperialism, to increase the standing army." Simpson then said, "If I have read correctly the history of our country," the founders warned us to "beware of establishing . . . a large standing army; and the immortal Jefferson said the reliance of a republican government should be on its citizen soldiery."

This commentary by Simpson was quite possibly the most effective by the Kansas Populist during his third and final term. He closed by saying:

> I hope this bill will be defeated; but if we get into actual hostility with Spain, as I hope we will not, we will again rest upon the strong arm of the citizens of this Republic to defend its honor.

> But if that war does come, I hope and trust we will be able to put it upon a high plane as defenders of civilization, as defenders of a free country, and the right for a struggling people to establish that kind of a government and govern themselves, and not be put on the low plane of stealing the territory of some other country. . . . I am for my country, and to a certain extent I am for my country right or wrong; but when that motto trenches upon right and justice, I draw the line. . . . And in this struggle which they say is about to come we must say to the world we are now going to enter [to] . . . prevent Spain from digging up the barbarities of the sixteenth century and flaunting them in our face, that we will fight this battle on that line, and we will give to the Republic of Cuba that is struggling to free itself the same rights that we have declared in our Declaration of Independence—life, liberty, and the pursuit of happiness and the right to govern themselves. [Applause.][35]

President McKinley kept the pressure on Spain to the last, getting virtually everything the administration seemed to want by way of concessions; nonetheless, the president presented Congress with his war message on 11 April. From that point to the actual declaration of war, passed on 25 April, nearly everyone had their say. In the House on 13 April, a joint resolution authorizing the use of the navy and army to end the hostilities in Cuba was passed 325 to 19. Among the Populists, only Milford Howard and Jerry Simpson voted no; William Greene from Nebraska did not vote; all the others favored the measure.

In the Senate, the Teller amendment, the famous imperial disclaimer, was agreed to by a voice vote, declaring, "The United States hereby disclaims any disposition or intention to exercise sovereignty, jurisdiction, or control over said island except for the pacification thereof, and asserts its determination when that is accomplished, to leave the government and control of the island to its people." This amendment was added to the original Senate resolution by a vote of sixty to twenty-eight. The joint resolution, thus amended, passed sixty-seven to twenty-one. Finally, at 1:15 A.M. on 19 April, the conference committee worked out a version of the joint resolution that retained the Teller amendment but included no statement regarding the recognition of an independent government in Cuba, a proviso that McKinley opposed and the cautious friends of Cuba desired. On 22 April, McKinley implemented a blockade, and in a message to Congress three days later, he called for a declaration of war, which promptly passed on that date and was signed later the same day by the president.

Once the war was under way, the Populists found themselves caught up in a debate about how it was to be financed. They were all staunchly opposed to the administration's plan to sell interest-bearing bonds as the primary method of paying for the war.[36] They would have preferred to finance on a pay-as-you-go basis, primarily by means of an income tax. Their plea that Congress not "mortgage future generations to carry on a war," as Marion Butler put it, would not be heeded. The bond bill passed in the House by a vote of 181 to 131, with all Populists registering a no vote.[37]

In just a matter of weeks—113 days, actually—"the splendid little war," to borrow John Hay's overworked description, was all but over. In the process, the door was thrown wide open to a potential empire, with island possessions extending from the Caribbean Sea out across the Pacific Ocean to the Philippine archipelago on the coastline of the Asian continent. It was all there for the taking. It was a small war but a huge force for change, ultimately loaded with serious consequences for America's future course. It was to be far more complicated than anyone had imagined. It was a golden opportunity in the eyes of those with imperial designs, but a Pandora's box to those who earnestly believed that an imperialistic republic—a democratic one, at least—was an "impossible hybrid." However that may be, the debate that opened late in 1895 regarding the Cuban struggle for independence culminated by August 1898 in a preliminary agreement, later confirmed in the Treaty of Paris, whereby Spain not only granted Cuban independence but also released to the United States, as outright possessions, the Philippines, Puerto Rico, and Guam. With that outcome, the nation entered a new phase of an ongoing debate between two large segments of the American population whose visions of America's role at home and in the world were as much at odds as the visions of the Populists and their most determined foes from 1890 on, and for quite similar reasons.[38]

HAWAIIAN ANNEXATION AND THE "BLIGHTING SEASON"

Those differences emerged clearly in the congressional debate that accompanied the move to annex Hawaii by joint resolution during June and July 1898. Some historical accounts would lead one to believe that the islands were annexed in the context of the war with barely a murmur, as the nation was consumed by a huge rush of nationalistic pride and military fervor. Such was not the case. Most of the arguments that would be made over the annexation of the Philippines had already surfaced during this debate. This was especially the case on the side of those who opposed annexation. The Populists were more divided, however, by the vote over Hawaiian annexation than they would be in the case of the Philippines. The House division on 15 June resulted in eight Populist yeas and seven nays, with six not voting. In the Senate, on 6 July, only James Kyle, who had by then gone over formally to the Republicans, voted for annexation. William Allen cast the lone Populist vote in the Senate against annexation. Harris, Turner, Heitfeld, and Butler voted present. The resolution passed forty-two to twenty-one, with twenty-six not voting.[39]

In the House debate, John Bell delivered a major address for the opposition. He said that if what was going on foreshadowed what he feared, "it photographs a dismal future for the weak republics of the Western Hemisphere and the individual poor of our country." This "new policy would necessarily break down the cardinal landmarks in the Declaration of Independence and make us but a part and parcel of the caste-ridden governments of Europe from which our forefathers fled." Then, after addressing a range of pro-annexation arguments in an impressive fashion, Bell asserted, "This war is *the blighting season of democracy* in the United States. Every indication is that the [country] will unfold itself in the early morning of the twentieth century into the greatest military and naval power and into the most regal and resplendent aristocracy that the world ever beheld. The mentally dwarfed inhabitants of the tropics will be the servants of those in temperate climates. . . . I shall deprecate the fulfillment of this unwelcome prophecy."[40]

A substitute resolution in the House, stating that the United States would "view as an act of hostility any attempt" by "Europe or Asia to take or hold possession of the Hawaiian Islands," but which also contained "a guarantee of the independence of the people," was defeated 204 to 96. Ten Populists voted for this measure and six against it, with five not voting.[41]

Senator Allen was one of only a handful of congressmen to question the method of annexation by joint resolution. He saw it as a blatant, unconstitutional maneuver concocted merely "to destroy the necessity of having a two-thirds [Senate] majority for a treaty." He even found himself agreeing with George Hoar on this issue. Beginning with this debate, the senior Republican senator from Massachusetts gradually emerged as a leading anti-imperialist. Allen indicated that he agreed with Hoar's statement that if the nation were to take the imperialistic road it would "seriously impair our usefulness to our own people if not eventually destroy the Government itself." In the debate, Allen also said that he took it "for granted" that a vote for the joint resolution would signify support for "imperialism and a policy of colonial acquisition." As he saw it, "it will be well understood . . . that the annexation of the Hawaiian Islands is the first act in the drama of colonization that is to go on until we have made a portion of our country the Philippine Islands, amounting to 1,400 in number, Cuba, Puerto Rico, and every little dimple in either the Atlantic or Pacific Ocean."[42]

Actually, several days before Allen's remarks, Georgia's Senator Alexander Clay registered a strong claim to being the most astute and prophetic member of the Senate on this particular subject. He said: "Mark my prediction, the annexation of the Hawaiian Islands is but the first step to accomplish the grand scheme of conquest. We are dispatching an army to take possession of the Philippines, which must necessarily be multiplied many times before our purpose is accomplished." Strange things are happening, he said; quite a few people have been duped. The Georgia senator was not at all pleased to be among their number. "When this war began," he continued, " it was said that its primary purpose was to free Cuba. . . . I thought this war was begun for the purpose of giving liberty to the people of Cuba, . . . and I gave it my loyal support. . . . I had no idea that this war was begun to acquire and annex the Sandwich Islands. I had no idea that we began this war to take charge of the Philippine Islands. . . . We are beginning a departure here which is liable at some time in the future to involve this country in ruin."[43]

For certain, the nation had arrived at a major crossroads by the closing months of 1898. It was indeed the "blighting season," as Bell had said, not only for democracy but also for Populism. Yet some crucial decisions had yet to be made. Was the United States to become a full-fledged imperial nation with a far-flung colonial empire of its own? Or would it forgo that extracontinental role and content itself with extending its influence by moral example and, above all, by peaceful, noncolonial means? These were critical questions indeed. With the economy on the rebound and the short and successful war at an end, the voters rewarded the Republican party in November with an even larger majority as they turned out of office a number of Populists and Democrats. As fate would have it, however, the key debate and the crucial decisions regarding these matters would fall to the lame-duck session of this Fifty-fifth Congress.

8

The Road to Empire, 1898–1903

> *[It] would be a brave man who would assert . . . that the Republican party of to-day has anything in common with the Republican party of Abraham Lincoln's day. That great man, if he could come back to earth, would not recognize it as the party which honored him and which he honored . . . ; which has had its sentiment so shriveled and shrunken that on all occasions it prefers the dollar to the man, and which has so little regard for liberty and the sacred principles upon which our free institutions are founded that at this moment it is endeavoring to drown in a sea of human blood the aspirations of a friendly and allied people fighting for liberty and independence. . . . It stands to-day not for a pure and simple administration of this Government in the interest of the common people . . . , but it stands for the material interests of the nation, for the corporations, for the trusts, and for the enormous aggregations of capital.*
>
> George Turner, *Congressional Record,* 57th Cong., 1st sess., 16 April 1902, 4210

Five weeks into the war with Spain, William Allen had taken notice of what he called a "tidal wave of patriotism rolling over the country." He acknowledged that people like himself who had taken the lead in support of the Cuban struggle for independence were being pushed to the rear while the same men who had been ready to "compromise everything for peace," even to the point of permitting the "women and children of Cuba to starve by the thousands, . . . have put themselves at the head of the procession."[1] For certain, a powerful dynamic had been unleashed for American territorial expansion and dominance, setting the stage for one of the more significant debates in one of the most important lame-duck sessions in congressional history.

That session commenced on 5 December 1898, and although the treaty formally concluding the war and annexing the Philippines and the debate over imperialism would eclipse everything else, other matters were also at issue. The story of Populism itself continued to unfold in significant ways. In early June, as the measure to fund the war by selling interest-bearing bonds worked its way through Congress, Marion Butler called attention to a press release indicating that a Populist had supported that measure in the Senate. Butler stated that that was not the case; the vote was by Senator James Kyle. "He is a Republican," said Butler. "They can get his vote when they need it. . . . Let it be known from now on that the Republican party has a majority in the Senate—a majority in all branches of the Government, and is therefore responsible for all legislation that is enacted." Kyle responded by saying, in effect, that there were Populists he liked and Populists he did not like. Those he disapproved of, and with whom he had not associated and would not associate, were "socialists and other classes—whose very aim, in my judgment, is to undermine American institutions." He then indicated that he would place Butler in the undesirable category with those who have done "more to injure the cause of reform in America, as well as the world, than any other class of men of whom I have knowledge." He went on to defend the support he had received from Republicans back in South Dakota, making his reelection to a second term possible. It was, he said, the result of his "conservative course during the past six years and because I made my campaign for reelection on an antisocialistic platform."[2]

All this certainly exposed a significant division within an already shaken Populist camp. Kyle's final defection was no revelation, given his long record of vacillation. What was surprising was his determined opposition to socialism, given that he had earlier made one of the more persuasive defenses of the public-ownership aspects of the Populist program. It was, however, a division that increasingly rankled Populists at all levels. Government ownership nonetheless continued to be one of the main issues championed by the Populists in Congress. It came out most prominently in the cases of the proposed canal in Nicaragua, the oceanic cable to the Hawaiian Islands, and, of course, the nation's troubled railroads.

"ESTABLISHING A DUAL DEFINITION OF LIBERTY"

The debate over annexation and imperialism in the Senate began slowly, with Senator George Hoar making a major address on 9 January 1899 in response to an earlier pro-annexation oration by Senator Orville Platt of Connecticut. Hoar quoted one of his state's illustrious former senators, Charles Sumner, in support of the proposition that the Declaration of Independence was—or at least ought to have been—"coequal with the Constitution." He said that he did not want to see his country "begin the twentieth century where Spain began the sixteenth." To annex the Philippines was to nullify the Monroe Doctrine. "Every European nation, every European alliance," would then have "the right to acquire dominion in this hemisphere when we acquire it in the other."[3]

Illinois Senator William Mason, another Republican, spoke the next day to urge passage of a resolution he had introduced a few days earlier, which stated:

"Whereas all just powers of government are derived from the consent of the governed: Therefore, be it Resolved by the Senate of the United States, That the Government of the United States of America will not attempt to govern the people of any other country in the world without the consent of the people themselves, or subject them by force to our dominion against their will."[4]

The next day, Allen offered a resolution of his own aimed at getting the Senate to go on record against the use of force in the Philippines without a declaration of war.[5] Long, impassioned antiannexation speeches followed, as well as more resolutions. On 19 January, Senator George Turner of Washington rose to support a resolution introduced earlier by Senator George Vest of Missouri, which attempted to put the Senate on record as opposed to holding any territory as a colony. Turner had voted for Hawaiian annexation, making an exception in that case for trade and defensive reasons and because he saw "statehood, either as an independent State or by connection with one or the other of the great Pacific Coast States," as a logical and likely outcome. For the Philippines he would make no such exception; it would mean "a permanent colonial system," and "every drop of blood shed in the Revolutionary War was a protest against such a system, which meant then, as it means now, taxation without representation, government in opposition to the consent of the governed, large standing armies quartered at the expense of colonies, and ignorant and incompetent and venal administration." After saying that he was not a "strict constructionist of the Constitution," he added, "I am, I believe, a liberal nationalist. But there are bounds to my liberality. I draw the line at that vain and boastful spirit which seems to be abroad in the land."[6]

In the House on 24 January, John Bell, one of only five Populist incumbents to win reelection the previous November, delivered a major address in opposition to the military spending bill under consideration, seeing it as having been designed "for imperial purposes." Referring to the increase in peacetime expenditures for the military, Bell reminded the House of the cost of the Civil War. "The immediate expenses were but a pittance to the expenses from 1865 to the present time. To-day $140,000,000 per annum for a pension roll, and it is to go on for a generation." As far as he was concerned, money spent for "a thorough development of the arid West would give far greater increase to commerce, with greater aid to American manufacturers, than all the commerce of the West Indies and the Orient combined." Besides, it would be "an absolute injury to the Filipinos to be relieved of the control of Spain and put in the control of the United States." The islands, he insisted, also posed a threat to organized labor, as well as to the sugar beet industry, which was important in his state.

All the talk about "civilizing" and "Christianizing" the people of the islands was "folly," said Bell. "They have been controlled and completely dominated by the church for centuries." He asked, did it not take "centuries and a complete change of environment to civilize a human being? We have tried for centuries to civilize the aborigines of this country and have them about purified and about all laid away in the grave." The Colorado Populist closed by saying that he was "opposed to paying twenty millions for the mythical sovereignty of Spain over the Philippines without it [being] . . . distinctly understood that we are doing it for the Filipinos and that they are to repay it out of the revenues of the Philippines." Likewise, he was "opposed to policing and further building up the island of Cuba unless it is distinctly understood that this is to be done for the Cubans and that the expenses in toto are to be returned." Beware, he said, of the "patriotic frenzy" that has come over the country.[7]

Simpson and William Greene followed Bell that day with speeches. Taken together, the group laid out the Populist position against the imperial course that the McKinley administration was seeking to accommodate with the military appropriations bill. The next day, Freeman Knowles also made a strong anti-imperialist statement. The South Dakota Populist, one of the victims of the "tidal wave of patriotism," asked those on the imperialist side: "What kind of 'blessings of law and liberty' is it that we are going to extend to the people of these islands? Is it the same kind which these same 'expansionists' are now extending to our own laboring classes?" All the "talk" he had been hearing about "extending the blessing of law and liberty to people 10,000 miles away, while our own laboring classes are reduced to absolute serfdom," was preposterous. What did it all signify? "Has our high and lofty purpose of humanity, promulgated in the declaration of war against Spain, degenerated into a land-grabbing war of conquest? Did we first play the hypocrite and afterwards play the hog?" The answers were all too obvious to Knowles. He warned that if the military appropriations bill under consideration "becomes a law it is the beginning of the end of the Republic."[8]

In the House, Cyrus Sulloway, a New Hampshire Republican, just about said it all for the new imperialists, and perhaps with a bit too much candor. We would no longer be a "hermit nation, isolated from the rest of mankind. . . . We are interested in every part of the globe that has commerce or conditions such that it can be developed." The nation needed "greater power to protect and extend our rights." Besides, "the mighty will and wish of a great people, in their sovereign right, can not be chained and bound by written law or treaties."[9]

Surprisingly, George White, the sole African American congressman, announced that he favored "the acquisition of all the territory that is within our grasp as a result of the war."[10] The North Carolina Republican apparently saw no contradiction between the fight he waged for his own people's freedom at home and the move to dominate and suppress others abroad.

Kansas Populist William Vincent followed White and had no problem linking military appropriations to oppression. The Kansan had also lost his bid for reelection and seemed to be in no mood to mince words. He said that it was "a significant fact that since the era of corporation rule set in and since our beneficent social system developed the tramp, the lockout, and the strike, the Army has never been called out to suppress or hold in check the corporation, but always to suppress the striker." It was obviously his fear that the move to enlarge the standing army was ultimately aimed at holding in check political dissidents at home.

As regards the civilizing mission he had heard talked about so much, Vincent said that he would "submit that our experience with the American Indians is not such as to encourage us in undertaking to civilize a people 8,000 miles away, who, according to our opponents, are much inferior and less deserving." In addition, "the race problem . . . which was shown to be such a perplexing one in some parts of our country ought to be sufficient without inviting new ones of still greater magnitude." In effect, said Vincent, the administration was asking the country "to repudiate the Declaration of Independence, and later on, I suppose, we will be expected to substitute therefor some famous Spanish state paper." Perhaps they should substitute one of General Valeriano "Butcher" Weyler's *reconcentrado* orders (Weyler was the Cuban revolution's most notorious military tyrant). Make no mistake about it, added the Kansan, "forcible annexation means government without the consent of the governed; it means continued oppression to those who have so bravely fought against it; it means injustice from every standpoint; it means increased taxation; it means an increase in the standing Army; it means that we are going 8,000 miles from home to invite trouble; it means everything that is bad and nothing that is good, and it is a public confession to all the world that the war with Spain was fought under false pretenses."[11]

Later that day, Nebraska Populists William Stark and Samuel Maxwell also delivered speeches against the drive for empire, as did Curtis Castle. Castle's was quite a stem-winder, as was his style, but considering the fact that he was closing out his congressional career, he may well have assigned special significance to this effort. The California Populist argued that what was occurring was a conspiracy "using territorial expansion as a stalking horse to foist an army upon an unwilling people." The purpose, he said, was "ostensibly to destroy the liberties of an alien people and an alien race. Ostensibly, yes, ostensibly, but in reality to overthrow the liberties of the patient and long-suffering wage-earners of this country." Prior to entering upon this "evil" course, he said,

> let us first burn every copy of the Declaration of Independence; let us raze the monument at Bunker Hill; let us destroy the tombs of Washington and Jefferson and let us send back to France her noble gift of "Liberty Enlightening the World." Let us break down all the altars of Liberty, and in their stead erect the alter of Mammon. The great masses of our people may be deceived for the time being, avarice may sometimes obscure their sense of justice, but when the sober second thought comes no friend of human freedom will volunteer to traverse half the globe to kill men who fought for freedom. The deed is unnatural; it is horrible, and the exploiting class who advocate it do so that they may destroy the liberties of the people of this country. . . . It is folly to dream of maintaining our liberties and at the same time crush the liberties of other people. Truth forbids that we claim the inalienable right of liberty in America and deny its exercise in the Philippines. No sophistry

> can make wrong right, or the worse the better cause. We are debarred from establishing a dual definition of liberty.[12]

In the course of the debate, James A. Norton, an Ohio Democrat who had earlier played a prominent role in Iowa politics, recalled, logically enough, Kansas Republican Senator John J. Ingalls's infamous remark from the 1890 election to make his case against imperialism and the Republicans generally. They stood, he said, for "wholesale" plunder. "It was officially announced some years ago by one high in Republican councils that 'the Ten Commandments have no place in politics,' and in perfect accord with that statement has been the Republican course, until it has laid its hands on as many rights of the people as it could grasp, has ignored the Constitution, and enthroned treason." These were rather strong words, especially coming from a congressman who had been employed for quite some time as a lawyer in the legal department of the Baltimore and Ohio Railroad.[13]

Another Democrat, John F. Fitzgerald of Massachusetts, delivered one of the session's more eloquent and thoughtful speeches. Among other things, Fitzgerald said that the issue confronting the American people was "whether they are to continue . . . as a peaceable republic or a conquering empire." Which will it be? "Imperialism unquestionably means incessant warfare with other nations of the East." He asked, "What justification is there for any member of Congress to vote for a policy which will compel the men who enlisted in our Army to fight for the cause of freedom and humanity in Cuba to fight now against the cause of freedom and humanity in the Philippine Islands?" Midway through this speech, the Massachusetts congressman (the only New England Democrat to survive the Republican landslide of 1894), received what the House secretary described as "loud and long-continued applause."

In Fitzgerald's view, "might did not make right," as was implied over and over again on the imperialistic side of the debate. "I am . . . one of those who prefer that civilization which develops and spreads through the practices of justice and freedom and truth"—the brand of civilization defined so well by one of "our great writers," Lord Chief Justice Russell, whom he quoted: " 'Civilization is not dominion, wealth, material luxury; nay, not even a great literature and education widespread—good though those things be. Its true signs are thought for the poor and suffering, chivalrous regard and respect for women, the frank recognition of human brotherhood, irrespective of race, color, or nation or religion; the narrowing of the domain of mere force as a governing factor in the world, the love of ordered freedom, abhorrence of what is mean and cruel and vile, ceaseless devotion to the claims of justice. Civilization in that, its true, its highest sense, must make for peace.' "[14]

On 30 January, Jeremiah Botkin addressed the House to oppose the military appropriations bill. It was the Kansas Populist's most effective speech. He wanted it understood that the "greatest menace to our free institutions" was what he called a "growing imperialism of capital." As he saw it, "about the only standing army" the country needed was one that was "sufficient to drive from the capitals of our nation and our several States the lobbies of the great corporations and trusts . . . , thus leaving our lawmakers unhampered in their efforts to legislate for the whole people." He quoted from President McKinley's last annual message to remind the House that the president had conceded that "forcible annexation" would be "criminal aggression." He then referred to the declaration of war, emphasizing the disclaimer regarding control over the territories to be freed. Make no mistake about it, said Botkin, "if it be the purpose of the administration to conquer the Filipinos by the force of arms and hold them in perpetual subjection . . . , a hundred thousand men will be found altogether insufficient long to satisfy the insatiable maw of that awful god of war enthroned under a tropical sun." He acknowledged that "every true American" would likely be willing to "die to make men free," but he did not think "any considerable number of American citizens will be found willing to enter a standing army which is confessedly to be used to acquire by conquest new territory thousands of miles away in another hemisphere, to subjugate its population, and to recklessly carry our flag into the very storm centers of the Old World's controversies and probable wars. It is absolutely un-American to organize an army for such purposes."

For those who talked about Christianizing the country's new subjects, Botkin, a Methodist minister, deplored the stand of what he called "many zealous propagandists of the religion of Jesus" on behalf of "criminal aggression in the Philippines"—regrettably including, he said, a number of "eminent ministers in the church to which I have the honor to belong." What the country needed was a settlement in accord with the Golden Rule. Do not be deluded, said Botkin. "You can not shoot the religion of Jesus into the Filipinos with 13-inch guns, nor punch it into them with American bayonets."[15]

Charles Barlow of California spoke after Botkin and opposed the measure under consideration for a variety of reasons, including a concern captured by his references to the "mongrel hordes of Asia" and the "Asiatic hordes of the East." He was against "colonial possessions." What was needed, he said, was an improvement in the situation at home. He urged the House to maintain the country's hemispheric separation and the integrity of the Monroe Doctrine and not to violate the noble and wise tradition of not having a "standing army." At the end, he posed a question for the House: "Are we not straining at a gnat and swallowing a camel?"[16]

Missouri's Champ Clark had never been accused of being a shrinking violet, and in this debate, the popular Democrat again made his presence felt, coming out strongly against the administration's imperialistic policies:

> I repeat it now, . . . and history will confirm the statement, that the Democrats and Populists in this House took the Republican party by the scruff of its neck and dragged it into the Spanish war. . . . The difference is this: We

> dragged you into a war to free a neighboring people struggling bravely for liberty; you are dragging us into a war to enslave a distant people who are struggling bravely for liberty. [Applause.]
>
> Your reluctance in patriotism then, your hoggishness in trying to monopolize its honors and glories now, reminds me of a Poland China sow that my father used to tell me about when I was a child, which was so bashful they had to pull her ears off to get her to the trough, and so greedy they had to pull her tail off to get her away from it. [Loud laughter.][17]

Albert May Todd of Michigan and Thomas Jefferson Strait of South Carolina, elected in 1896 on fusionist tickets, engaged on the anti-imperialistic side. Todd, in fact, offered a fairly comprehensive statement of the opposition position regarding imperialism and, in the process, quoted a person he identified as one of the founders of the Republican party, Albert Williams, in support of his contention that his "once beloved party has passed into the hands of those who seek to destroy human freedom." Strait had printed along with his speech an anti-imperialistic Thanksgiving sermon delivered by Henry Van Dyke, pastor of the Brick Presbyterian Church in New York City. It was Van Dyke who said, "When imperialism comes in at the door democracy flies out the window." There was no question in the minister's mind (nor in those of any of the Populists, with the possible exception of Harry Skinner, who apparently had gone over to the Republicans by this time), that "an imperialistic democracy is an impossible hybrid."

Todd, Strait, Botkin, and nearly all the Populists seconded Van Dyke's conclusion that the question confronting the nation at that moment was "vaster, more pressing, more fraught with incalculable consequences" than any previous crisis, including that which followed the American Revolution and the Civil War. The country must not, Van Dyke had insisted, "sell its birthright for a mess of pottage."[18]

Opposition to America's new course was extremely unpopular in many areas. Jerry Simpson, who had lost his race in 1898 primarily because of the war's afterglow, conceded that that was the case in his district; still, he was no less determined in his opposition. Just before the vote in the House on the military appropriations bill, Simpson said that several congressmen, on and off the floor, had admitted that the move to create a 100,000-man army was aimed, in part, to "suppress domestic violence," should that need arise. "That is what they want it for," said Simpson, "along with a scheme for colonial empire, and to place on the throne in this country William McKinley, President of the United States, Emperor of the West Indian Islands and of the Philippines, and then get a standing army to enforce the power of this new empire. EMPIRE! Do gentlemen understand the meaning of the word 'empire' as applied to a republic? It means that we are taking the first step toward that strong centralized power that will finally result in this Republic being turned into an empire."[19]

On 31 January 1899, to no one's surprise, the army appropriations bill passed. The yeas were 168 and the nays 126; 4 answered present; 53 members did not vote. Among the Populists and Fusionists, only Harry Skinner supported the bill; all the others cast negative votes, except for Charles Martin, James Gunn, and Nelson McCormick, who did not vote.[20]

"A DECLARATION OF WAR AGAINST THE PHILIPPINE PEOPLE"

On 1 February 1899, the Senate debate leading up to the treaty ratification vote got under way in earnest; the critical decision would be made in the upper chamber. Joseph Rawlins, a Utah Democrat, let it be known that the "mere idea of expansion, of extending our borders, does not alarm me so much as some of the startling doctrines advanced in its justification."

Both sides advanced some unusual justifications. At one point, Wisconsin Senator John Spooner referred to Ben Tillman as the "Senator from Aguinaldo" because Tillman, a leading opponent of Philippine annexation, did not agree with Spooner's portrayal of the Filipino leader. The South Carolinian responded with this curious mixture of arguments: "Coming, not as a 'Senator from Aguinaldo,' but as a Senator from Africa, if you please, South Carolina, with 750,000 colored population and 500,000 whites, I realize what you are doing, while you do not, and I would save this country from the injection into it of another race question which can only [lead to] . . . bloodshed and a costly war and the loss of lives of our brave soldiers. I would save the country the disgrace of having our flag float over a battlefield drenched with the blood of patriots fighting for liberty and self-government shed by American soldiers."[21]

It was a mixed blessing, no doubt, but Senator Tillman was one of the most outspoken opponents of the treaty and Philippine annexation, and his arguments were heavily laden with racial arguments. Attitudes regarding race, as has long been recognized, came into play on both sides of the debate. John Daniel, a Virginia Democrat, told the Senate that if the treaty were ratified, "we will be the United States of America and Asia." They were being asked, he said, "to annex to the United States a witch's caldron"—a caldron of "mixed races, Chinese, Japanese, Malay Negritos" and make "it a part of our great, broad, Christian, Anglo-Saxon, American land. . . . Not in a hundred years, nay, not in a thousand years, can we lift the Philippine Islands and the mixed races" of that area to the "level of civilization" enjoyed in this land. "This treaty," said Daniel, "is not a treaty of peace except in formal ceremony with Spain. It is a declaration of war against the Philippine people."[22]

On 4 February, Senator Allen presented a resolution declaring that ratification did not mean that the country was declaring its intention to annex the Philippines. The Nebraska Populist, in accord and in touch with William Jennings Bryan, had decided to vote for ratification but was dead set against annexation. The principles of the Declaration were, he insisted, universal, and he particularly deplored as "novel and startling"—a "monstrous doctrine"—views expounded on the Senate floor suggesting otherwise. "I have no doubt," said Allen, "that in permanently acquiring territory we would do so with the view of incorporating its inhabitants into our population as citizens. . . . We have no power . . . to hold the Filipinos as vassals. We have no right to deprive them . . . of the right of self-government."[23]

Fighting between American and Filipino forces broke out on Saturday evening, 4 February, almost as Allen spoke. By Monday, that development had its effect on Congress. In a speech of 6 February, Allen referred to the beginning of hostilities. He accepted the official American version of events, calling it a "treacherous assault" on our troops.[24] Clearly, Allen's support for ratification was strengthened by the outbreak of hostilities; no doubt, others were swayed by that development as well. The fighting certainly put the opponents of annexation in a difficult situation.

Donelson Caffery of Louisiana was one of the few senators whose opposition to annexation was such that he refused to be silenced by that development. Said Caffery, mixing his metaphors rather freely, "I do not see that the blood that flowed yesterday lies entirely upon the heads of those people. I see, if any fault lies anywhere, that it is a joint fault, and lies as well at the doors of the United States as upon the heads of the Filipinos."

Allen interrupted Caffery at that point to register his agreement with the McKinley administration's version of events. Caffery replied: "Very well. I say that on account of the relations that have existed between these people and the United States such an occurrence, although deplorable, was likely to happen. We were there as conquerors. We did not bear the message of peace and kindness to these people. We bore the message of subjugation."[25]

Others, like Delaware's George Gray, a Democrat, viewed the matter in a very different light. After the fighting commenced, they were even more determined, as Gray put it, not to make "concessions to them while they are shooting down . . . Americans who have stood by them and have given them the hope for this great boon of liberty and of decent, orderly government."[26]

The Treaty of Paris was ratified on 6 February 1899 by a vote of fifty-seven to twenty-seven, only one vote in excess of the two-thirds vote required among those present. No doubt, William Jennings Bryan's support for ratification had made the difference. Among the fifty-seven voting for the treaty were fifteen Democrats and Populists. Somehow, Bryan hoped to win a separate battle on behalf of Philippine independence and against the imperial course. It was a hope that would ultimately be fulfilled, more or less, but not quite the way Bryan and his allies would have hoped, and certainly not within the time frame they would have preferred.[27]

Just before the vote, Arthur Gorman, a prominent Democratic leader from Maryland, said that he believed a decision to annex the Philippines "would be more disastrous" than the Civil War and worse even than slavery, "because of which the whole land was deluged in blood and brother turned against brother." He predicted: "I believe that if the pending treaty is ratified and we attain a cession of the sovereignty of those islands, it will be only the beginning of a war that will cost us hundreds, yes thousands, of lives of our splendid specimens of intelligent young manhood and millions and millions of money, and that when we shall have, as we will, driven them at the point of the bayonet to submit to the authority of the American nation, with all the accompanying destruction, the whole archipelago will then be a pest to the America union."[28]

For certain, the great debate had only just begun, as was the case with the undeclared war that would not be declared over until July 1902. In the interval, the nation would deploy more than 125,000 troops and sustain 4,200 battle deaths, with another 2,800 wounded. According to one analyst, "This represented a casualty rate of 5.5 percent, one of the highest of any war in American history." The Filipinos would suffer far more dearly, with casualties in the 16,000 to 18,000 range, with more than 200,000 additional deaths brought on by disease, famine, and other war-related causes. On top of all that, of course, were the financial costs of the war—incalculable perhaps, but by no means insignificant on either side. One estimate put the immediate cost to the United States at "more than $400,000,000."[29] But perhaps the most severe damage of all would derive from the heavy blow inflicted on the nation's self-image. To many, America had been the land that above all others stood for "that glorious privilege of which we have boasted for more than a hundred years—the right to govern ourselves." That was how Jerry Simpson put it. This was "the lesson we taught the world," said Simpson. It was our great boast, and "we have turned it into a disgrace and a shame that will darken the pages of the history of this great Republic."[30]

America had taken the wrong road—or was it the glory road, as imperialists would have us believe? Regardless, all that remained was to rationalize the departure. That process had already begun in Congress with the imperialist side of the debate. Philippine annexation and imperialism continued to be discussed in the House and Senate right up to the close of the Fifty-fifth Congress. Occasionally, there were even some lighter moments worthy of note. At one point, Joseph Cannon of Illinois, one of the Republican leaders and later House Speaker, commented that if Simpson and others had delivered their speeches in Manila, "they would have been arrested, tried by a drumhead court-martial, and shot." This drew "applause on the Republican side." Instantly, Simpson and several others were on their feet seeking recognition. Simpson finally got the floor and produced one last gem of that famous wit. Said he, in response to how he might have been dealt with in Manila: "That may be true and it may not be true. I do not know, in choosing between two difficulties of this kind, whether I would rather be court-martialed and shot in Manila or be shot with an old muzzle-loading brass Cannon like that I was shot with a few moments ago." That drew "great laughter," and Simpson went on to make an eloquent statement on behalf of free speech. He also went out of his way to make it clear that his criticism was directed at the administration and not at the soldiers who were doing the fighting and dying in the Philippines. "I say to-day that the soldiers who have fallen recently and those who have fallen from the State of Kansas, in defense of the policy of the administration, for the subjugation of these people—that the blood of these brave soldiers deserves to rest, and will rest upon the President of the United States, the Commander in Chief of the Army."[31]

On 1 March, William Allen delivered what he thought would be his last speech. (Actually, the Nebraskan would return quite unexpectedly the following December to serve out the term of another senator that ran until 1901.) In it, Allen accurately reminisced about his years in the Senate and defended his record as a Populist. Bringing his senatorial career up to date, he roundly condemned the administration's imperialistic course. He warned, "If the Republican party shall undertake to hold permanently the Philippines without the consent of the American people, and without the consent of the Filipinos, they will be guilty of overturning the very foundation on which this Republic rests."[32]

Over on the House side, John Allen, a loquacious Mississippi Democrat, made some remarks (partly in jest) containing more truth than even he could have imagined. He had recently heard it said that even though members "attached a great deal of importance to what [they did] . . . our speeches and predictions would soon be forgotten and . . . Government would go on about the same as if we had not spoken." That was only true, he said, of the "average" congressman, and he did not include himself in that category. "I speak with the confident expectation that a hundred years from now, when questions of war and expansion agitate this country, as they do to-day, the statesmen of that day will search with eagerness the musty volumes of the *Congressional Record* of the Fifty-fifth Congress."[33] The Mississippi wit was probably wrong about statesmen making such a search, but historians certainly have looked to the record of this pivotal Congress to understand why and how America made the choices it did in those years, although a much closer examination of the role of the Populist delegation would have added greatly to our understanding.

From the perspective of 100 years, one might make a strong case that the country has paid a heavy price for this crucial decision made long ago. Some historians, myself included, would seriously contend that the road selected at that time led straight to the debacle called the Vietnam War. However that may be, in spite of a prominent tendency to use the word *history* as a synonym for words like *done, finished, dead,* and *irrelevant,* history is not quite like that; we continue to pay the price for critical decisions made—and not made—in our past, even when they have been conveniently erased from our collective memories.[34] This may especially be the case when a society makes large and critical choices such as those made during the crises of the 1890s—choices that ultimately were terribly wrong or led precisely to where the losers predicted they would lead.

THE REAR GUARD

As previously indicated, Populist numbers dwindled significantly beginning with the 1898 election—down to fourteen in the Fifty-sixth Congress and nine in the Fifty-seventh. Also during this time, individual Populists, one after the other, moved to new political homes; except for James Kyle and Harry Skinner, who aligned with the Republicans during the Fifty-fifth Congress, Populists moved to the Democratic camp. Only William Neville and William Allen of Nebraska continued to identify themselves as Populists to the end of their tenure (although they too eventually became Democrats). In spite of their meager numbers, however, this rear guard of the movement had much to say on a variety of subjects worthy of being placed before the bar of history.

George Turner of Washington State—a Republican in his politics from nearly the founding of the party until the revolt of the 1890s, when he became first a silver Republican, then a Fusionist, a Populist, and ultimately a Democrat—remained quite active to the end of his term in 1903. Early in February 1900, the onetime "carpetbagger" participant in Alabama's Reconstruction government announced in the Senate that he believed that the Democratic party had "rejuvenated itself" and had by then "stepped into the shoes of the Republican party as the true exponent of the principles of Abraham Lincoln."[35] For a time after 1899, Turner was one of the primary opponents of the arguments made in the Senate by the administration's leading exponent of imperialism, Albert Beveridge of Indiana. Early on, Beveridge became known far and wide for his no-holds-barred, unqualified defense of the nation's new imperial role in the world. Americans (defined, by and large, as white, Anglo-Saxon Protestants) were simply "God's chosen people," "the sovereign power among the nations," and he was the number-one salesman for the nation's new imperial wares. Over and over Beveridge proclaimed, "Our day as the master people of the world has dawned."[36]

In one of his responses to Beveridge, Turner insisted, "Liberty knows no clime, no color, no race, no creed. Its principles as embodied in the immortal Declaration of Independence, comprehend all time, past, present, and future, and embrace all peoples to whom Almighty God has vouchsafed the instinct of association and the capacity, however limited, for orderly government." He went on to agree with Beveridge's contention that the American Indians did not "possess" the "instinct or the capacity" for "orderly government," but insisted "the same thing can not be said of Filipinos." He spoke of what he called the possible "boomerang effect" of America's imperial policies. Arguments advanced to support subjugation—or advanced in support of greater freedoms for the subjugated—could very well start an unanticipated firestorm at home. He concluded by saying, "Let us pray that it may . . . not be said of the American people now, to be repeated in the future in derogation of freedom, that they who have sat so long at the feet of Liberty were the first in their blindness to plunge a dagger into the heart of her youngest and latest devotee."[37]

George Hoar, a respected elder among the Republicans, was probably even more effective in his replies to the young senator from Indiana. After listening intently to one of Beveridge's pontifical speeches, Hoar said, "God who made of one blood all the nations of the world has made all the nations of the world capable of being influenced by the same sentiments and the same motives." The "love of liberty," said Hoar, "does not depend on the color of the skin, . . . it depends on humanity. These men are God's children." Addressing himself directly to Beveridge, Hoar said that he had "heard his eloquent description of wealth and glory and commerce and trade." Much in it was "calculated to excite the imagination of the youth seeking wealth or the youth charmed by the dream of empire." But "I listened in vain for the words Right, Justice, Duty, Freedom—they were absent."[38]

While the imperial surge was working its will on Congress and the nation, southern state governments, dominated by whites, were moving, one after the other, to put an end to black male suffrage, a move that was soon followed by an even more systematic effort to institutionalize white supremacy throughout southern society and beyond and to put in place, by law, an elaborate caste system. Justice John Marshall Harlan had predicted in the *Plessy* case that the Supreme Court's 1896 decision would lead to "aggressions, more or less brutal and irritating, upon the rights of colored citizens, " encouraging "the belief that it is possible, by means of state enactments, to defeat the beneficent purposes which the people of the United States had in view when they adopted the recent amendments of the Constitution." Discounting some earlier sporadic efforts to limit the franchise by means of literacy tests, registration requirements, and other such devices in the voting area, Florida led off in 1889 by adopting a poll tax; Mississippi followed in 1890 with a more elaborate plan involving a revision of the state's constitution; then came South Carolina in 1895, followed by Louisiana in 1898, North Carolina in 1900, Alabama in 1901, Virginia in 1902, Texas in 1904, Georgia in 1908, and Oklahoma in 1910. Populists had denounced this development in their 1896 platform. It was, of course, to no avail. As one writer so aptly put it, by the turn of the century, "colorphobia was a disease of epidemic proportions in the United States."[39] Horrible reports of lynching, mutilation, torture, and burnings began to make their way into the journalistic record.[40] According to one study, 4,743 *recorded* lynchings occurred in the United States between 1882 and 1968. African Americans made up a growing percentage of those being killed by mobs, growing "from 46 percent in 1882 to an average of 89 percent between 1900 and 1910, with seven of the eleven years showing rates above 90 percent." In addition, a number of "African American sympathizers" were the victims of mob violence.[41]

Because this was such a widespread and deplorable development, one would think that any and all moves to counter the trend ought to receive recognition and due credit. On 16 January 1900, Allen presented to the Senate a petition, signed by more than 3,200 colored citizens of the United States, solemnly protesting widespread and growing violations of their rights; they especially wanted something to be done about "the barbarous custom of lynching and burning of colored men." Allen noted that the Fourteenth Amendment surely provided ample constitutional authority for the government to act. "It is within the power of the Congress of the United States," he said, "to enact laws to protect citizens of the United States, white or black, and it is within the power of the executive branch of the Government to enforce those statutes on every foot of every State, Territory, and District within the jurisdiction of this country."[42]

Several weeks later, Marion Butler took up the same issue by introducing the following resolution in the Senate: "*Resolved*, That an enactment by constitution or otherwise, by any State which confers the right to vote upon any of its citizens because of their descent from certain persons [classes of], and excludes other citizens because they are not descended from such persons or classes of persons, having all other qualifications prescribed by law, in the opinion of the Senate, is in violation of the Fourteenth and Fifteenth Amendments to the Constitution of the United States and of a fundamental principle of our republican form of government."[43] This was aimed at defeating the grandfather clause that was to be voted on in North Carolina later that year as part of an effort aimed at taking the vote away from black males and ultimately denying the civil liberties of all blacks. Butler delivered an impressive speech on behalf of his resolution. This courageous move would in no way slow the move toward disfranchisement, however. Unbelievably, it would even take until 1915, in *Guinn v. United States,* for the Supreme Court to declare this outrageously transparent scheme unconstitutional.

Butler, George White, and the few remaining Populists from North Carolina were certainly in danger of having a significant portion of their constituency disappear. Remarks by White in February 1900 regarding the Philippine question seemed to indicate that the nation's only black congressman, who had once been in favor of annexation, was having second thoughts about his party's imperial ways—either that or he was taking advantage of the situation to send his party a message. He asked, "Should not a nation be just to all of her citizens, protect them alike in all their rights, on every foot of her soil—in a word, show herself capable of governing all within her domain before she undertakes to exercise sovereign authority over those of a foreign land . . . ?" White also surveyed the treatment blacks had received over the preceding thirty-five years. Since the end of slavery, he said, "fully 50,000 of my race have been ignominiously murdered by mobs, not 1 per cent of whom have been made to answer for their crimes in the courts of justice, and even here in the nation's Capital—in the Senate and House—Senators and Representatives have undertaken the unholy task of extenuating and excusing these foul deeds, and in some instances they have gone so far as to justify them."[44]

Congressmen had indeed done just as White said, and the most notorious offender was Benjamin Tillman. In several heated exchanges, the South Carolinian bragged about how his fellow whites had killed people of color in his state and had taken the vote away from them by any and all means at their disposal. At one point, while the Senate was discussing, in executive session, the appointment of a black man to a government post, Tillman became highly agitated, beat his fists in the air, and roared, "You can keep up that kind of thing until you compel the people of the South to use shotguns and kill every man you appoint." When George Hoar commented that he would not dare make such a threat in open session, Tillman replied, "Open the door right now and see whether I will admit it or not." He was not a man to bluff; he was, in fact, well known for a variety of "reckless truth-telling" that many of his colleagues found quite shocking and intimidating.[45]

One of the low points of the ongoing but sporadic congressional debate over imperialism came two years later, in February 1902, as the Roosevelt administration moved to follow up on the report of McKinley's Philippine Commission, which confirmed that colonial status had been imposed on the Filipinos, just as the anti-imperialists had predicted. As this process worked its way through Congress, Senator Tillman was again in the headlines. At one point, after protesting "the addition" of "9,000,000" more "colored people" to the population and the costs of the war, Tillman asked, "Why did you not spend your $400,000,000 helping to do something to relieve the Southern States of the incubus of negro domination by colonizing some of them away from here?" Earlier, he had also defended William Jennings Bryan against the charge of being solely responsible for swaying enough votes to ratify the treaty of annexation by suggesting that Republicans had engaged in some vote trading of their own. He then indicated that his state's junior Democratic senator, John McLaurin, was likely one of those who had been won over.

Tillman went on to explain what he viewed as McLaurin's perfidy: "After having told us in confidence that he would not vote for it, he did; and since then he has been adopted by the Republican caucus and put upon committees as a member of that party, and has controlled the patronage in South Carolina." Somewhat later, McLaurin entered the Senate, obtained the floor on a question of personal privilege, and labeled Tillman's account "a willful, malicious, and deliberate lie." The record then states: "At this point Mr. Tillman advanced to Mr. McLaurin of South Carolina; and the two Senators met in a personal encounter." In fact, they engaged in a fistfight and scuffle on the floor of the Senate until they were pulled apart by the doorkeeper and several nearby senators. The doors were then closed, and contempt proceedings commenced immediately. The vote on the motion passed sixty-one to zero. Tillman and McLaurin were then given a chance to apologize. Six days later, Tillman received a twenty-day suspension; McLaurin was suspended for five days. Thus the two South Carolina senators hold the dubious distinction of being only two of four senators in the twentieth century to be chastised in this manner.[46]

As for Populism, the high point of the debate over imperialism came with William Neville's extraordinary speech castigating Republicans and Democrats for their selective denial of basic human rights to people under their control. In this respect, no one laid claim to the Lincoln mantle more clearly than did this Nebraskan—who clearly was the last Populist congressman. His was a message for the ages, and one worth repeating: "Nations should have the same right among nations that men have among men. The right to life, liberty, and the pursuit of happiness is as dear to the black and brown man as to the white; as precious to the poor as to the rich; as just to the ignorant as to the educated; as sacred to the weak as to the strong, and as applicable to nations as to individuals, and the nation which subverts such right by force is not better governed than the man who takes the law into his own hands."[47]

In the upper chamber, William Allen and George Turner both waged a vigorous fight against imperialism. The two were as one in their belief and insistence that the Republicans had "dishonored the nation in their greed for power and spoils." Turner predicted, "Abraham Lincoln, who would not know one of these leaders as a Republican if he could come back to earth and should meet him in the middle of the street, declared that it was possible to fool some of the people all the time and all of the people some of the time, but it was not possible to fool all the people all of the time. There will come an awakening some time, be assured of it."[48]

Unlike Allen, Turner and several other Populists from the West coast may have bought into the racial distinctions (possibly as an expedient) that were so popular on both sides of the major-party aisle. In opposing a move to end Chinese exclusion under consideration in April 1902, Turner made the following pitch for support:

> We appeal with especial confidence to our friends from the South, who have in their body politic a growing cancer second only in virulence to that which would be fastened on the Pacific coast by a further propulsion to their shores of the pagan hordes of China. The Caucasian and the Mongolian are as far apart as the Caucasian and the Ethiopian. We have had the race problem with us from the beginning as the result of the presence of the Ethiopian. It kept us in turmoil for half a century and came near destroying the integrity of the Republic. . . . How it will end no man can foresee, but one thing is certain, since the black man is nonassimilable and can not reach up to the standard of the Caucasian, nor pull the latter down to the level of the Ethiopian, he will remain a disturbing factor in our nationality so long as he remains one of its constituent elements.[49]

Senator Henry Heitfeld, an Idaho Populist who uttered precious few words for the record during his six years in the Senate, chose this topic, Chinese exclusion, to break his long silence. His advice was, "We have the door closed; let us keep it closed."[50]

As the proponents of empire completed their work with the passage of the Philippine government bill, it was Republican Senator George Hoar who asked, in so many words, What will we write on this generation's hall of fame? "Must we engrave on that column, 'We repealed the Declaration of Independence. . . . *We [have] crushed the only republic in Asia.* We made war on the only Christian people in the East. We converted a war of glory to a war of shame. We vulgarized the American flag. We introduced perfidy into the practice of war. We inflicted torture on unarmed men to extort confessions. We put children to death. We established reconcentrado camps. We devastated provinces. We baffled the aspirations of a people for liberty.' "[51]

On the House side, William Neville made a final pronouncement as the Philippine government bill was speeding on its way to passage: "I was once a Republican," he said. "It was many years ago, and my consolation is that that party came into power because it advocated man's humanity to man, as a means to produce the greatest good to the greatest number, and I got out of the party when I foresaw that it would go out of power advocating man's inhumanity to man, as a means to produce the greatest misery to the greatest number."[52]

But of course the winners in the Great Debate were absolutely convinced that American imperialism was different—a "new imperialism," they loudly proclaimed, perhaps not even imperialism at all. It was more like a case of the nation simply "extending civilization" to the benighted heathens. And they certainly would applaud Theodore Roosevelt's reasoning from an 1899 article: "Every expansion of civilization makes for peace. In other words, every expansion of a great civilized power means a victory for law, order, and righteousness." Roosevelt wrote further, "If the men who have counseled national degradation, national dishonor, by urging us to leave the Philippines and put the Aguinaldan oligarchy in control of those islands, could have their way, we should merely turn them over to rapine and bloodshed until some stronger, manlier power stepped in to do the task we had shown ourselves fearful of performing. But, as it is, this country will keep the islands and will establish therein a stable and orderly government, so that one more fair spot of the world's surface shall have been snatched from the forces of darkness."[53] It was, after all, the season for "the white man's burden." And the struggle in the Philippines, President Roosevelt insisted, should be called the "War to Extend Anglo-Saxon Progress and Decency."[54]

It was also the season for a growing concern about what was to be done about huge corporate monopolies in the form of trusts—the "octopus," the "beast," or the "iron heel," as they soon came to be called in popular jargon. That issue again came to the front after the spectacular corporate merger movement that commenced in 1897 and continued to accelerate until 1904. The few surviving Populist congressmen picked up on the trend, seeing it as ample justification for their approach to the economy: some in order to make a case for more effective regulatory action; others to make one for public ownership of key sectors of the nation's economy.

Kansas' last Populist to be sent to Congress was Edwin Ridgely, first elected in 1896 and reelected in 1898 from the southeastern corner of the state, which had proved itself to be the most radical of recruiting grounds. This was the same area that had already been established as the base for the soon to be nationally acclaimed socialist weekly *The Appeal to Reason,* published in the small county-seat town of Girard, in Crawford County. The area was also involved in a building socialist movement that was plainly evident in Populist-Democratic party politics in Kansas after 1898, especially in the 1900 gubernatorial campaign of John Breidenthal.

Ridgely—as was the case with the entire Populist delegation—was a determined foe of imperialism. In the debate prompted by the McKinley administration's move to commit the country formally to the gold standard, he made this revealing comment: "Socialists are multiplying by the hundreds of thousands throughout the nation. This bill will recruit their ranks by millions. . . . We are by this very bill unwittingly hastening and making the establishment of socialism an absolute certainty. As one who believes in the fundamental principles of socialism I take a degree of satisfaction in seeing this bill enacted . . . , knowing that it will hasten the overthrow of the present system of capitalism."[55] Later, when a bill dealing with the trusts was under consideration, the Kansan let it be known that there was but one legitimate remedy: "Government ownership and State ownership." He would agree with his party's candidate for governor in 1900, who insisted that regulation would not work: "You might as well try to regulate a coyote or a rattlesnake," John Breidenthal said in a speech delivered in William Allen White's hometown of Emporia. "You cannot supervise them and you cannot control them. My remedy is to allow the people to run these businesses themselves, but you say that is socialism. Well, maybe it is."[56]

Near the end of his tenure, Senator Butler still urged that same fundamental Populist solution in the Senate. As he put it, the nation needed to remove the conditions that produced the trusts by having "the three greatest instruments of commerce—money, transportation, and the transmission of intelligence—in their modern form, operated as public functions at cost, without discrimination against any and with equal opportunities to all."[57]

William Harris was just as concerned about the ever-growing problem of corporate consolidation but was more inclined to put his faith in regulatory reform, as were growing numbers of Americans who called themselves "progressives." Anticlimactic as it was, the Kansas senator's last major effort in that direction was aimed at promoting the passage of the oleomargarine bill then before Congress. One opponent of the measure minced no words when he said that its "purpose [was] . . . to enrich one class at the expense of another and to destroy an industry in order to do it." Harris nonetheless delivered a long and effective speech making a case for why oleomargarine needed to be regulated in order to safeguard the production of butter. That regulatory measure would become law and a year later would be upheld in a rather murky decision by the Supreme Court.[58]

Several years before his term expired in 1903, Harris appealed for "progressive" bipartisan support in his bid for reelection by the Kansas legislature, which he failed to obtain. In 1906, however, the former senator was the Democratic and reform nominee for governor. The ex-Virginian was, as ever, a popular figure, having demonstrated his attachment to the "middle-ground" reform agenda. In the course of that campaign, he also publicly confessed to having considerable "admiration" for President Theodore Roosevelt, who, according to him, had "adopted a great many" of the Democratic party's "best ideas." Said Harris, "There is a good deal of Democracy permeating through the ranks of the Republican party." Harris's campaign came within nearly 2,000 votes (0.4 percent) of winning in a state where the Republicans had decisively reasserted their dominance eight years earlier.[59]

That same year witnessed the significant beginnings—albeit belated—of a major reform movement within the Kansas Republican party. At about the same time, William Allen White was editorializing in his *Emporia Gazette* about how "funny" it was that his contemporaries had "all found the octopus; an animal whose very existence we denied ten or a dozen years ago." In retrospect, White went so far as to concede that he had been a "reactionary" back in the 1890s, and "the Populists had the germ of a great truth which the country was not prepared to accept." They were just "too early in the season," said White, "and [their] . . . views got frost bitten."[60]

For better or worse, the "frost bitten" Populists would have to settle for having played a significant educational role at a vital turning point in the nation's history—a role that was nowhere more vital than on the floor of Congress. As we have seen, their message was delivered. But was it received? Certainly not in the way they would have had it. Perhaps that was because congressional Populists confronted somewhat the same challenge experienced by that noted American author and social democrat Upton Sinclair. Beginning with his 1905 journey to the Chicago stockyards to gather material for his soon-to-be-famous novel *The Jungle,* Sinclair in effect took up where the Populists left off and began a long battle for "suffering humanity."[61] After having fought the "good fight" through the depths of the Great Depression, with much less success than he would have hoped, he arrived at the sobering conclusion that it was "difficult" if not impossible to get people to listen to an argument when their livelihood "depended on their not understanding it."[62] But has that not been at the heart of the problem since the crisis of the 1890s, growing stronger with each passing decade? And will it not be with us into the indefinite future?

Epilogue

Late in March 1898, as the nation girded itself for a war that everyone knew was just ahead, several states began to take steps of their own to prepare for action. In Kansas that effort was led by John Leedy, the state's second and last Populist chief executive.[1] The governor had issued a call for a company of volunteers. Afterward, he could not forgo the opportunity to poke fun at a favorite target of the Populists—that mighty "artificial person" called a corporation. At a press conference, Leedy made this offhand remark: "I have received scores of volunteer applications from farmers, merchants, and mechanics all over the State, but so far I haven't received a notice from one corporation that is ready to give its services to the country." Possibly with tongue in cheek, he added: The Court has ruled that "corporations were persons, like you and me and the rest of the people in these United States, and had the same rights as natural born citizens." Consequently, "I feel that the *Supreme court individuals* are slighting the State by failing to signify their willingness to go in defense of the government, and believe that with the same rights as natural born citizens, they should show some of the same patriotism."[2]

Like most people, then and later, Governor Leedy was probably not fully appreciative of just how complete the victory of that "artificial person" over the "natural citizen" had been in the contest for those inalienable rights that many Americans cherished. They could hardly be said to have the "same rights." By 1898, thanks to a series of judicial determinations over the previous twenty-five years, corporations had been awarded, certainly in Fourteenth Amendment terms, what amounted to first-class citizenship, whereas whole categories of real people had, in effect, been consigned to second- or even third-class citizenship. Corporate America had indeed captured "the cultural high ground," as Lawrence Goodwyn so aptly put it.[3]

The governor's taunt had been prompted by the business community's less-than-enthusiastic support for Cuban intervention; however, once the war had begun and the road to an empire was thrown open, there were no more avid sponsors of imperialism (or "the large policy," to use one of their preferred euphemisms) than those within the business community.[4]

The prospect of huge new markets in the Far East being made more accessible by the country's annexation of Hawaii and the Philippines also had a strong effect on the agricultural community. As has been noted by foreign policy specialists, it resonated in such a way as to create an approach later labeled "insular imperialism."[5] America's island possessions were viewed primarily as stepping stones on the way to the great and mythical Asian market. This aspect of America's imperialism was clearly highlighted by Nebraska Populist Roderick Sutherland in the debate over annexation that took place in February 1900. In one of his anti-imperialistic speeches, Sutherland hit on what he called the "real object" of those seeking to annex the Philippines: it was "not benevolent assimilation, not the ultimate good of the inhabitants, nor the betterment of this country, . . . the hidden motive is the presence of sufficient military and naval strength to enable the capitalists of England and America at the proper time to invade China with railroads, open up the territory containing 500,000,000 people to the planting of factories, where can be found the cheapest labor on earth, and thus make China the workshop of the world."[6]

Could that have been what it was all about? Who would deny that the economic component was powerful and carried an appeal that cut across sectional, urban, rural, and class lines? In the end, even the strongest foes of imperialism would likely have conceded that expansion of trade by peaceful, nonmilitary means was a desirable and legitimate goal. Surely, what separated the imperialists from the anti-imperialists involved the element of force and dominance and, above all, the denial of self-determination and the negation of principles thought to be at the very core of American values. It was the implicit—occasionally even explicit—denial of a common humanity that troubled congressional Populists. Many anti-imperialists, as Christopher Lasch pointed out long ago, "did not challenge the central assumption of imperialist thought: the natural inequality of men." Among those who did, one finds the Populists strongly represented. As we have seen, however, they were not altogether free of race-based biases. We should take care, however, to keep such matters in perspective. As Lasch also noted, "It is not possible to condemn anti-imperialists for holding certain opinions on race unless one is willing to condemn the entire society of which they were a part. The fact is . . . the atmosphere of the late nineteenth century was so thoroughly permeated with racist thought (reinforced by Darwinism) that few [white?] men managed to escape it. The idea that certain cultures and races were naturally inferior to others was almost universally held by educated, middle-class, respectable Americans—in other words, by the dominant majority."[7]

America's emergence as a full-fledged imperial power was by no means an aberration, a brief and uncharacteristic interlude; it was a logical product of forces, ideas, and developments that were years in the making. According to the broader and, I think, most historically honest definition, borrowed from two specialists on the subject, imperialism boils down to this: "the extension of sovereignty or control, whether direct or indirect, political or economic, by one government or society over another, together with the ideas justifying or opposing this process. Imperialism is essentially about power [or dominance] both as end and means. . . . Underlying all forms of imperialism is the belief—at times *unshakable* [and usually unconscious]—of the imperial agent or nation in an inherent right, based on moral superiority as well as on material might, to impose its [presumptively] preeminent values and techniques on the [allegedly] 'inferior' indigenous nation or society."[8] Taking this definition as a guide, one can certainly make a strong case that American Indians, Mexicans, African Americans, women generally, and even radical Populist farmers, among others, served as early punching bags for the imperialistically minded. It is also true that among the Populists themselves a significant element shared or ultimately came to share some of the same notions that made one an imperialist. Among their congressional colleagues, the most prominent convert to imperialism was their first senator, William Peffer. After leaving office in 1897, the Kansan soon dissociated himself from the People's party. Just as Ronald Wilson Reagan, years later, liked to say about his departure from the Democratic party, Peffer would contend that the party had left him. In 1898, he agreed to become a gubernatorial candidate of the Kansas Prohibition party. Following that, Peffer made his return to the Republican fold, becoming a supporter of and an apologist for American imperialism. In 1900, he came out with a book on the subject called *Americanism and the Philippines*.[9]

Populism's first senator also wrote and published a history of Populism that was serialized in the *Chicago Tribune* from May to July 1899.[10] The story he told was, not surprisingly, heavily laden with his special version of events. The memoir was nonetheless revealing, scrupulously honest, and informative regarding the meaning of Populism—particularly at the congressional level.

As he returned to his original political home, Peffer remained steadfast in his belief that the Democratic party had undergone no significant changes with the ascendancy of Bryan's supporters. "[The] . . . Democratic party and the People's party are antipodal," he insisted. Apparently, he also managed to convince himself that the following highly dubious proposition was valid: "Populists and Republicans do not differ at the foundation." He stated, "The Republican party believes the national government may do anything anywhere within the boundaries of the union that will promote the general welfare, and Populists believe the same, but Democrats do not."[11] An insurgent revolt within the Republican party, followed by Theodore Roosevelt's presidency and his later leadership of a short-lived Progressive party revolt, had yet to occur to work the kind of changes within the GOP that might lend a degree of credence to such a claim. Nevertheless, Peffer was not off base in his interpretation of what Populism had signified, only as regards its legitimate heirs.

After 1897, however, among Populist senators, none more clearly articulated the meaning of the movement than the young senator from North Carolina, Marion Butler. In 1905, four years after his term ended, Butler also joined the Republicans. As such, he was an avid supporter of the brand of politics that came to be associated with Theodore Roosevelt. His choice of the Republican party was logical, given the fact that the North Carolina Democratic party was such a bitter foe and more truly a polar opposite than was the case beyond the South. Not long before he died in 1938, it was said that Butler was seriously considering writing a history of Populism. One suspects that it would have made an interesting and useful companion to Peffer's account. In lieu of that, Butler left us one of the richer collections of Populist materials, one that still has not been explored to the extent that it merits.

On 29 January 1901, George White, one of Butler's fellow North Carolinians, delivered a long and emotional farewell address to the House. White had been defeated, as had Butler and the remaining Tarheel Populists, as a result of the tactics employed throughout much of the South aimed primarily at taking the vote away from American citizens of African descent. In this speech, White laid out in detail how that had been accomplished and warned of a day of reckoning: "He that sheddeth man's blood, by man shall his blood be shed," said White. He also offered what he called a "recipe for the solution of the so-called American negro problem." It was, of course, a problem of white racism. He advised: "Treat him as a man; go into his home and learn of his social conditions; learn of his cares, his troubles, and his hopes for the future; gain his confidence; open the doors of industry to him; let the word 'negro,' 'colored,' and 'black' be stricken from all the organizations enumerated in the federation of labor." Be done with "race hatred, party prejudice, and help us to achieve nobler ends, greater results, and [to] become more satisfactory citizens to our brother in white."

White conceded that his address was "perhaps the negroes' temporary farewell to the American Congress; but let me say, Phoenix-like, he will rise up some day and come again." He said he spoke on behalf of "an outraged, heart-broken, bruised, and bleeding, but Godfearing people" and that "the only apology that I have to make for the earnestness with which I have spoken is that I am pleading for the life, the liberty, the future happiness, and manhood suffrage of one-eighth of the entire population of the United States. [Loud applause.]"[12]

White was and apparently remained a Republican. As indicated, nearly all the congressional Populists established their new political home within the Democratic party. They convinced themselves that it had managed to regenerate itself as a result of the political revolt of the 1890s. And despite the glaring contradiction of the American version of apartheid—the lowering of a racial iron curtain throughout American society—the Republican party's defense of imperialism made this particular adaptation much easier and more logical than otherwise would have been the case.

In addition, the strong identification of Republicans with the nation's ongoing economic revolution—well advanced by the turn of the century in fashioning a new urban-industrial, corporate America—figured prominently in decisions made about future political homes. That reality was definitely a factor in determining Peffer's course. Soon after he left the Senate in 1897, the Kansan briefly became the editor of his state's major Populist weekly. In his first editorial, he announced that the paper would remain Populist and would continue to support the party's principles as outlined in its national platforms; however, he put his readers on notice that he now saw the need for "applying them along conservative lines." "This world is too big," he said, "for men to recreate it. Too many things are now established to make it possible or even desirable that all needed changes should be immediately and at once completely wrought."[13]

For others such as George Turner—and they were far more numerous—the Republican party's close identification with the emerging corporate order was ample reason for a move to the Democratic party. In Turner's view, the Grand Old Party had come to stand "for the material interests of the nation, for the corporations, for the trusts, and for the enormous aggregations of capital." His old hero had insisted that Republicans were for "both the man and the dollar; but in cases of conflict, the man before the dollar." By the turn of the century, however, it was obvious to Turner that Lincoln's party much preferred the dollar to the man.[14] To make this move, the Washington Populist would have to amend his concept of humanity (if not that, at least put on blinders) while associating with a political organization that had become a party of reform for whites only throughout the South and beyond.

But of course that would be the nature of the new reform movement that had begun to pick up steam as the nation entered the new century. Its adherents could call themselves "progressives" and at the same time subject black Americans to a retrogression in status and not send listeners into convulsions of laughter (flunking the giggle test) simply because the nation was well on its way to abandoning its earlier, more liberal commitment to the philosophy of inherent natural rights proclaimed in the Declaration of Independence. As it has been said, "the right to liberty" was no longer "natural" or innate, a gift from God or nature's God, inherent in each and every person solely because he or she was a human being. The "politically correct" position of that day insisted that rights and the idea of liberty and freedom had become dependent on one's "readiness" to enjoy the benefits of such rights. As never before, human rights were made contingent on a variety of factors. Above all, said Lasch, they hinged on a "pseudo-Darwinian hierarchy of cultural stages, [with people] being unequal in the capacity for enjoyment of the rights associated with self-government."[15]

Populism was not without flaws in this area, as we have seen, but the movement and its congressmen waged a significant fight against this illiberal transformation, which was the fundamental and least understood crisis of the 1890s. To be sure, it was a losing battle, but did they ultimately win the war of ideas? Or is that a work still in progress? However that may be, the nation was the immediate loser. The "retreat from idealism" represented by this transformation was a national—if not an international— phenomenon. White racism, sexism (in the form of male supremacy), possessive individualism, hypercapitalism, and imperialism were the key ingredients in the mind-set that frustrated and enervated the Populist movement.[16] Without question, this particular plague of isms reached into the Populist camp; it was, however, *far more* prominently represented in the camp of the anti-Populists, where there were far fewer antidotes.

As indicated previously, the whole phenomenon may well have been merely symptomatic of a more fundamental change at work within Western civilization and beyond, signifying a decided shift on the scale of values to what might be called the inhumane preference: one that confirmed and sanctioned the belief that human rights were not universal and certainly not transcendent; one in which systems and material objects are given—or simply assume by default—priority, while at the same time capital accumulation becomes the sine qua non of progress, a crucial and seminal transvaluation of cultural norms that was right at the core of the crisis of the nineties. That being the case, genuine Populism—as opposed to that pseudo version we continue to hear so much about (the one that focuses on political style and ignores or is confused about substance)—will likely continue to have a high degree of relevance for humanity, while at the same time becoming increasingly more remote and unattainable in the modern world. After all is said and done, perhaps the Populist moment was a classic case of that well-known and prophetic "tide in the affairs of men" that moves in and out, undisturbed and unheeded, taking with it the promise of a "rendezvous with destiny."

Appendix A. Profiles of Populists in Congress at Election

FIFTY-SECOND CONGRESS, 1891–1893

Senators *(average age 48.00)*

William Peffer. Topeka, Kans. Born 10 Sept. 1832, Cumberland Co., Pa. Editor/publisher. Age 59 at election.

James Kyle. Aberdeen, S.D. Born 24 Feb. 1854, Xenia, Ohio. Clergyman. Age 37 at election.

Representatives *(average age 48.56)*

William Baker. Lincoln, Kans. Born 19 Apr. 1831, Centerville, Pa. Farmer. Age 59 at election.

Benjamin Clover. Cambridge, Kans. Born 22 Dec. 1837, Jefferson, Ohio. Farmer. Age 53 at election.

John Davis. Junction City, Kans. Born 9 Aug. 1826, Springfield, Ill. Farmer/editor. Age 64 at election.

Kittel Halvorson. Stearns Co., Minn. Born 15 Dec. 1846, Telemarken, Norway. Farmer. Age 44 at election.

Omer Kem. Broken Bow, Nebr. Born 13 Nov. 1855, Hagerstown, Ind. Farmer. Age 35 at election.

William McKeighan. Red Cloud, Nebr. Born 19 Jan. 1842, Millville, N.J. Farmer/judge. Age 48 at election.

John Otis. Topeka, Kans. Born 10 Feb. 1838, Danby, Vt. Farmer. Age 52 at election.

Jeremiah Simpson. Medicine Lodge, Kans. Born 31 Mar. 1842, Prince Edward Island. Sailor/rancher. Age 48 at election.

Thomas Watson. Thomson, Ga. Born 5 Sept. 1856, Thomson, Ga. Attorney/landlord. Age 34 at election.

FIFTY-THIRD CONGRESS, 1893–1895

Senators

William Allen. Madison, Nebr. Born 28 Jan. 1847, Midway, Ohio. Attorney/judge. Age 46 at election.

Representatives *(average age 46.5)*

John Bell. Montrose, Colo. Born 11 Dec. 1851, Sewanee, Tenn. Attorney/judge. Age 41 at election.

Haldor Boen. Fergus Falls, Minn. Born 2 Jan. 1851, Sondre Aurdal, Norway. Farmer. Age 41 at election.

Marion Cannon. Ventura, Calif. Born 30 Oct. 1834, Morgantown, Va. Farmer. Age 58 at election.

William Harris. Linwood, Kans. Born 29 Oct. 1842, Luray, Va. Engineer/rancher. Age 51 at election.

Lafayette Pence. Denver, Colo. Born 23 Dec. 1857, Columbus, Ind. Attorney. Age 35 at election.

Thomas Hudson. Fredonia, Kans. Born 30 Oct. 1839, Jamestown, Ind. Attorney. Age 53 at election.

FIFTY-FOURTH CONGRESS, 1895–1897

Senators

Marion Butler. Clinton, N.C. Born 20 May 1863, Clinton, N.C. Editor/publisher. Age 32 at election.

Representatives *(average age 44.33)*

Alonzo Shuford. Newton, N.C. Born 1 Mar. 1853, Newton, N.C. Farmer. Age 36 at election.

William Strowd. Chapel Hill, N.C. Born 7 Dec. 1832, Chatham Co., N.C. Farmer. Age 62 at election.

Harry Skinner. Greenville, N.C. Born 25 May 1855, Hertford, N.C. Attorney. Age 39 at election.

Milford Howard. Fort Payne, Ala. Born 18 Dec. 1862, Rome, Ga. Attorney. Age 32 at election.

Albert Goodwyn. Robinson Springs, Ala. Born 17 Dec. 1842, Robinson Springs, Ala. Planter/landlord. Age 51 at election.

Charles Martin. Raleigh, N.C. Born 28 Aug. 1848, Youngsville, N.C. Attorney/clergyman/professor. Age 46 at election.

FIFTY-FIFTH CONGRESS, 1897–1899

Senators *(average age 45.67)*

William Harris. *See* Fifty-third Congress. Age 55 at election.
Henry Heitfeld. Lewiston, Idaho. Born 12 Jan. 1859, St. Louis, Mo. Farmer/rancher. Age 36 at election.
George Turner. Spokane, Wash. Born 25 Feb. 1850, Edina, Mo. Attorney. Age 46 at election.

Representatives *(average age 47.58)*

Charles Barlow. San Luis Obispo, Calif. Born 17 Mar. 1858, Cleveland, Ohio. Publisher/farmer. Age 38 at election.
Curtis Castle. Merced, Calif. Born 4 Oct. 1848, Galesburg, Ill. Physician. Age 48 at election.
Jeremiah Botkin. Winfield, Kans. Born 24 Apr. 1849, Atlanta, Ill. Clergyman. Age 47 at election.
Mason Peters. Kansas City, Kans. Born 3 Sept. 1844, Kearney, Mo. Attorney/merchant. Age 52 at election.
Edwin Ridgely. Pittsburg, Kans. Born 9 May 1844, Lancaster, Ill. Merchant. Age 52 at election.
William Vincent. Clay Center, Kans. Born 11 Oct. 1852, Dresden, Tenn. Merchant. Age 44 at election.
Nelson McCormick. Phillipsburg, Kans. Born 20 Nov. 1847, Waynesburg, Pa. Attorney. Age 49 at election.
Freeman Knowles. Deadwood, S.D. Born 10 Oct. 1846, Harmony, Maine. Publisher/attorney. Age 49 at election.
Samuel Maxwell. Fremont, Nebr. Born 20 May 1825, Syracuse, N.Y. Attorney/judge. Age 71 at election.
William Stark. Aurora, Nebr. Born 29 July 1853, Mystic, Conn. Attorney/judge. Age 43 at election.
Roderick Sutherland. Nelson, Nebr. Born 27 Apr. 1862, Scotch Grove, Iowa. Attorney. Age 34 at election.
William Greene. Kearney, Nebr. Born 3 Oct. 1849, Ireland, Ind. Attorney/judge. Age 47 at election.
John Fowler. Clinton, N.C. Born 8 Sept. 1866, Clinton, N.C. Attorney. Age 30 at election.
John Kelley. Flandreau, S.D. Born 27 Mar. 1853, Portage City, Wis. Publisher/editor. Age 43 at election.
James Gunn. Boise, Idaho. Born 6 Mar. 1843, County Fermanagh, Ireland. Editor. Age 53 at election.
Jehu Baker. Belleville, Ill. Born 4 Nov. 1822, Lexington, Ky. Attorney. Age 74 at election. First elected as a Republican in 1864.
Albert Todd. Kalamazoo, Mich. Born 3 June 1850, Nottawa, Mich. Manufacturer/chemist. Age 46 at election.
John Rhea. Russellville, Ky. Born 9 Mar. 1855, Russellville, Ky. Attorney. Age 41 at election.

James Callahan. Kingfisher, Okla. Born 19 Dec. 1852, Salem, Mo. Clergyman/farmer. Age 43 at election.

FIFTY-SIXTH CONGRESS, 1899–1901

Representatives

John Atwater. Fearington, N.C. Born 27 Dec. 1840, Fearington, N.C. Farmer. Age 58 at election.

FIFTY-SEVENTH CONGRESS, 1901–1903

Representatives *(average age 54.33)*

William Neville. North Platte, Nebr. Born 19 Dec. 1843, Nashville, Ill. Attorney/judge. Age 55 at election.

Thomas Glenn. Montpelier, Idaho. Born 2 Feb. 1847, Bardwell, Ky. Attorney. Age 51 at election.

Caldwell Edwards. Bozeman, Mont. Born 8 Jan. 1841, Sag Harbor, N.Y. Rancher. Age 57 at election.

Appendix B.
Populists in Congress, Alphabetically

*Allen, William Vincent. Nebraska, 1893–1899, 1899–1901
Atwater, John Wilbur. North Carolina, 1899–1901
Baker, Jehu. Illinois, 1897–1899
Baker, William. Kansas, 1891–1897
Barlow, Charles Averill. California, 1897–1899
Bell, John Calhoun. Colorado, 1893–1903
Boen, Haldor Erickson. Minnesota, 1893–1895
Botkin, Jeremiah Dunham. Kansas, 1897–1899
*Butler, Marion. North Carolina, 1895–1901
Callahan, James Yancey. Oklahoma (delegate), 1897–1899
Cannon, Marion. California, 1893–1895
Castle, Curtis Harvey. California, 1897–1899
Clover, Benjamin. Kansas, 1891–1893
Davis, John. Kansas, 1891–1895
Edwards, Caldwell. Montana, 1901–1903
Fowler, John Edgar. North Carolina, 1897–1899
Glenn, Thomas Lewis. Idaho, 1901–1903
Goodwyn, Albert Taylor. Alabama, 1896–1897
Greene, William Laury. Nebraska, 1897–1899
Gunn, James. Idaho, 1897–1899
Halvorson, Kittel. Minnesota, 1891–1893
*Harris, William Alexander. Kansas, 1893–1895, 1897–1903
*Heitfeld, Henry. Idaho, 1897–1903
Howard, Milford Wriarson. Alabama, 1895–1899
Hudson, Thomas Jefferson. Kansas, 1893–1895
Kelley, John Edward. South Dakota, 1897–1899
Kem, Omer Madison. Nebraska, 1891–1897
Knowles, Freeman Tulley. South Dakota, 1897–1899
*Kyle, James Henderson. South Dakota, 1891–1901
Martin, Charles Henry. North Carolina, 1896–1899

Maxwell, Samuel. Nebraska, 1897–1899
McCormick, Nelson B. Kansas, 1897–1899
McKeighan, William Arthur. Nebraska, 1891–1895
Neville, William. Nebraska, 1899–1903
Otis, John Grant. Kansas, 1891–1893
*Peffer, William Alfred. Kansas, 1891–1897
Pence, Lafayette. Colorado, 1893–1895
Peters, Mason Summers. Kansas, 1897–1899
Rhea, John Stockdale. Kentucky, 1897–1901
Ridgely, Edwin Reed. Kansas, 1897–1901
Shuford, Alonzo Craig. North Carolina, 1895–1899
Simpson, Jeremiah. Kansas, 1891–1895, 1897–1899
Skinner, Harry. North Carolina, 1895–1899
Stark, William Ledyard. Nebraska, 1897–1903
Strowd, William Franklin. North Carolina, 1895–1899
Sutherland, Roderick Dhu. Nebraska, 1897–1901
Todd, Albert May. Michigan, 1897–1899
*Turner, George F. Washington, 1897–1903
Vincent, William Davis. Kansas, 1897–1899
Watson, Thomas Edward. Georgia, 1891–1893

*U.S. senators

Listed here are fifty different congressmen, elected for a total of seventy-two terms: forty-three Populists to sixty-four House terms, and seven Populists to eight Senate terms (fractional, appointed terms are not included). Only James Kyle and John Bell managed to serve ten years: Kyle in the Senate, Bell in the House. Neither did so, entirely, as Populists; both returned to their original political homes before leaving Congress—Bell to the Democrats, Kyle to the Republicans. In the House, only Bell of Colorado was elected to more than three terms—five consecutive terms in his case. William Baker of Kansas and Omer Kem and William Stark of Nebraska all were elected to three consecutive terms. After Bell, William Allen of Nebraska and William Harris of Kansas had the longest tenures as Populists; both served eight years. It is not coincidental that the three with the longest tenure were Populist/Democratic Fusionists, ultimately declaring themselves Democrats.

In his study of the Populists in the House,[1] Marquette University professor Karel Bicha lists Jehu Baker, John Rhea, Albert Todd, and Thomas Jefferson Strait as Populists. Baker, Rhea, and Todd—but not Strait, who called himself an Alliance Democrat—identified themselves as Fusionists. The sketches provided by congressmen for the *Biographical Directory,* however, are not altogether reliable and must be verified by other means. Several Populists who became Democrats did not even acknowledge their earlier Populist connection (John Bell, Populist speaker for a time, is a prominent example, and note the case of Albert Goodwyn below). It is quite possible that Baker, Rhea, and Todd were elected as Fusionists but immediately joined the Democrats in Congress. I include them on this list with that caveat attached. Strait, incidentally, was a forty-five-year-old physician when elected to Congress and had served previously in the South Carolina senate.

For the record, I asked Lawrence Goodwyn, a prominent historian of Populism, via telephone in 1990, whether he was related to Alabama's Albert Taylor Goodwyn. After what seemed a pregnant pause, his response was "yes." Apparently, Albert Goodwyn was his great-grandfather. On close examination we discover that Congressman Goodwyn was a southern Fusionist, the candidate of his district's Republicans, Jeffersonian Democrats, and Populists; while in Congress, he briefly allied with the Republicans. One historian concluded that he was "the foremost advocate of fusion."[2] Apparently, in 1894, Goodwyn also supported, for a time, a silver Democrat who was the encumbent in Alabama's Seventh Congressional District.[3] Those familiar with the literature may recognize the irony in that revelation. Incidentally, in the *Biographical Directory,* Goodwyn indicated that he successfully "contested as a Democrat, the election of James E. Cobb." Albert Goodwyn's son, Tyler Goodwyn, was also a leader among the Alabama Populists and a highly regarded editor of the Populist *Reform Advocate* in Wetumpka. After the demise of Populism, Tyler Goodwyn returned to the Democratic party, where he became a prominent leader. According to Sheldon Hackney, the younger Goodwyn "became one of the most respected spokesmen for railroad and corporation interests in the state. In 1907 he led the legislative opposition to [Governor Braxton] Comer's Progressive program."[4] His father, however, was said to have returned to the Democratic party, becoming a strong supporter of William Jennings Bryan and Braxton Comer's progressive Alabama regime; he also later held several appointive positions under Democratic administrations.[5]

NOTES

1. Karel D. Bicha, *Western Populism: Studies in an Ambivalent Conservatism* (Lawrence, Kans.: Coronado Press, 1976), 108.
2. William Warren Rogers, *The One-Gallused Rebellion: Agrarianism in Alabama* (Baton Rouge: Louisiana State University Press, 1970), 297.
3. See D. Alan Harris, "Campaigning in the Bloody Seventh: The Election of 1894 in the Seventh Congressional District," *Alabama Review* 27 (April 1974).
4. Sheldon Hackney, *Populism to Progressivism in Alabama* (Princeton, N.J.: Princeton University Press, 1969), 116.
5. Louise Goodwyn Mustin, "Albert Taylor Goodwyn," master's thesis, University of Alabama, 1936, 75.

Appendix C.
Populists by Congress

FIFTY-SECOND CONGRESS, 1891–1893

Senators

William A. Peffer, Kansas
James H. Kyle, South Dakota (Independent)

Representatives

William Baker, Kansas
Benjamin H. Clover, Kansas
John Davis, Kansas
John G. Otis, Kansas
Jeremiah Simpson, Kansas
Kittel Halvorson, Minnesota (Farmers' Alliance)
Omer Kem, Nebraska (Independent)
William A. McKeighan, Nebraska (Independent)
Thomas E. Watson, Georgia (Alliance Democrat)

FIFTY-THIRD CONGRESS, 1893–1895

Senators

William A. Peffer, Kansas
James H. Kyle, South Dakota
William V. Allen, Nebraska

Representatives

Haldor E. Boen, Minnesota
John C. Bell, Colorado
Lafayette Pence, Colorado

Marion Cannon, California (Populist/Democrat)
William Baker, Kansas
John Davis, Kansas
William A. Harris, Kansas (Populist/Democrat)
Thomas J. Hudson, Kansas(Democrat/Populist)
Jeremiah Simpson, Kansas (Populist/Democrat)
Omer M. Kem, Nebraska
William A. McKeighan, Nebraska (Democrat/Populist)

FIFTY-FOURTH CONGRESS, 1895–1897

Senators

William A. Peffer, Kansas
James H. Kyle, South Dakota
William V. Allen, Nebraska
Marion Butler, North Carolina

Representatives

William Baker, Kansas
Omer M. Kem, Nebraska
John C. Bell, Colorado (Populist/Democrat)
Milford W. Howard, Alabama
Albert T. Goodwyn, Alabama (Republican/Populist)
Harry Skinner, North Carolina
Charles H. Martin, North Carolina
William F. Strowd, North Carolina
Alonzo C. Shuford, North Carolina

FIFTY-FIFTH CONGRESS, 1897–1899

Senators

William V. Allen, Nebraska
Marion Butler, North Carolina
William A. Harris, Kansas (Democrat/Populist)
Henry Heitfeld, Idaho (Populist/Democrat)
James H. Kyle, South Dakota (Republican/Populist)
George F. Turner, Washington (Silver Republican/Populist/Democrat)

Representatives

Milford W. Howard, Alabama
Jehu Baker, Illinois (Fusionist)
Charles A. Barlow, California (Populist/Democrat)

Curtis H. Castle, California (Populist/Democrat)
John C. Bell, Colorado (Democrat/Populist)
Jeremiah Botkin, Kansas (Populist/Democrat)
Mason S. Peters, Kansas (Democrat/Populist)
Edwin R. Ridgely, Kansas (Populist/Democrat)
William D. Vincent, Kansas
Nelson B. McCormick, Kansas (Populist/Democrat)
Simpson, Jeremiah, Kansas (Populist/Democrat)
Samuel Maxwell, Nebraska (Populist/Democrat)
William L. Stark, Nebraska (Democrat/Populist)
Roderick D. Sutherland, Nebraska (Populist/Democrat)
William L. Greene, Nebraska (Populist/Democrat)
Harry Skinner, North Carolina
John E. Fowler, North Carolina
William F. Strowd, North Carolina
Charles H. Martin, North Carolina
Alonzo C. Shuford, North Carolina
John E. Kelley, South Dakota (Populist/Democrat)
Freeman T. Knowles, South Dakota
James Gunn, Idaho
Albert May Todd, Michigan (Fusionist Democrat)
John Stockdale Rhea, Kentucky (Fusionist Democrat)
James Yancey Callahan, delegate, Oklahoma Territory (Populist/Democrat)

FIFTY-SIXTH CONGRESS, 1899–1901

Senators

William A. Harris, Kansas (Populist/Democrat)
William V. Allen (December 1899–1901)
James H. Kyle, South Dakota (Republican)
Marion Butler, North Carolina
Henry Heitfeld, Idaho (Populist/Democrat)
George F. Turner, Washington (Populist/Democrat)

Representatives

John W. Atwater, North Carolina
John C. Bell, Colorado (Democrat/Populist)
Edwin R. Ridgely, Kansas (Populist/Democrat)
William L. Stark, Nebraska (Democrat/Populist)
Roderick D. Sutherland, Nebraska (Populist/Democrat)
William L. Greene, Nebraska (died 11 March 1899)
William Neville, Nebraska (succeeded William L. Greene on 4 December 1899)
John S. Rhea, Kentucky (Fusion Democrat)

FIFTY-SEVENTH CONGRESS, 1901–1903

Senators

William A. Harris, Kansas (Fusionist/Democrat)
James Kyle, South Dakota (Republican by 1897)
George Turner, Washington (Fusionist/Democrat)
Henry Heitfeld, Idaho (Fusionist/Democrat)

Representatives

John C. Bell, Colorado (Democrat by 1902)
William L. Stark, Nebraska (Fusionist/Democrat)
William Neville, Nebraska (last Populist)
Thomas L. Glenn, Idaho (Fusionist/Democrat)
Caldwell Edwards, Montana (Fusionist/Democrat)

Appendix D.

The Oz Story and Populism

For years, the academic community has accepted the view, advanced by Henry Littlefield, that L. Frank Baum's famous children's book *The Wonderful Wizard of Oz* was a pro-silver, Populist parable inspired by the 1896 battle of the standards.[1] It turns out that although some of the book's broader outlines were almost certainly inspired by the contest over the monetary system, it is much more likely that the story was never intended to be a pro-Populist or even a pro-silver parable.[2] Instead, Baum apparently amused himself by writing a subtle yet ingenious anti-Populist, gold-standard tract in the form of a highly suggestive and enormously successful children's story.[3] Regardless, *The Wonderful Wizard of Oz* was destined to become much more than its author claimed in the preface: a "story . . . written solely to please children of today."[4]

Although skeptical, I, too, accepted Littlefield's interpretation until I actually examined the book for use in a college history class some years ago.[5] It then became apparent that the old view was considerably amiss. The most startling discovery was that the character of the Wicked Witch of the West most likely was modeled after the specter created in the minds of conservatives like Baum by Populism itself—or the left-wing persuasion generally, which could appropriately be made to encompass pre-Populist radical agrarianism and post-Populist socialism and communism—an early manifestation of the antiradical persuasion. My judgment then—based in part on erroneous positions attributed to Baum by Littlefield—was that the creator of Oz was probably a pro-Bryan, pro-silver Democrat but definitely not pro-Populist.[6] But this was before I was made aware of the even more critical judgment of one of Baum's biographers, Michael Patrick Hearn, who came to the conclusion that there was no evidence that "Baum's story" was "in any way a Populist allegory."[7] Subsequently, thanks to Hearn's comments and other writings, it became even clearer that Baum was not pro-Populist or even a pro-Bryan Democrat but was a tough-minded, pro-McKinley Republican, as the poem that heads Chapter 4 clearly demonstrates.

Hearn also concluded that Littlefield's interpretation had "no basis in fact." But I think that the Oz interpreter was not that far off base, for the great battle over silver and gold, commencing in 1893 and culminating with the 1896 presidential campaign, simply had to be a major source of inspiration. Although it had abated considerably, the issue was still being contested when Baum wrote his story sometime before April 1900. This "modernized fairy tale," as he called it, clearly had quite a different etymology than its author and others would have us believe. In the final analysis, the confusion mirrored that which had emerged by the 1960s over the meaning of Populism itself. Littlefield, like a number of prominent 1950s revisionist writers on Populism, managed to blur the distinction between two major varieties of agrarianism (one radical and democratic, the other conservative to reactionary), and even more so the distinction between Populism and Bryanism.

Baum's road to the Emerald City, the *apparent* seat of power in the Land of Oz, was "paved with yellow bricks." In her quest to return home, Dorothy was advised by the good Witch of the North to follow that Yellow Brick Road to seek the aid of Oz, the Great Wizard. In roundabout fashion, Dorothy would ultimately be returned to her beloved Kansas, after killing the Wicked Witch of the West at the behest of Oz, and without the magic slippers she had taken from the dead Wicked Witch of the East, disposed of inadvertently when Uncle Henry and Aunt Em's house fell to earth in Munchkinland after being carried to the heavens by a Kansas cyclone.[8] All that and more seems to have been suggested by Baum's commitment to a monetary system with a gold base. As noted, Populists and their silver allies were determined to discontinue or, at a minimum, to reconstruct that gold-standard thoroughfare by adding an appropriate number of silver bricks to its surface (such as in a ratio of sixteen to one), but in the end, they found themselves acting more like speed bumps on the Yellow Brick Road.

NOTES

1. Henry M. Littlefield, "The Wizard of Oz: Parable on Populism," *American Quarterly* 16 (spring 1964): 47–58. See also Martin Gardner and Russel B. Nye, *The Wizard of Oz and Who He Was* (East Lansing: Michigan University Press, 1957); Raylun Moore, *Wonderful Wizard, Marvelous Land* (Bowling Green, Ohio: Bowling Green University Popular Press, 1974); Carol Bilman, "L. Frank Baum: The Wizard behind Oz," *American History Illustrated* 20 (Sept. 1985): 43–48; and William R. Leach, "The Clown from Syracuse: The Life and Times of L. Frank Baum," introductory essay for *The Wonderful Wizard of Oz by L. Frank Baum* (Belmont, Calif.: Wadsworth, 1991), 1–34. Leach revealed that Baum and his wife did not like Kansas. About Baum's stint as an editor in South Dakota in 1890 and 1891, Leach wrote: "What did not matter to him was the plight of the farmer. Nor did he care much about the Indians who in the early 1890s were fighting in the region against the threat of annihilation. For years Baum-specialists and historians have argued that Baum felt much sympathy for the misery of the farmer and for the Populist revolt against exploitation by the railroads and banks. But Baum wrote nothing about Populism in his newspaper, although given the intensity of the Populist dissent around Aberdeen, one might logically have expected him to say something. His thoughts on the Indians were grim." According to Leach, "Four related subjects reappear repeatedly in *The Pioneer:* the local theater, theosophy/mind cure, middle-class feminism, and America's technological and economic abundance. These subjects formed something of a new cultural totality for Baum, a new way of being that departed fundamentally from the traditional agrarian and religious world in which most Americans were born and raised." Basically, the research by Leach suggests that Baum was an early adherent of what would

come to be called "progressive," which, except for his "middle-class feminism," was quite like the muscular-conservative-jingoistic brand of progressivism championed by Theodore Roosevelt, one suspects.

2. It is entirely possible that Baum's position was similar to that of Samuel McCall, a Republican congressman from Massachusetts, who said in the repeal debate that he believed "in bimetallism so far as it can be maintained on the gold standard, which is our present standard" (*Congressional Record,* 53rd Cong., 1st sess., 16 Aug. 1893, 395).

3. The record regarding Baum's anti-Populism and conservatism (or support for what I call the inhumane preference for systems over people and cultures) has since been filled in even more. One defining piece of information comes from the *Aberdeen Saturday Pioneer,* the newspaper edited by Baum for a time while the People's party was being formed in South Dakota. Baum made this revealing statement not long before the massacre of Wounded Knee, which took place there on 29 December 1891, proving that he was not quite the "gentle soul" that many have assumed: "The nobility of the Redskin is extinguished, and what few are left are a pack of whining curs who lick the hand that smites them. The Whites, by law of conquest, by justice of civilization, are masters of the American continent, and the best safety of the frontier settlements will be secured by the total annihilation of the few remaining Indians. Why not annihilation? Their glory has fled, their spirit broken, their manhood effaced; better that they should die than live the miserable wretches that they are." A few days after the massacre, Baum wrote another editorial urging this course: "we had better, in order to protect our civilization, follow it up . . . and wipe these untamed and untamable creatures from the face of the earth" (quoted in David E. Stannard, *American Holocaust: The Conquest of the New World* [New York: Oxford University Press, 1992], 126–27).

4. L. Frank Baum, *The Wonderful Wizard of Oz* (New York: Ballantine Books, 1956).

5. My investigation of Baum's book was sparked by my use of an excellent and highly popular college history textbook that has gone through four editions featuring a version of the story quite like the one advanced by Littlefield. See Robert A. Divine, T. H. Breen, George N. Fredrickson, and R. Hal Williams, *America, Past and Present,* 4th ed., vol. 2 (New York: HarperCollins, 1995), 6209–21. See also R. Hal Williams, *Years of Decision: American Politics in the 1890s* (New York: John Wiley and Sons, 1978), 105–6.

6. Gene Clanton, *Populism: The Humane Preference in America, 1890–1900* (Boston: Twayne Publishers, 1991), 149–50.

7. *New York Times,* 10 Jan. 1991, A-26.

8. Incidentally, the Kansas cyclone was most likely Baum's way of depicting the economic collapse that suddenly became national in 1893 (perhaps conjoined in his mind with the Coxey movement of early 1894), and Grover Cleveland would appear as the best candidate for Oz, the "humbug" and the implied agent or front man for the money power. This particular interpretation would have been so much easier had Baum simply made Oz's hometown Buffalo instead of Omaha, but then that would have robbed the story of some of its protean qualities. Because of how he responded to the economic crisis, President Cleveland was perceived by many, including a significant number of Republicans, as the agent of the eastern money power.

It is all too easy to fall into the trap of interpreting the cyclone as Populism or as the silver movement generally. In devising his parable, Baum seems to have been inspired at this point by what suddenly came over the country with the panic of 1893—an economic cyclone, of sorts. The Scarecrow as the farmer (who is off to see the Wizard to get some brains but does the smart thinking for the group) and the Tinman as the laborer (who is out to get a heart but is the most caring pilgrim of them all) are perfect fits. In the biggest switch for those familiar with the Littlefield interpretation, the Cowardly Lion (off to see the Wizard to get some courage but ultimately the most courageous of the lot), contrary to what many of us so fondly believed, would be better read as an ordinary businessman (even William McKinley would make a better fit) rather than William Jennings Bryan. The symmetry would thus be improved: the farmer, the laborer, and the businessman.

In quick order, here are a few other likely representations that seem appropriate: Dorothy as the innocent, little miss everybody; Oz for ounce (as in 1 oz. of gold); Toto for what he seemed to represent in the story, from in toto perhaps, the loving critter who had it (all) together; and the Wicked Witch of the West as Populism. We should not fail to note the silver whistle she wears around her neck (nor perhaps even the close resemblance to "Pitchfork" Ben Tillman in the original drawing done by W. W. Denslow), which seems to depict the enticing nature of Populism's inclusion of the silver plank in the Omaha platform, something that enabled her to beguile the Winkies (western farmers) and get them into her clutches. And we should note what happens to the Wicked Witch of the West when Dorothy pours a bucket of water on her: Just as in the case of Populism, once major segments of the Democratic and Republican parties took up the monetary issue, she/it simply melted away (a meltdown of Populism). As Littlefield also noted, other portions of the story simply were not intended to fit this single theme of a battle over the monetary system; thus one needs to be careful not to be led down false paths.

Notes

PREFACE

1. See Richard Hofstadter, *The Age of Reform: From Bryan to F.D.R.* (New York: Vintage Books, 1955), and Michael Kazin, *The Populist Persuasion: An American History* (New York: Basic Books, 1995).

INTRODUCTION

1. See Kermit E. Opperman, "The Political Career of William Alexander Harris," master's thesis, University of Kansas, 1938; Clyde Leon Fitch, "William A. Harris of Kansas: His Economic Interests," master's thesis, Kansas State Teacher's College, Emporia, 1967; O. Gene Clanton, *Kansas Populism: Ideas and Men* (Lawrence: University Press of Kansas, 1969); Peter H. Argersinger, *Populism and Politics: William Alfred Peffer and the People's Party* (Lexington: University Press of Kentucky, 1974); William A. Peffer, *Populism: Its Rise and Fall,* edited, introduced, and annotated by Peter H. Argersinger (Lawrence: University Press of Kansas, 1992); and *Biographical Directory of the American Congress 1784–1961* (Washington, D.C.: U.S. Government Printing Office, 1961).

2. Karel D. Bicha, *Western Populism: Studies in an Ambivalent Conservatism* (Lawrence, Kans.: Coronado Press, 1976), 110. Harris's father had also been a lawyer, editor of the *Spectator,* the *Constitution,* and the *Washington Union,* all in the nation's capital, and a diplomat (chargé d'affaires to the Argentine Republic, 1846–1851). See *Biographical Directory.*

3. John Grant Otis rose to the rank of colonel, serving as paymaster general on the military staff of Governor Charles Robinson.

4. For a different treatment of the differences between Peffer and Harris, see Peter H. Argersinger, *The Limits of Agrarian Radicalism: Western Populism and American Politics* (Lawrence: University Press of Kansas, 1995), p. 26 especially.

5. *Advocate* (Topeka), 3 Feb. 1897.

6. By the time Harris made his remarks, the Supreme Court had put its stamp of

approval on what amounted to a judicial revolution—under way since 1873—in the interest of the so-called artificial person, i.e., corporations. The Constitution, especially its seminal Fourteenth Amendment, had been interpreted in such a fashion as to award what amounted to first-class citizenship to corporations, while whole categories of real people—with women and black Americans as the primary victims—were relegated to second-class citizenship or worse. It is a development that still fails to receive the kind of treatment it deserves in historical accounts.

7. *Congressional Record,* 56th Cong., 1st sess., 6 Feb. 1900, 1589–90. There were four others in the House who in part owed their election to the People's party, but they thought of themselves as Fusionists and were on their way to becoming Democrats. Neville alone identified himself as a member of the People's party: thus the designation "the last congressional Populist."

8. An earlier version of this material (including two chapters that detailed the philosophical origins of the Populist movement) was deposited in manuscript form with the Kansas State Historical Society, Topeka, under the title "The Origins of Populism: A Centennial Essay." For an abbreviated version of that discussion, see Gene Clanton, *Populism: The Humane Preference in America, 1890–1900* (Boston: Twayne Publishers, 1991). For additional material bearing in various ways on the same subject, see Thomas W. Riddle, *The Old Radicalism: John R. Rogers and the Populist Movement in Washington, 1891–1900* (New York: Garland Publishing, 1991); Lawrence Goodwyn, *Democratic Promise: The Populist Moment in America* (New York: Oxford University Press, 1976); Bruce Palmer, *"Man Over Money": The Southern Populist Critique of American Capitalism* (Chapel Hill: University of North Carolina Press, 1981); Steven Hahn, *The Roots of Southern Populism: Yeoman Farmers and the Transformation of the Georgia Upcountry, 1850–1890* (New York: Oxford University Press, 1983); Worth Robert Miller, *Oklahoma Populism: A History of the People's Party in Oklahoma Territory* (Norman: University of Oklahoma Press, 1987); Norman Pollack, *The Just Polity: Populism, Law, and Human Welfare* (Urbana: University of Illinois Press, 1987); and Norman Pollack, *The Humane Economy: Populism, Capitalism, and Democracy* (New Brunswick, N.J.: Rutgers University Press, 1990).

Regarding the larger traditions at issue here, see Robert McCloskey, *American Conservatism in the Age of Enterprise, 1865–1910* (New York: Harper Torchbooks, 1964); Sidney Fine, *Laissez Faire and the General-Welfare State: A Study of Conflict in American Thought, 1865–1901* (Ann Arbor: University of Michigan Press, 1966); Clinton Rossiter, *Conservatism in America: The Thankless Persuasion* (New York: Vintage, 1962); Garry Wills, *Inventing America: Jefferson's Declaration of Independence* (New York: Vintage, 1979); Garry Wills, *Lincoln at Gettysburg: The Words That Remade America* (New York: Simon and Schuster, 1992); Richard K. Matthews, *The Radical Politics of Thomas Jefferson: A Revisionist View* (Lawrence: University Press of Kansas, 1986); R. Jeffrey Lustig, *Corporate Liberalism: The Origins of Modern American Political Theory, 1890–1920* (Berkeley: University of California Press, 1982); and John L. Thomas, *Alternative America: Henry George, Edward Bellamy, Henry Demarest Lloyd and the Adversary Tradition* (Cambridge: Harvard University Press, 1983).

9. Vernon L. Parrington, *The Beginnings of Critical Realism in America, 1860–1920,* vol. 3, *Main Currents in American Thought* (New York: Harcourt, 1958), 285–86.

CHAPTER ONE. POPULIST CONGRESSMEN AND THEIR AGENDAS

1. Sol Miller was a major leader among the state's Republicans.

2. See O. Gene Clanton, *Kansas Populism: Ideas and Men* (Lawrence: University Press of Kansas, 1969), for a more comprehensive treatment of the political and ideological context that produced Miller's attack.

3. See Hortense Marie Harrison, "The Populist Delegation in the Fifty-second Congress, 1891–1893," master's thesis, University of Kansas, 1933; Richard N. Kottman, "An Analysis of the People's Party Delegation in Congress, 1891–1897," master's thesis, University of Iowa, 1954; James C. Malin, "At What Age Did Men Become Reformers?" *Kansas Historical Quarterly* 29 (autumn 1963): 250–66; Clanton, *Kansas Populism*; Karel D. Bicha, *Western Populism: Studies in an Ambivalent Conservatism* (Lawrence, Kans.: Coronado Press, 1976); and Peter H. Argersinger, *The Limits of Agrarian Radicalism: Western Populism and American Politics* (Lawrence: University Press of Kansas, 1995).

I did not set out to do an institutional study of Congress, although it is hoped that the closer look at the Populist delegations of the 1890s provided by this study will shed some light on this important subject. Readers are urged to consult the work of Peter Argersinger, especially "No Rights on This Floor: Third Parties and the Institutionalization of Congress," *Journal of Interdisciplinary History* 22 (spring 1992): 655–90, for some important pioneering work in this area. This excellent study was republished in Argersinger, *Agrarian Radicalism*, 213–45.

4. I have not investigated the previous career of Jehu Baker, but given the influence of what is called an old radicalism, Baker's pre-Populist years in Congress (1865–1869, 1887–1889), and his career generally, this might be a highly revealing case study. Could it be he fits the mold of the genuine Radical Republican? On the other hand, he may have been a bit of a rascal like Ignatius Donnelly in that earlier period. See *Biographical Directory of the American Congress, 1784–1961* (Washington, D.C.: Government Printing Office, 1961) for a thumbnail sketch of Baker.

5. Kottman somehow missed Georgia's Tom Watson, who served in the first of his three Congresses. Had Watson been included, Kottman's findings would have been tilted even more in favor of youth, education, experience, and quality. With C. Vann Woodward's prominent biography available since the late 1930s, it is difficult to understand how Watson escaped notice. In the Fifty-fourth Congress, Kottman omitted Charles Martin and Albert Goodwyn. These last two entered late and thus were more easily missed. As in the case of Watson, their data would have altered his statistics in a positive fashion.

6. Kottman, "Congress, 1891–1897," 10–11. At about the same time that Kottman's thesis was completed, Richard Hofstadter published his prize-winning, devastating essay on Populism in *The Age of Reform: From Bryan to F.D.R.* (New York: Vintage, 1955), described recently and appropriately as a "think piece" more "than a well-researched interpretation of Populism (see Worth Robert Miller, "A Centennial Historiography of American Populism," *Kansas History* [spring 1993]: 59). One can only wonder whether that contributed to Kottman's work on the Populists in Congress failing to receive the recognition it seemed to deserve. Incidentally, Kottman revealed that his thesis topic was suggested by a young University of Iowa assistant professor by the name of Allan Bogue. Fourteen years later, Bogue would become the Frederick Jackson Turner Professor of History at the University of Wisconsin, where he would direct, among numerous other important graduate

studies, one by Peter H. Argersinger dealing with Senator Peffer and the Populist movement. Kottman went on to earn his Ph.D. in American diplomatic history at Vanderbilt University in 1958 and eventually joined the faculty at Iowa State University.

7. *Biographical Directory;* Argersinger, *Agrarian Radicalism,* 236–38; Kottman, "Congress, 1891–1897," 18–19; and Bicha, *Western Populism,* 106–9.

8. See Allan G. Bogue et al., "Members of the House of Representatives and the Process of Modernization, 1789–1960," *Journal of American History* 63 (September 1976): 275–302. Jack London, in his 1907 novel *The Iron Heel,* asserted that the railroads had in their employ "forty thousand lawyers." It would be interesting to know how many of these people made it to Congress in the late nineteenth century.

9. The major source of information here was the *Biographical Directory of the American Congress.* Of course, these autobiographies must be cross-checked with other sources.

10. Lawrence Goodwyn, *Democratic Promise: The Populist Movement in America* (New York: Oxford University Press, 1976), 81–82; Gene Clanton, *Populism: The Humane Preference in America, 1890–1900* (Boston: Twayne Publishers, 1991), 8–11.

11. Argersinger, *Agrarian Radicalism,* 237.

12. William McKeighan of Nebraska, a farmer, held the position of probate judge but was not a lawyer. He had run unsuccessfully for Congress in 1888 as a Democrat before being elected in 1890 as an Independent.

13. Kottman, "Congress, 1891–1897," 15.

14. In 1870, 7,993 males received bachelor's or first professional degrees in the United States; that same year, the age bracket twenty to twenty-four encompassed 1,835,945 (male and female), and the age bracket twenty-five to twenty-nine encompassed 1,515,671 (male and female). The graduation figures for males in 1871 was 10,484; in 1872, 6,626; in 1873, 9,070; in 1874, 9,593; in 1875, 9,905; and in 1876, 9,911. Seven thousand male students are said to have graduated from high school in 1870. I leave it to the reader to compute the percentages. See *Historical Statistics of the United States* (Washington, D.C.: Bureau of the Census, 1975).

15. One cannot speak for the situation in all the states with quite the authority as in Kansas (especially in a substantive sense), wherein the major leadership, consisting of eighty-nine men and women, was identified and profiled, in addition to virtually *all* the members (Democrats, Republicans, and Populists) of five different legislatures from 1891 to 1899. See Clanton, *Kansas Populism,* 64–65, 251, and passim; see also Scott G. McNall, *The Road to Rebellion: Class Formation and Kansas Populism, 1865–1900* (Chicago: University of Chicago Press, 1988), which seemed to corroborate Clanton's earlier work. Robert W. Cherny's *Populism, Progressivism, and the Transformation of Nebraska Politics, 1885–1915* (Lincoln: University of Nebraska Press, 1981) revealed a background and profile similar to that of Kansas, in addition to pointing to a relationship between Progressivism and Populism not unlike the situation in Kansas, especially if we take into consideration Clanton's 1977 comparative study of Populism and Progressivism in that state (see "Populism, Progressivism, and Equality: The Kansas Paradigm," *Agricultural History* 51 [July 1977]: 559–81.) Worth Robert Miller's equally solid study, *Oklahoma Populism: A History of the People's Party in the Oklahoma Territory* (Norman: University of Oklahoma Press, 1987), 212–18, profiled the territorial legislatures, revealing a background quite like that of the Kansas legislatures. Miller did not single out a

major leadership. What he discovered about Oklahoma, however, appears not to have deviated significantly from the case of Kansas and Nebraska. Miller came to this conclusion: "The collective biography [of Oklahoma Populist leaders] validates the Populists' contention that their party . . . was a party of the people" (217).

16. One North Carolina historian said this about Nathaniel Macon: "Elected to the House of Representatives in 1791, Macon began a quarter-century of congressional membership and soon became North Carolina's foremost enunciator of Jeffersonian principles" (Hugh Talmage Leffler, ed., *North Carolina History Told by Contemporaries* [Chapel Hill: University of North Carolina Press, 1965], 141).

For the record, those with college degrees included these congressmen: William Baker, Waynesboro College in Pennsylvania; Marion Butler, the University of North Carolina in Chapel Hill; Curtis Castle, Northwestern University in Evanston, Illinois, and the College of Physicians and Surgeons in Keokuk, Iowa; Albert Goodwyn, South Carolina College in Columbia (study terminated by enlistment in the Confederate Army) and the University of Virginia in Charlottesville; William Harris, Columbian College (now George Washington University) in Washington, D.C., and the Virginia Military Institute in Lexington; Thomas Jefferson Hudson, Wabash College in Crawfordsville, Indiana, and the University of Cincinnati; James Kyle, the Univesity of Illinois in Urbana, Oberlin College in Ohio, and the Western Theological Seminary in Allegheny, Pennsylvania; Charles Martin, Wake Forest College in Winston-Salem, North Carolina, the University of Virginia, and the Southern Baptist Theological Seminary in Louisville, Kentucky; Lafayette Pence, Hanover College in Indiana; Harry Skinner, the University of Kentucky in Lexington; and William Stark, Mystic Valley Institute in Connecticut.

Although not graduating, sixteen additional Populist congressmen attended college: William Allen, Upper Iowa University in Fayette; Jehu Baker, McKendree College in Lebanon, Illinois; Haldor Boen, St. Cloud Normal College in Minnesota; Jeremiah Botkin, De Pauw University in Greencastle, Indiana; John Davis, Illinois College in Jacksonville; John Fowler, Wake Forest College and the University of North Carolina; Thomas Glenn, Commercial College, Evansville, Indiana; William Neville, McKendree College; John Otis, Burr Seminary in Manchester, Vermont, Williams College in Williamstown, Massachusetts, and Harvard University in Cambridge, Massachusetts; Mason Peters, William Jewell College in Liberty, Missouri; John Rhea, Bethel College in Russelville, Kentucky, and Washington and Lee University in Lexington, Virginia; William Vincent, Kansas Agricultural College in Manhattan; Alonzo Shuford, Newton College in North Carolina; Roderick Sutherland, Amity College in College Springs, Iowa; Albert Todd, Northwestern University; and Thomas Watson, Mercer University in Macon, Georgia.

17. William A. Peffer, *Populism: Its Rise and Fall,* edited, introduced, and annotated by Peter Argersinger (Lawrence: University Press of Kansas, 1992), 185.

18. Unfortunately, some years back when I read this commentary by Allen, I made no note of it, but be assured, it is in the *Congressional Record.* Perhaps someone like David Holscher, a graduate student at the University of Nebraska, Omaha, who is researching Senator Allen's career, will recover this material for his thesis.

19. Four Kansans (William Baker, Benjamin Clover, T. J. Hudson, and Mason Peters), two from the Far West (Marion Cannon of California and Caldwell Edwards of Montana, a transplanted New Yorker), and no southerners were among those old enough to have served in the Civil War but who apparently did not.

20. Albert Goodwyn's granddaughter indicated that the rank of captain was awarded while he was a prisoner in the North; however, she made no mention of a special award. See Louise Goodwyn Mustin, "Albert Taylor Goodwyn," master's thesis, University of Alabama, 1936.

21. The Goodwyns owned thousands of acres of land; exactly how much is unknown, but at one point, Albert Goodwyn found it necessary to sell "25,000 acres" to keep his plantation solvent. His granddaughter said this: "Albert believed that to labor with the hands in the fields was degrading. He had grown to manhood in a social condition which left all manual labor to slaves and he could not quite readjust himself to the new era. In his later years he often voiced a regret that he had not allowed his sons to work on the farm. He himself, although a farmer all his life, never did manual labor" (ibid., 27–29). In this insight, one can see the sharp difference between some southern Populists and most of those who made up the party beyond Dixie.

22. Albert Goodwyn's son, Tyler Goodwyn, was also a leader of the Alabama Populists. He was the editor of the *Reform Advocate,* a Populist newspaper published in Wetumpka. See Appendix B for more information concerning the Goodwyns.

23. See *Biographical Directory;* Mustin, "Albert Taylor Goodwyn," 15; and William Warren Rogers, *The One-Gallused Rebellion: Agrarianism in Alabama* (Baton Rouge: Louisiana State University Press, 1970), 234.

24. A rare event was the election of a Confederate veteran to Congress as a Republican, which happened in the case of Daniel Lindsay Russell from North Carolina, who served one term from 1879 to 1881; Russell would also be elected governor of his state in 1896 as a result of Populist-Republican fusion politics.

25. Bogue et al., "Members of the House, 1789–1960," as referenced in Argersinger, *Agrarian Radicalism,* 237.

26. The studies by Miller and Cherny referred to earlier in note 15 are important regarding religion. Miller wrote this: "Although religion may have been important to party choice in the Midwest, Civil War–Reconstruction loyalties and race were the overwhelming bases of partisan choice in the late-nineteenth-century South. . . . During the Populist era, . . . rural-urban cleavage and the type of agriculture rivaled sectionalism as the most important indices of partisan choice" (*Oklahoma Populism,* 207). Sheldon Hackney's *Populism to Progressivism in Alabama* (Princeton, N.J.: Princeton University Press, 1969) and Barton C. Shaw's *The Wool-Hat Boys: Georgia's Populist Party* (Baton Rouge: Louisiana State University Press, 1984) are also helpful in determining who the Populists were. In addition, all the older state studies contain vital information, albeit random and incomplete, regarding the background of Populist leaders.

27. Clanton, *Kansas Populism,* 65–66; Mustin, "Albert Taylor Goodwyn," 85–86. Mustin also revealed that the subject of "Lincoln was one subject about which he was utterly intolerant. About him he could see not one redeeming feature. Whenever Lincoln's name was mentioned in his presence he snorted, and when he himself mentioned his name he always accompanied it by the phrase 'devil incarnate.'" His wife was a Christian Scientist, and it was said that "he could never reconcile himself" to her religious beliefs. The founder of the religion, Mary Baker Eddy, was invariably referred to as "that old witch," and "in her he could see no more good than he could see in Lincoln" (ibid., 83, 86).

28. Regarding the meaning of Populism, see these important recent studies: Goodwyn, *Democratic Promise;* Bruce Palmer, *"Man Over Money": The Southern Populist*

Critique of American Capitalism (Chapel Hill: University of North Carolina Press, 1981); Norman Pollack, *The Just Polity: Populism, Law, and Human Welfare* (Urbana: University of Illinois Press, 1987); Norman Pollack, *The Humane Economy: Populism, Capitalism, and Democracy* (New Brunswick, N.J.: Rutgers University Press, 1990); Clanton, *Humane Preference*; Robert C. McMath, Jr., *American Populism: A Social History, 1877–1898* (New York: Hill and Wang, 1993); Argersinger, *Agrarian Radicalism*; and William F. Holmes, ed., *American Populism* (Lexington, Mass: D. C. Heath, 1994).

29. Clanton, *Kansas Populism,* 65; Cherny, *Nebraska Politics,* 71.

30. Ibid.; see also "In Defense of Freedom of Conscience: A Cooperative Baptist/Secular Humanist Declaration," *Free Inquiry* 16 (winter 1995–96): 4.

31. See Clanton, *Kansas Populism,* 67.

32. Quoted in ibid., 69, and in Michael Brodhead, *Persevering Populist: The Life of Frank Doster* (Reno: University of Nevada Press, 1969), 121–22. Brodhead's biography is an excellent study of a truly unusual and remarkable Kansas Populist.

33. Milford W. Howard, *If Christ Came to Congress* (New York, 1964), 97, 4.

34. The 1964 edition of Howard's book has an introduction written by Harvey Wish. See also William T. Stead, *If Christ Came to Chicago* (Chicago, 1894); and Milford W. Howard, *The American Plutocracy* (New York: Holland Publishing Company, 1895). Sheldon's book, as of 1933, was estimated to have sold 23 million copies, according to Wish's introduction to *If Christ Came to Congress*. Regarding the phrase "rugged individualism," see Louis Filler, *A Dictionary of American Social Reform* (New York: Philosophical Library, 1963). Hoover denied being the author of the label but did say that he "would be proud to have invented it" (*The Challenge to Liberty* [New York: Charles Scribner's Sons, 1934], 54). In fact, the extreme version of laissez-faire economics, as well as its Gospel of Wealth corollary, was much less ambiguously expounded by Andrew Mellon, who was secretary of the treasury during the Harding, Coolidge, and Hoover administrations.

35. Quoted in Clanton, *Kansas Populism,* 65–66.

36. Carl N. Degler, *The Other South: Southern Dissenters in the Nineteenth Century* (New York: Harper and Row, 1974), 319 ff.; Sheldon Hackney, *Populism to Progressivism in Alabama.*

37. Quoted in D. Alan Harris, "Campaigning in the Bloody Seventh: The Election of 1894 in the Seventh Congressional District," *Alabama Review* 27 (Apr. 1974): 136. The larger quote is worth repeating here: "It will give you some idea of this bitterness when I state that my own father would not hear me speak and said he would rather make my coffin with his own hands and bury me than to have me desert the Democratic party. This has been more than thirty years ago but some of the old feeling still slumbers and I have never been and never will be forgiven for my fall from grace" (from David Alan Harris, "The Political Career of Milford W. Howard, Populist Congressman from Alabama," master's thesis, Alabama Polytechnic Institute, 1957), p. 58.

38. One of the documents in the Butler collection revealed this top-thirteen ranking: (1) Texas, 238,962; (2) Kansas, 163,111; (3) North Carolina, 155,700; (4) Georgia, 96,888; (5) Alabama, 85,181; (6) Nebraska, 83,134; (7) Colorado, 71, 683; (8) Illinois, 59,743; (9) California, 51,304; (10) Missouri, 41, 213; (11) South Dakota, 37, 181; (12) Iowa, 34,917; and (13) Michigan, 30,012.

39. J. H. Davis to Marion Butler, 25 Mar. 1897, Marion Butler Papers (no. 114), Southern Historical Collection, Chapel Hill, N.C.

40. Ibid. Lawrence Goodwyn wrote this about Davis's later career as a Texas Democrat: "He became a prohibitionist and white supremacist, worked for the Ku Klux Klan, and won election for one term as a Congressman in 1916 [*sic*], taking the old seat that had been denied him by Harrison County methods in 1894. As late as 1939, the white-bearded Davis could be heard on the streetcorners of Dallas, making flamboyant speeches on the need to control Wall Street and the necessity for white supremacy" (*Democratic Promise*, 559–60).

I have taken Davis's quote out of context. He wrote this to Butler: "I am in the middle of the road but not the road that leads to disruption and destruction of our party and the loss of a cause which has cost me so much labor [,] suffering and financial sacrifice." Here Davis would disagree absolutely with Goodwyn's later interpretation. Davis saw the "ultra" (his word) Texas antifusionist position leading to what Goodwyn contends fusionist politics led to in Texas and nationally. Frankly, I believe that Davis has the better case. Incidentallly, Davis had the nickname "Cyclone" officially added to his name in 1932, when he was eighty-one. For interesting material regarding this "electrifying" Texas Populist, probably the most traveled speaker among all the Populists, see Worth Robert Miller, "James Harvey 'Cyclone' Davis," *Handbook of Texas* (forthcoming), and "Harrison County Methods: Election Fraud in Late Nineteenth Century Texas," *Locus* 7 (spring 1995): 111–28.

41. James Yancy Callahan, the Populist-Democratic delegate from Oklahoma Territory, was not included in the southern contingent. Callahan was born in Missouri, had a common school education, became a minister, moved to Kansas in the 1880s and then to Oklahoma Territory in 1892, settled near Kingfisher, and became a farmer prior to his election. Regarding Callahan, see Miller, *Oklahoma Populism,* passim.

42. Actually, Howard had almost no formal schooling outside the home and the church until he was fourteen. See Harris, "Milford W. Howard," 1–10.

43. *Biographical Directory;* Marion Butler Papers, Southern Historical Collection, Chapel Hill, N.C. Marion Butler's life is long overdue for treatment. As of now, we have only the good three-part article covering his presenatorial years by James L. Hunt, "The Making of a Populist: Marion Butler, 1863–1895," *North Carolina History* 42 (Jan., Apr., July 1985). Several years back, Norman Pollack told me that he had already written a lengthy manuscript focusing on Marion Butler; I should think that study will make its way into print. A fresh and thoroughly researched study of North Carolina Populism is also badly needed.

44. Skinner was an attorney with a law degree from the University of Kentucky. He was also singularly distinguished in another area: his brother had been elected to three congressional terms in the 1880s as a Democrat.

45. *Congressional Record,* 52nd Cong., 1st sess., 27 Jan. 1892, 599.

46. K. D. Bicha's chapter on the Populists in the House in *Western Populism* is entitled "The Futilitarians."

47. The idea here was inspired in part by Carlos Schwantes's discussion in *Radical Heritage: Labor, Socialism, and Reform in Washington and British Columbia, 1885–1917* (Seattle: University of Washington Press, 1979), 65. The record demonstrates that Populists proved themselves much better suited to "education and agitation" than to governing; studies of Kansas, Colorado, and Washington support that conclusion. We should not lose sight of the fact, however, that an extremely bitter counterattack orchestrated by anti-Populists

(prototypes for some individuals and groups that are, ironically, identified in the 1980s and 1990s as "populist") account for much of their difficulty.

48. David F. Noble, *America by Design: Science, Technology, and the Rise of Corporate Capitalism* (New York: Oxford University Press, 1977), xxii; emphasis added. The people, Herbert Marcuse has written, "are themselves an integral part and factor of technology, not only as the men who invent or attend to machinery, but also as the social groups which direct its application and utilization. Technology, as a mode of production, as the totality of instruments, devices, and contrivances which characterize the machine age, is thus at the same time a mode of organizing and perpetuating (or changing) social relationships, a manifestation of prevalent thought and behavior patterns, an instrument for control and domination" (quoted in ibid.).

49. Ibid., xx. Historians puzzled by why Populism was fairly strong in Nebraska, Kansas, and Oklahoma Territory and points west but not in the states of the Old Northwest should pay attention to this "paralyzing web of instrumentality." Although Jeffrey Ostler reminded us of the importance of one-party dominance as an explanatory factor, especially when a state's politics was without a serious reform challenge led by Democrats, he might well benefit from Noble's important observation. From it might come greater appreciation of why Frederick Jackson Turner was so "prophetic" when he predicted that the Populist phenomenon in the West, to quote Ostler, had about as "much chance of spreading eastward as the Sioux Indians had of conquering Turner's native Wisconsin" (Jeffrey Ostler, *Prairie Populism: The Fate of Agrarian Radicalism in Kansas, Nebraska, and Iowa, 1880–1892* [Lawrence: University Press of Kansas, 1993], 175).

50. Regarding the organization and expansion of the People's party, see Clanton, *Humane Preference,* 57– 85. Much of the current debate among historians of Populism is the result of one school of interpretation focusing too exclusively on the southern Alliance background of the movement and another focusing too exclusively on the party phase of the phenomenon. In my view, one must pay equal attention to both in coming to grips with the origin and meaning of Populism.

51. Regarding the origin of the name, see John D. Hicks, *The Populist Revolt: A History of the Farmer's Alliance and the People's Party* (Lincoln: University of Nebraska Press, 1961), 238; George T. Tindall, "Populism: A Semantic Identity Crisis," *Virginia Quarterly Review* 48 (1972): 501–18; and Clanton, *Humane Preference,* 70–71.

52. In the interest of length, I forgo a detailed account of the organizational and third-party background pertinent to the origins of Populism. For that, the reader is urged to refer to "Tillers and Toilers: The Origins of Populism, 1872–1890," in Clanton, *Humane Preference,* 1–23. See also Robert C. McMath, Jr., *Populist Vanguard: A History of the Southern Farmers' Alliance* (Chapel Hill: University of North Carolina Press, 1975); and Goodwyn, *Democratic Promise.*

53. *Idaho World* (Idaho City), 24 Aug. 1894, quoted in David B. Griffiths, *Populism in the Western United States, 1890–1900,* vol. 2 (New York: Edwin Mellen Press, 1992), 637.

54. I remind the reader that I do not believe that "free market" is appropriate terminology to describe what went on in the Gilded Age. "Neomercantilism" would be a more accurate label.

55. For the record, Hamlin Garland later indicated in a letter that he had "conspired" with Jerry Simpson "in St. Louis to get the land plank into the People's Party platform"

(Annie L. Diggs, *The Story of Jerry Simpson* [Wichita, Kans.: Jane Simpson Publisher, 1908], 248).

56. Missing this aspect of Populism, combined with a tendency to ignore or misinterpret the nature of anti-Populism in the 1890s, can lead one to the conclusion that the right-wing persuasion identified by such labels as "Reaganism/Gingrichism" and the related New Right phenomenon that began, in a significant way, with Barry Goldwater in the early 1960s grew out of a degenerated Old Left rather than an Old Right. This is what Michael Kazin has done in his otherwise credible recent study *The Populist Persuasion: An American History* (New York: Basic Books, 1995); see also my review essay of the same in *Gateway History* 16 (winter 1995–96): 58–59.

57. One reader, early on, responded to this segment by saying that I was being "too politically correct" in handling gender bias and white racism. That may be, but I believe that raising the issue of "political correctness" is for many people in the 1990s merely a clever way of trying to restore historical amnesia about such issues. It seems to me that the delegates at Omaha in 1892 were themselves bowing to an earlier version of political correctness that made white racism and gender bias all too respectable.

58. *Advocate* (Topeka), 6 July 1892.

59. Regarding Mary Lease's unflattering racial views, see her book *The Problem of Civilization Solved* (Chicago: Laird and Lee Publishers, 1895). Regarding disfranchisement, see these classic studies: Rayford Logan, *The Betrayal of the Negro: From Rutherford B. Hayes to Woodrow Wilson* (New York: Collier Books, 1965); C. Vann Woodward, *The Strange Career of Jim Crow* (New York: Oxford University Press, 1966); and J. Morgan Kouser, *The Shaping of Southern Politics: Suffrage Restriction and the Establishment of the One-Party South, 1880–1910* (New Haven, Conn.: Yale University Press, 1974).

60. Failure to make legitimate distinctions between the Alliance movement and the People's party, coupled with the failure to heed the qualification agreed to by the Populists themselves, led to the subtreasury system looming much too large in Lawrence Goodwyn's influential interpretation of Populism. Although Robert McMath's entrée to Populism was based even more heavily than Goodwyn's on his study of southern Alliance history, he correctly described the Omaha platform as "the clearest and most unadulterated expression of Populist political thought"; yet he too failed to note this important qualification regarding Populism's primary economic objective and the relationship of the subtreasury plan to that goal. As a matter of fact, considering how important the plan was to the southern Alliance, the subtreasury idea receives surprisingly little coverage in McMath's general history of Populism. See McMath, *American Populism: A Social History,* 166 ff.; see also McMath's *Populist Vanguard.*

61. Hicks, *Populist Revolt,* 439–44.

CHAPTER TWO. POPULIST STYLE AND SUBSTANCE

1. When Simpson came on the floor, the secretary interjected this comment: "Mr. Simpson appeared on the floor of the House, after a long and serious illness, and was loudly applauded" (*Congressional Record,* 53rd Cong., 3rd sess., 22 June 1894, 6733). Apparently, only two official photographs of Simpson exist. The first shows him healthy and robust at the time he was first elected; the second was obviously taken after Simpson's

illness, and the difference is striking. After his illness, Simpson may have taken to carrying some whiskey with him, for those well-known "medicinal purposes," which set up this interesting exchange on the floor in January 1895 with Joseph Sayers, who later became governor of Texas: "MR. SIMPSON: Do I understand the gentleman to say that they have no illicit distilleries in Texas? / MR. SAYERS: We have none in Texas. / MR. SIMPSON: That is because you have no hills there to hide in. [Laughter.] / MR. SAYERS: Possibly so; but in Texas we do not carry whisky around in walking canes as in Kansas. [Laughter.] We do not pretend to be a prohibition State and then violate the law in every nook and corner, as they do in Kansas. / MR. SIMPSON: You Texans carry it around inside of you. [Laughter.]" (ibid., 25 Jan. 1895, 1370).

2. For a polar opposite view of Simpson's performance, see Karel Denis Bicha, "Jerry Simpson: Populist without Principle," *Journal of American History* 54 (Sept. 1967): 291–306. See also O. Gene Clanton, "Jerry Simpson: A Critique of Bicha's 'Populist without Principle' " (unpublished manuscript), Kansas State Historical Society, Topeka, Kans., 1968. Much of the material at issue here regarding Simpson can be found in Myron C. Scott's solidly researched master's thesis "A Congressman and His Constituents: Jerry Simpson and the Big Seventh," Kansas State College, Fort Hays, 1959.

3. Mississippi Democrat Hernando Money referred to Simpson in October 1893 as the "Sage from Medicine Lodge"; in February 1895, Jonathan Dolliver, the Republican leader from Iowa, also used that expression.

4. That is exactly what I did, and the task took more time than I care to recall. My liberal use of quotations from these proceedings was necessary because of the long-standing misconceptions and misinformation that have been put on the record.

5. O. Gene Clanton, *Kansas Populism: Ideas and Men* (Lawrence: University Press of Kansas, 1969), 84 ff.

6. *Congressional Record*, 52nd Cong., 1st sess., 11 Mar. 1892, 2001 ff.

7. See Annie L. Diggs, *The Story of Jerry Simpson* (Wichita, Kans.: Jane Simpson Publisher, 1908), 45. My note to this particular exchange was misplaced, but the exchange occurred just as Diggs reported it.

8. *Congressional Record*, 52nd Cong., 1st sess., 8 Apr. 1892, 3114.

9. Ibid., 1654.

10. Ibid., 4037.

11. Ibid., 20 Jan. 1894, 1119.

12. In the 1890s, apparently the word "scapeless" was used in the same way as "spineless"; it is hard to imagine Simpson as a demagogue, and even harder to see him as one without backbone.

13. *Congressional Record*, 52nd Cong., 1st sess., 21 May 1892, 4521–29. The claim that it was Victor Murdock, a journalist and later a longtime occupant of Simpson's old seat, who coined the "Sockless" label in the aftermath of Simpson's famous debate with "Prince" Hallowell in the 1890 campaign rests largely on this offhand reference by Simpson to "every little red-headed editor out in my part of the country." Murdock was red-headed and certainly never denied having been the originator of the label; apparently, Simpson believed that he had been its creator. It is interesting that Simpson made such a mark that his opponents vied for the honor of having bestowed the nickname on him.

As in Snodgrass's comeback, Simpson was several times alluded to by conservative opponents as a "demagogue" (a charge that would be echoed in a few later historical accounts). That obviously set him to thinking. When Charles Grosvenor, a prominent Republican leader from Ohio, repeated the charge early in January 1894, Simpson responded by saying: To call me a "demagogue" is to forget "the courtesy due to every gentleman in this House." As "I understand the meaning of the word demagogue, it means one who falls in with a popular idea and the mob to get himself into position and place. I stood up in Kansas against this pernicious system of tariff taxation when Kansas was giving an 80,000 Republican majority. I stood almost alone in my county and fought it through. . . . If I had been a demagogue and had carried my wits and abilities, poor though they may be, to the same market to which the gentleman carried his I might have met with greater rewards and been now a part of the party that expects to run the Government in the future, as he is" (ibid., 53rd Cong., 2nd sess., 20 Jan. 1894, 1111).

14. See the exchange between Simpson and Joseph D. Taylor, Republican from Ohio, in this regard (ibid., 52nd Cong., 1st sess., 8 June 1892, 5165, 5165, and appendix, 343–46). Taylor, a person who would probably be called a "production farmer" in our time, was also president of two national banks.

15. *Congressional Record,* 53rd Cong., 2nd sess., 26 Jan. 1894, 1475.

16. Ibid., 12 Jan. 1894, 772; and Diggs, *Simpson,* 144.

17. *Congressional Record,* 52nd Cong., 1st sess., 23 May 1892, 4563; for John Davis, see ibid., 5730–31, and appendix, 609–20.

18. Ibid., 4223–25. Regarding Watson, see ibid., 7 July 1892, 5862; regarding Peffer, ibid., 5822–23; regarding Simpson, ibid., 5 Aug. 1892, 712.

19. Ibid., 28 May 1892, 4803, 4821, 5034; ibid., 52nd Cong., 2nd sess., 17 Feb. 1893, 1760.

20. Ibid., 52nd Cong., 2nd sess., 21 Feb. 1893, 1972.

21. C. Vann Woodward, *Tom Watson: Agrarian Rebel* (New York: Oxford University Press, 1963), 241.

22. *Congressional Record,* 52nd Cong., 2nd sess., 28 Jan. 1893, 917–18. I made a few minor grammatical changes in this quote for the sake of readability; apparently this was, in the main, an extemporaneous speech by Watson.

23. Watson to Butler, 23 Dec. 1895, Marion Butler Papers, Southern Historical Collection, Chapel Hill, N.C. The Watson Papers are also housed in the Southern Historical Collection, and although they are not extensive, they confirm Watson's antisocialist views. The Watson letters to Butler, however, are most revealing.

24. Lawrence Goodwyn, *Democratic Promise: The Populist Movement in America* (New York: Oxford University Press, 1976), 392. Bruce Palmer recognized and noted Watson's pre-1896 apostasy, cautiously, in his well-researched and balanced study *"Man Over Money": The Southern Populist Critique of American Capitalism* (Chapel Hill: University of North Carolina Press, 1981).

25. For the record, the terminology used in text was developed in a long list of courses I have taught over the years, endeavoring to understand and explain the meaning and origins of right-wing extremism in American history. Among the better books on the subject are Seymour Martin Lipset and Earl Raab, *The Politics of Unreason: Right-Wing Extremism in America, 1790–1970* (New York: Harper and Row, 1970); Michael Paul Rogin, *The Intellectuals and McCarthy: The Radical Specter* (Cambridge: MIT Press, 1967); David H. Bennett, *The Party of Fear: From Nativist Movements to the New Right in American History* (Chapel Hill: University of North Carolina Press, 1988); and M. J.

Heale, *American Anticommunism: Combatting the Enemy Within, 1830–1970* (Baltimore: Johns Hopkins University Press, 1990).

26. *Congressional Record,* 52nd Cong., 2nd sess., 20 Jan. 1893, 908.

27. Ibid., 880–81.

28. Ibid., 15 Feb. 1893, appendix, 49–50.

29. Ibid., 3 Mar. 1893, 2595–96.

30. Ibid., 53rd Cong., 3rd sess., 7 Feb. 1895, appendix, 283.

31. Ibid., 15 Feb. 1895, 2242.

32. Ibid., 2 Mar. 1895, 3094–95.

33. On 18 January 1894, McKeighan said this in the debate over the protective tariff bill: "The whole system is one which is intended to and does in fact make a few thousand people rich, [on] . . . the theory that if we would only make them rich enough they will be able to take care of all the rest of the community. This is a very old theory, which despots and oligarchies have always maintained. 'Take care of the rich and they will take care of the poor' " (ibid., 52nd Cong., 2nd sess., 1020 ff).

34. For a more comprehensive assessment of the Populist position, see Gene Clanton, " 'Hayseed Socialism' on the Hill: Congressional Populism, 1891-1895," *Western Historical Quarterly* 15 (Apr. 1984): 139–62.

35. *Congressional Record,* 52nd Cong., 1st sess., 21 Jan. 1892, 470.

36. Clanton, *Kansas Populism,* 85.

37. *Congressional Record,* 52nd Cong., 1st sess., 12 July 1892, 6072–75.

38. Ibid., 5730–31. One should note that, according to Bicha, this was one area that Populists did not concern themselves with while in Congress.

39. Ibid., 22 July 1892, 6556. Peffer's suggestion that the national government had the power to protect its "citizens anywhere in the country" did not sit well with those whites intent on disfranchising and marginalizing black citizens of the United States. Sensitivity on that score would include most southern Democrats and, unfortunately, more than a few white Populists.

40. Ibid., 12 Mar. 1892, 3008.

41. Karel D. Bicha, *Western Populism: Studies in an Ambivalent Conservatism* (Lawrence, Kans.: Coronado Press, 1976), 116. As part of his effort to defeat an appropriation to finance a survey for a railroad to Central and South America, William Baker commented: "I am internally, externally, and eternally opposed to subsidies. . . . Believing such a proposition to be anti-Republican, anti-Democratic, anti-American, and contrary to the best interests of all or nearly all the people of this country" (ibid., 3 May 1892, 3894). The Populists were on record in the Omaha platform as being against any further subsidies to corporations. Thus, Baker's stand here was quite consistent with Populist doctrine. None of them, not even McKeighan, were hostile to assistance to individuals in need, nor were they against particular programs that would assist farmers and laborers. This is an important distinction as regards the meaning of Populism. Bicha, however, used this comment by Baker to support his case of their being unqualified proponents of a government of minimal scope.

42. I must stress here that William Allen was not in the same camp as McKeighan, despite Lawrence Goodwyn's widely circulated notion that the Nebraskan "was a Populist in name only" (see *Democratic Promise,* 392, passim). On other occasions, McKeighan virtually endorsed, point by point, the entire Omaha platform, except for the subtreasury

plan. See *Congressional Record,* 53rd Cong., 1st sess., 6 Apr. 1892, 3009, and 18 July 1892, 6377.

43. *Advocate* (Topeka), 15 Sept. 1894. Doster's idea of the role of government was very close to that advanced by Abraham Lincoln on 1 July 1854. At that time, Lincoln quoted an unidentified writer to this effect: "The legitimate object of government is 'to do for the people what needs to be done, but which they can not, by individual effort, do at all, or do so well, for themselves' " (*The Collected Works of Abraham Lincoln,* vol. 2, edited by Roy P. Basler [New Brunswick, N.J.: Rutgers University Press, 1955]).

44. *Advocate* (Topeka), 5, 12, and 19 Sept. 1894.

45. For Kem's remarks, see *Congressional Record,* 53rd Cong., 3rd sess., 10 Aug. 1894, 8395–99.

46. Ibid., 53rd Cong., 2nd sess., 12 Jan. 1894, 777.

47. Ibid, 52nd Cong., 1st sess., 17 Feb. 1892, 1250–51.

48. Ibid., 54th Cong., 1st sess., 30 Dec. 1895, 425.

49. Ibid., 53rd Cong., 3rd sess., 22 June 1894, 6709.

50. Ibid., 52nd Cong., 1st sess., 31 Mar. 1892, 4126, appendix, 30–32. In this speech by Clover, one finds one of the more obvious examples of what Richard Hofstadter called rhetorical anti-Semitism among the congressional Populists. Actually, examples of this kind were not frequent, even when one includes the mere use of the name Rothschild or the Shakespearean Shylock imagery. Speaking in the debate over repeal of the silver act, Lafayette Pence used the expression to "Jew down" in reference to haggling over price. At one point, North Carolina Populist Alonzo Shuford asked, "Why should 70,000,000 of Americans bend the knee to the alien Jews of London?" Still later, William Greene of Nebraska in a more serious abuse of the Jewish stereotype referred to the "hook-nosed Jews of Wall Street." But the worst case encountered, an example of full-blown anti-Semitism, did not come from a Populist but from a pro-silver Democrat from Wyoming by the name of Henry A. Coffeen, a former college teacher and apparently a banker. He made his blatant remarks in support of a bill to repeal, temporarily, the 10 percent tax on state bank notes, a measure that the Populists opposed as contrary to the goal of a national and public banking system. Those few Populists who engaged in the use of rhetorical anti-Semitism were by no means alone and probably were not even the major offenders. One of their allies in Congress for a time, Joseph Sibley from Pennsylvania, a charismatic Democrat elected with Populist support, actually came to the defense of Jews in the debate over the Chinese Exclusion Act. (See *Congressional Record,* 54th Cong., 1st sess., 12 Feb. 1896, appendix, 122–26; 55th Cong., 2nd sess., 31 Jan. 1898, appendix, 48–50; 53rd Cong., 3rd sess., 5 June 1894, 876–78; 53rd Cong., 1st sess., 14 Oct. 1893, 2525–26.) My findings on this subject add support to Walter Nugent's excellent treatment of this subject in *The Tolerant Populists: Kansas, Populism and Nativism* (Chicago: University of Chicago Press, 1963). Perhaps it is worth adding here that I also encountered numerous examples of anti-black, white racist attitudes—primarily by southern Democrats, however, and none at all by Populists.

CHAPTER THREE. GROVER CLEVELAND'S SPECIAL SESSION

1. Among the general studies treating late-nineteenth-century politics, these have been most instructive: J. Rogers Hollingsworth, *The Whirligig of Politics: The Democracy*

of Cleveland and Bryan (Chicago: University of Chicago Press, 1963); Paul W. Glad, *McKinley, Bryan, and the People* (Philadelphia: J. B. Lippincott, 1964); Carl N. Degler, *The Age of the Economic Revolution, 1876–1900* (Atlanta: Scott, Foresman, 1968); Ray Ginger, *Age of Excess: The United States 1877–1914* (New York: Macmillan, 1965); Robert H. Wiebe, *The Search for Order, 1877–1920* (New York: Hill and Wang, 1967); Samuel T. McSeveney, *The Politics of Depression: Political Behavior in the Northeast, 1893–1896* (New York: Oxford University Press, 1972); Vincent P. DeSantis, *The Shaping of Modern America: 1877–1920* (Arlington Heights, Ill.: Forum Press, 1973, 1989); Walter T. K. Nugent, *From Centennial to World War: American Society, 1876–1917* (Indianapolis: Bobbs-Merrill, 1977); R. Hal Williams, *Years of Decision: American Politics in the 1890s* (New York: John Wiley and Sons, 1978); H. Roger Grant, *Self-Help in the 1890s Depression* (Ames: Iowa State University Press, 1983); and Nell Irvin Painter, *Standing at Armageddon: The United States, 1877–1919* (New York: W. W. Norton, 1987).

2. Quoted in Williams, *Years of Decision,* 71–72.

3. *The Autobiography of William Allen White* (New York: Macmillan, 1946), 187. Also see Glad, *McKinley, Bryan, and the People,* 70–71. Regarding Francis Amasa Walker, see Sidney Fine, *Laissez Faire and the General-Welfare State: A Study of Conflict in American Thought, 1865–1901* (Ann Arbor: University of Michigan Press, 1966), 73 ff. Fine tells us that Walker's economics was transitional in nature: "He was unwilling to accept either a program of unqualified laissez faire or a program calling for state action. Of the two, however, he found laissez faire more to his liking." That is also a fair description of the prevailing economic theory of the Gilded Age: a muddled middle position that benefited primarily those who were positioned best to take advantage of the situation. Laissez-faire became "no intervention in the economy, except to aid our interests."

4. Painter, *Standing at Armageddon,* 116–17; Glad, *McKinley, Bryan, and the People,* 71; Grant, *1890s Depression,* 7–8.

5. *Congressional Record,* 53rd Cong., 1st sess., 8 Aug. 1893, 205; Williams, *Years of Decision,* 75 ff.

6. Ginger, *Age of Excess,* 164.

7. *Congressional Record,* 52nd Cong., 1st sess., 26 May 1892, 4215.

8. Ibid., 53rd Cong., 1st sess., 8 Aug. 1893, 217.

9. Ibid., 11 Aug. 1893, 252.

10. Ibid., 12 Aug. 1893, 278.

11. Ibid., 279.

12. Ibid., 18 Aug. 1893, 486 ff.

13. Ibid., 13 Sept. 1893, 437.

14. Ibid., 298–99, 338–39, 784–90; appendix, 7 and 11 Oct. 1893, 289–329.

15. Ibid., 11 Oct. 1893, appendix, 312.

16. Ibid., 14 Aug. 1893, 326–27.

17. Ibid., 338.

18. Ibid., 24 Aug. 1893, 858–62.

19. The debate in the House began on 8 August and by 26 August it was revealed that 170 speeches had already been delivered.

20. Some of the material here regarding the question of silver was first written by

me for Howard R. Lamar, ed., *The Reader's Encyclopedia of the American West* (New York: Thomas Y. Crowell, 1977), and is reprinted here with permission. For much more extensive coverage, consult these sources, among others: Robert P. Sharkey, *Money, Class, and Party: An Economic Study of the Civil War and Reconstruction* (Baltimore: Johns Hopkins University Studies in Historical and Political Science, Series 77, 1959); Irwin Unger, *The Greenback Era: A Social and Political History of American Finance, 1867–1879* (Princeton, N.J.: Princeton University Press, 1964); Walter T. K. Nugent, *The Money Question during Reconstruction* (New York: W. W. Norton, 1967); Walter T. K. Nugent, *Money and American Society, 1865–1880* (New York: Free Press, 1968); Nugent, *Centennial to World War;* and especially Nugent's essay in Wayne Morgan, ed., *The Gilded Age: A Reappraisal,* 2nd ed. (Syracuse, N.Y.: Syracuse University Press, 1970). I am likewise indebted to Degler, *Age of the Economic Revolution,* for certain insights here regarding the money question, and for certain other insights coming by way of counterreasoning.

21. Nugent, *Money Question,* 87.

22. John Hicks mistakenly identified Sarah Emery as a Kansas woman; others—such as Richard Hofstadter—who drew much of their material from Hicks's classic study took that false linkage to build their case for a special kind of conspiratorial-mindedness. About that and Sarah Emery, see Hofstadter, *The Age of Reform: From Bryan to F.D.R.* (New York: Vintage Books, 1955), 75 ff.

23. The best discussion of the role of Emery and this whole issue of how silver came to be demonetized is contained in Nugent, *Money and American Society*, 162–71. As Nugent points out (168), there was not only a legend about how silver was demonetized but also a "counter-legend"created by the proponents of a gold standard. This legend, wrote Nugent, became "the 'orthodox' legend because it was accepted very uncritically by financial historians who should have known better. But they were prone to believe and propagate it because they worked under virtually the same rhetorical and ideological presuppositions as the respectable, monometallist lawmakers of the seventies."

24. Stanley L. Jones, *The Presidential Election of 1896* (Madison: University of Wisconsin Press, 1964), 12.

25. Paolo E. Coletta, *William Jennings Bryan: Political Evangelist, 1860–1908* (Lincoln: University of Nebraska Press, 1964), 140. The two most recent biographies of Bryan, by Robert W. Cherny, *A Righteous Cause: The Life of William Jennings Bryan* (Boston: Little, Brown, 1985), and LeRoy Ashby, *William Jennings Bryan: Champion of Democracy* (Boston: Twayne Publishers, 1987), seem to underestimate the role of this special session in boosting Bryan's career: Cherny does not even mention Bryan's important role in it; Ashby devotes a paragraph to the event and treats it as being somewhat important in his rise to prominence.

26. *Congressional Record,* 53rd Cong., 1st sess., 16 Aug. 1893, 408–11.

27. Ibid., 28 Aug. 1893, 1008.

28. Ibid., 2 Oct. 1893, appendix, 170–89.

29. Ibid., 30 Oct. 1893, 2958.

30. Ibid., 24 Aug. 1893, 840.

31. Ibid., 30 Oct. 1893, 2955–57.

32. Ibid., 2 Nov. 1893, 3077–78.

CHAPTER FOUR. SPEED BUMPS ON THE YELLOW BRICK ROAD

1. As quoted by Michael Patrick Hearn, letter to the editor dated 12 Dec. 1991, *New York Times,* 10 January 1992, A-26. This letter was called to my attention by Cynthia Miller, then editor of the University Press of Kansas. It was already my belief that L. Frank Baum's *The Wonderful Wizard of Oz* contains quite a different parable than we have been led to believe; that belief has since been greatly strengthened by further reading and analysis. The title to this chapter, incidentally, was meant to suggest that the Populists and their silver allies merely served to slow the nation's formal conversion to the gold standard. See Appendix D for additional remarks regarding the Oz story and the battle over the monetary standards.

2. Apparently, Peffer arrived at this figure simply by using the population count, one dollar per inhabitant.

3. *Congressional Record,* 53rd Cong., 2nd sess., 19 Dec. 1893, 384–87.

4. Ibid., 3 Jan. 1894, 583–85.

5. Ibid., 15 Jan. 1894, appendix, 49 ff.

6. Ibid., 51.

7. Ibid., 57–58.

8. Ibid., 18 Jan. 1894, 1026.

9. Ibid., 1093–94.

10. Ibid., 19 Jan. 1894, 1060.

11. Ibid., 24 Jan. 1894, appendix, 105–6, 1335; 27 Jan. 1894, 1551; 30 Jan. 1894, appendix, 601–15; 31 Jan. 1894, 1730; in the end, barbed wire was dropped from the free list, as was lumber, both of which had been added as a result of Populist initiative.

12. Ibid., 31 Jan. 1894, appendix, 293–98.

13. The record indicated ten Populists, but there were actually eleven, unless Marion Cannon is omitted from the list.

14. *Congressional Record,* 53rd Cong., 2nd sess., 1 Feb. 1894, 1796–97; R. Hal Williams, *Years of Decision: American Politics in the 1890s* (New York: John Wiley and Sons, 1978), 90 ff. The numbers here are off by one, but they were reported as given.

15. *Congressional Record,* 53rd Cong., 2nd sess., 7 Mar. 1894, 2681–84.

16. Ibid., 8 Mar. 1894, 2731.

17. Ibid., 9 Mar. 1894, 2789 ff.

18. Ibid., 12 June 1894, 6179–80.

19. Ibid., 6, 11, 12, and 13 Apr. 1894, appendix, 650–69.

20. More study of the response to Populism is needed. For a good beginning study in this area, see Greg Harness, "The Response to Populism in the Genteel Press, 1890–1900," master's thesis, Washington State University, Pullman, May 1996.

21. While considering the admission of Utah as a state, Michael Daniel Harter, an Ohio Democrat, drew laughter and applause with this line directed at Jerry Simpson: "I feel that we have already gone as far into the experiment of admitting States sparsely settled and wholly unentitled to statehood as we should go. I say let us digest, if we can digest, the infantile States we have admitted to the Union. . . . Let us for instance, get through with such enlightened States as Kansas! Let us have Kansas thoroughly civilized before we undertake any more" (*Congressional Record,* 2 Dec. 1893, 184). Regarding the Kansas situation, see O. Gene Clanton, *Kansas Populism: Ideas and Men*

(Lawrence: University Press of Kansas, 1969), and Walter Nugent, *The Tolerant Populists: Kansas, Populism and Nativism* (Chicago, Ill.: University of Chicago Press, 1963).

22. Quoted by Henry F. Pringle, *Theodore Roosevelt, a Biography* (New York: Harcourt, Brace and World, 1956), 114. Speaking on 3 March 1898, Curtis Castle mentioned Theodore Roosevelt's earlier suggestion that what ought to be done was to " 'stand up the leaders of the silver movement against a brick wall and shoot them to death.' " Castle utilized the comment in making his case for how corrupt the nation had become.

23. Ibid., 109.

24. See especially Donald L. McMurry, *Coxey's Army: A Study of the Industrial Army Movement of 1894* (Seattle: University of Washington Press, 1968), published originally in 1929; and Carlos A. Schwantes, *Coxey's Army: An American Odyssey* (Lincoln: University of Nebraska Press, 1985).

25. Schwantes, *Coxey's Army,* 274.

26. Ibid., 275.

27. Ibid., 278–79; see also Henry Steele Commager, *The American Mind: An Interpretation of American Thought and Character since the 1880's* (New Haven, Conn.: Yale University Press, 1950).

28. *Congressional Record,* 53rd Cong., 2nd sess., 19 Apr. 1894, 3843. Later, in an exchange with Senator David Hill, Allen said this: "I will make a charge for the benefit of the Senator from New York that I am prepared to prove, and I will go into court and prove it if need be. At the very day, or the day after Coxey and his unfortunate followers were taken to the common jail of this District, for trespassing on the grass of the Capitol grounds a certain railroad magnate of the United States was in a committee room at the other end of the Capitol, guarded by an officer of this Government, and sending into the House of Representatives to get Representatives to come to see him that he might tell them what he would do with reference to certain of the Pacific roads. . . . He was there to procure legislation regarding the Pacific roads by which this Government is to be buncoed out of a hundred million dollars if the scheme can be passed through Congress" (ibid., 22 June 1894, 6709). Incidentally, in this same exchange, Senator Orville Platt of Connecticut used the word "Populistic" in the same pejorative sense that it would be used, especially in the 1950s and later, to describe seamy mass sentiments—particularly as regards envy on the part of the have-nots toward the haves.

29. Ibid., 20 Apr. 1894, 3856.

30. Ibid., 26 Apr. 1894, 4107.

31. Ibid., 9 May 1894, 4518, 4570.

32. Ibid., 10 May 1894, 4568. See Russell R. Eliott, *Servant of Power: A Political Biography of Senator William M. Stewart* (Reno: University of Nevada Press, 1983), 172. Consistent with his book's title, the author writes that Stewart "joined the national People's Party in the latter part of 1893 solely to promote the cause of silver."

33. *Congressional Record,* 53rd Cong., 2nd sess., 10 May 1894, 4568.

34. Ibid., 4952. The gardening metaphor comes from a 1906 editorial by William Allen White; see Clanton, *Kansas Populism,* 243.

35. *Congressional Record,* 53rd Cong., 2nd sess., 1 June 1894, 5587.

36. Ibid., 11 May 1894, 4631.

37. Ibid., 5 June 1894, 5794–98.

38. See Gene Clanton, "The Origins of Populism: A Centennial Essay," unpublished manuscript, Kansas State Historical Society, Topeka, 1993, regarding Thomas Mendenhall and Edward Kellogg.

39. *Congressional Record,* 53rd Cong., 2nd sess., 6 June 1894, appendix, 926–28. The manner in which Cannon wrote this address might suggest that he had disassociated himself from the party he helped organize in California; perhaps he considered himself an Alliance congressman in the style of Populism as defined by Lawrence Goodwyn in *Democratic Promise: The Populist Moment in America* (New York: Oxford University Press, 1976). Toward the end of this Congress, Jerry Simpson referred to his party as comprising only ten members; without Cannon—the only one about whom there was any doubt—that figure would be correct.

40. *Congressional Record,* 53rd Cong., 2nd sess., 18 June 1894, 6444. See James W. Ely, Jr., *The Guardian of Every Other Right: A Constitutional History of Property Rights* (New York: Oxford University Press, 1998), regarding the sacred nature of property rights among many mainstream Americans.

41. Peter Argersinger has done an excellent job of showing how the Populist delegations were frustrated by traditional leadership and committee procedures and in showing how the Populists managed to overcome, at points, various obstacles to make their influence felt. See "No Rights on This Floor: Third Parties and the Institutionalization of Congress," in *The Limits of Agrarian Radicalism: Western Populism and American Politics* (Lawrence: University Press of Kansas, 1995), 213–45.

42. The phrase "1890s Populism" was used because of the need to distinguish between it and a prominent brand of pseudo-Populism that has loomed so large in explaining right-wing politics from Barry Goldwater and Ronald Reagan to Newt Gingrich and Pat Buchanan.

43. *Congressional Record,* 53rd Cong. 2nd sess., 20 June 1894, 6551.

44. Ibid., 19 June 1894, 931, 944. Apparently, Sibley meant what he said about principles being more important than party labels: In 1894 and 1896, Sibley would lose bids to return to Congress as a Democratic-Populist candidate; in 1898, he would be reelected as a Democrat but would then become the candidate of the Republican party in 1900, returning to Congress as a Republican for three more terms.

45. Perhaps we should remind ourselves that Grover Cleveland was likely the inspiration for the Great Wizard of Oz, who turned out to be a mere mortal and a "humbug" to boot; could it be that his humbuggery was not totally without effect, at least as far as historians are concerned? To this day Cleveland, in my opinion, remains in higher esteem than justified by the record.

46. *Congressional Record,* 53rd Cong., 2nd sess., 22 June 1894, 6684–90.

47. Ibid., 23 June 1894, 6768.

48. Ibid., 10 July 1894, 7230, 7284.

49. Ibid., 7543–44; in the House, only Lafayette Pence raised questions about the broad wording of the resolution approved there.

50. Ibid., 14 July 1894, 7468.

51. Clanton, *Kansas Populism,* 56–57. The Kansas legislature in 1891 selected Peffer to replace Ingalls.

52. *Congressional Record,* 53rd Cong., 2nd sess., 16 Aug. 1894, 8395–99.

53. In August, this measure by Davis and other emergency measures suggested by Populists came in for special attention and an attack led by James Pigott, a Connecticut

Democrat, who first published his speech in a capital newspaper and later had it inserted in the appendix of the *Record*. Pigott's speech and Davis's reply provide a convenient index to the various attempts by Populists to do something about the nation's economic crisis. By conflating Populist proposals, Pigott managed to put a large price tag on Populist programs.

54. Williams, *Years of Decision*, 93 ff.

55. According to the *Biographical Directory of the American Congress, 1784–1961* (Washington, D.C.: Government Printing Office, 1961), Clark was president of Marshall College in 1873–1874. In his memoirs, published in 1920, Clark made this statement: "My expulsion [from the University of Kentucky] . . . sent me to Bethany College, where I graduated with the highest honors in 1873, which fact more than all else made me president of Marshall College, West Virginia, at twenty-three—the youngest college president in America" (Champ Clark, *My Quarter Century of American Politics* [New York: Harper and Brothers, 1920], 1:98). I confirmed Clark's claim by calling Marshall University. Clark also included Simpson's name on a list of the most outstanding debaters in Congress. Some of the better known names on his list were Henry Clay, Daniel Webster, Thomas Hart Benton, John C. Calhoun, Steven A. Douglas, Abraham Lincoln, James G. Blaine, and William E. Borah.

56. *Congressional Record*, 53rd Cong., 3rd sess., 11 Dec. 1894, 5.

57. Ibid., 5 Dec. 1894, 41.

58. Ibid., 31 Jan. 1895, 1565.

59. Ibid., 12 Jan. 1895, 901.

60. Ibid., 6 Aug. 1894, 8239–40; 24 Aug. 1894, 8654; Arthur A. Ekirch, *The Decline of American Liberalism* (New York: Atheneum, 1967), 238; William Preston, Jr., *Aliens and Dissenters: Federal Suppression of Radicals, 1903–1933* (Cambridge: Harvard University Press, 1963).

61. In several decisions prior to the advent of congressional Populism, the Supreme Court had already conceded that government did indeed, if it chose, have the authority to build, own, and operate railroads, at least in the case of those extending beyond the boundary of a particular state. See *Peik v. The Chicago & Northwestern Railway* (1877) and Joseph Bradley's dissent in *Chicago, Milwaukee and St. Paul R.R. Co. v. Minnesota* (1890).

62. *Congressional Record*, 53rd Cong., 3rd sess., 6 Feb. 1895, 1820–21.

63. Ibid., 31 Jan. 1895, 1556, 1590–92.

64. Ibid., 24, 25 Jan. 1895, 1277, 1329.

65. Ibid., 8 Feb. 1895, 1937–40.

66. Ibid., 1931.

CHAPTER FIVE. METAMORPHOSIS, 1894 AND AFTERWARD

1. The parable in the dialogue ran as follows: "You can't patch up this old social system so as to do any permanent good," said he. "It's putting new cloth on an old garment. I've seen an old grist mill that was all awry—twisted all out of shape, every which way—but every part of it shared in the twist and was adjusted to the general snarled condition. Now, if some man had come in and said, 'This beam, or this upright, or this something or

other is crooked, is out of plumb,' and had fixed that particular part of the old mill just right, the old thing would have been thrown all out of gear and wouldn't have been fit to grind mud for a brick yard. Just so with the existing social system. It's all out of whack, so if you straighten up any particular part of it, the old thing will be all knocked out of gear, and we'll be worse off bye and bye. . . . You've got to overhaul the old mill all through, or you'd better let it be as it is. Patch work won't do any good. You've got to be satisfied with things as they are, or you've got to have socialism, one or the other. There's no middle ground—no room to tinker" (G. C. Clemens, *The Deadline* [Topeka, 1894]; Michael J. Brodhead and O. Gene Clanton, "G. C. Clemens: 'Sociable Socialist,' " *Kansas Historical Quarterly* [winter 1974]: 475–502).

2. Here I should note that I consider the informal fusion arrangements of the 1890 election to have made that election virtually a fusion campaign.

3. *Congressional Record,* 54th Cong., 1st sess., 30 Dec. 1895, 422–23.

4. Ibid., 25–26. Russell R. Elliott, *Servant of Power: A Political Biography of Senator William M. Stewart* (Reno: University of Nevada Press, 1983).

5. *Congressional Record,* 54th Cong, 1st sess., 13 Jan. 1896, 611.

6. Ibid., 14 Jan. 1896, 660–61.

7. Ibid., 16 Jan. 1896, 738–39.

8. Senator Tillman later said this about President Cleveland: "Republican in disguise, and the best friend of the money power that the United States has ever seen, because he accomplished more than any other man in its history has ever been able to accomplish to enslave the masses, to put the farmers in the poorhouse, and to fasten the manacles of gold upon the American people" (ibid., 55th Cong., 2nd sess., 28 Jan. 1898, 1162). It was a sentiment that all Populists would second.

9. Ibid., 54th Cong., 1st sess., 20 Dec. 1895, 262.

10. Apparently, Tillman's demeanor and looks were a bit frightening to some. At one point, a fellow senator actually remarked on the floor that he found Tillman's mannerisms and oratorical style fearful and intimidating. Regarding the evolution of the word "populist," see James Turner, "Understanding the Populists," *Journal of American History* 67 (Sept. 1980): 354–73; and Michael Kazin, *The Populist Persuasion: An American History* (New York: Basic Books, 1995).

Incidentally, it was Lawrence Goodwyn who coined the terminology "shadow movement" in reference to the silver fusionist effort that came on strong after 1893; Goodwyn also alluded to Tillmanism as a kind of shadow movement, although he did not develop the point as he did the former.

11. *Congressional Record,* 54th Cong., 1st sess., 16 Dec. 1895, 219.

12. Ibid., 10 Feb. 1896, 1563–65. On 21 February, speaking in support of this bill, Skinner said, "I did not introduce the bill either to popularize myself at home or to unpopularize myself on this floor, for I am a high-priced man; I believe in reasonable and even high salaries under proper circumstances. When we have the conditions out of which high prices can properly arise and be paid, this House will find me liberal in all respects." On another occasion, John Bell attempted, unsuccessfully by amendment, to reduce a government salary being acted on from $7,000 to $5,000 (ibid., 21 Feb. and 17 Mar. 1896, 2022, 2903).

13. Ibid., 8 May 1896, 4997.

14. Ibid., 1566.

15. Ibid., 10 June 1896, 6391.
16. Ibid., 19 Feb. 1896, 1926.
17. Ibid., 23 Jan. 1897, 1105.
18. Ibid., 24 Mar. 1896, 3139–40, and 7 Apr. 1896, 3651.
19. Ibid., 17 Apr. 1896, 4088, 4091–93.
20. Ibid., 7 Apr. 1896, 3651.
21. Ibid., 9 Apr. 1896, 3755.
22. Ibid., 1 May 1896, 4657–62.
23. Ibid., 5 May 1896, 4828.
24. Ibid., 6 May 1896, 4874.
25. Ibid., 9 May 1896, 5433.
26. Ibid., 23 May 1896, 5627.
27. Ibid., 15 May 1896, 5297–98.
28. Ibid., 3 June 1896, 6042.
29. Ibid., 20 May 1896, 5441.
30. Karel D. Bicha, *Western Populism: Studies in an Ambivalent Conservatism* (Lawrence, Kans.: Coronado Press, 1976), 127. See Gene Clanton, " 'Hayseed Socialism' on the Hill," *Western Historical Quarterly* 15 (Apr. 1984): 139–62, regarding government railways and labor-related issues and attitudes toward African Americans, Native Americans, and women. I would like to add that in the 55th Congress (1897–1899), Populists supported the move to establish an eight-hour day for laborers engaged in work for the federal government. Of particular importance is the discovery that John F. Fitzgerald, Democrat from Massachusetts, suggested at one point that the Populists join him in amending a bill to include a minimum wage of not less than twenty-five cents per hour; however, Fitzgerald did not formally move the amendment. Populists in the same Congress were also strongly supportive of a bill requiring arbitration between railroad corporations and their employees, when the businesses in question were engaged in interstate commerce (*Congressional Record,* 55th Cong., 2nd sess., 11 May 1898, 4795; 12 May 1898, 4858; 17 May 1898, 4984; 19 May 1898, 5052–53).

Although Indian policy was not nearly as prominent in phase two of congressional Populism (1897–1903), William Allen and John Kelley spoke out quite positively in support of fair treatment. On 10 and 11 February 1898, Senator Allen made a special effort aimed at undoing the heavy penalties imposed on the Sioux Indians in the aftermath of the Ulm massacre that had occurred in Minnesota during the Civil War (see ibid., 1618, 2658–60). There were also several instances of more negative commentary by other Populists. See statements by James Gunn of Idaho and James Callahan of Oklahoma in ibid., 26 Jan. 1898, 1049, 1052–53.

31. *Congressional Record,* 54th Cong., 2nd sess., 11 Feb. 1896, 1593.
32. Ibid., 13 Feb. 1896, 1642.
33. Ibid., 9 Apr. 1896, 3755.
34. Ibid., 3756.
35. Ibid., 22 Apr. 1898, 4411.
36. Ibid., 4412.
37. Ibid., 1 May 1896, 4668.
38. Ibid., 16 May 1896, 5329.
39. Ibid., 23 May 1896, 5614–15.

40. Allen had this speech added to his comments made on 7 January 1897; see ibid., 420–23.

41. Ibid., 8 and 11 Jan. 1897, 595–98, 601, 689.

42. Maldwyn Allen Jones, *American Immigration* (Chicago: University of Chicago Press, 1960), 247–77.

43. *Congressional Record,* 54th Cong., 2nd sess., 30 Mar. 1896, 2817–20.

44. Ibid., 14 May 1896, 5215.

45. Ibid., 20 May 1896, 5476, 5480–81.

46. Ibid., 2 Mar. 1897, 2667–68.

47. Ibid., 3 Mar. 1897, 2947.

48. The Wilson-Gorman tariff of 1894 had ended the "preferential" arrangement that had existed regarding Cuba's sugar crop. Deprived of a "free market" and confronted with a duty, the industry was devastated. See Vincent P. De Santis, *The Shaping of Modern America: 1877–1920* (Arlington Heights, Ill.: Forum Press, 1973, 1989), 124, and Lewis L. Gould, *The Spanish-American War and President McKinley* (Lawrence: University Press of Kansas, 1982), 20.

49. Harold U. Faulkner, *Politics, Reform, and Expansion, 1890–1900* (New York: Harper and Row, 1959), 219–20.

50. *Congressional Record,* 54th Cong., 1st sess., 4 Dec. 1895, 36–37.

51. Ibid., 20 Feb. 1896, 1972.

52. Richard Hofstadter, *The Age of Reform: From Bryan to F.D.R.* (New York: Vintage, 1955), 86–87.

53. *Congressional Record,* 54th Cong., 1st sess., 25 Feb. 1896, 2122–23.

54. Ibid., 28 Feb. 1896, 2250.

55. Ibid., 2 Mar. 1896, 2359.

56. Ibid., 17 Mar. 1896, 2865.

57. Ibid., 19 Mar. 1896, 2971.

58. Ibid., 3 Apr. 1896, 3549.

59. Ibid., 3555.

60. Ibid., 4 Apr. 1896, 3578.

61. Ibid., 3587.

62. Ibid., 3587–88.

63. Ibid., 3590.

64. Ibid., 3592.

65. Ibid., 3593. For a clever example of one southern Democrat's use of racial stereotypes and language, see the remarks by Representative Peter Otey, Virginia Democrat, former railroad president and banker, in the House, on 4 April 1896. Otey's was one of the rare instances of a congressman using the word "nigger" for the public record (ibid., 3593–95).

66. For a lively treatment of President McKinley's role in the coming of the war and its aftermath, see Gould, *Spanish-American War*. Among other things, Gould concluded that "Cleveland and his secretary of state, Richard Olney, pursued a course that was pro-Spanish; McKinley tilted toward the rebels." Overall, McKinley's "presidential leadership" in this whole episode, in his view, "was more courageous and principled than his critics realized."

CHAPTER SIX. POPULIST MELTDOWN, 1896–1897

1. Paolo E. Coletta, *William Jennings Bryan: Political Evangelist, 1860–1908* (Lincoln: University of Nebraska Press, 1964), 104 ff.

2. Robert W. Cherny, *A Righteous Cause: The Life of William Jennings Bryan* (Boston: Little, Brown, 1985), 54.

3. Coletta, *William Jennings Bryan,* and Cherny, *A Righteous Cause,* both recognized this connection between Bryan and New Deal–style reform. Bryan's statement was: "There are those who believe that, if you will only legislate to make the well-to-do prosperous, their prosperity will leak through on those below. The Democratic idea . . . has been that if you legislate to make the masses prosperous, their prosperity will find its way up through every class which rests upon them." Obviously, Howard's comments quoted at the beginning of this chapter show the influence of Bryan's famous remark.

4. See Worth Robert Miller, "The Worst Conglomeration I Ever Saw: Texas Populists and the Forging of the Bryan-Watson Ticket of 1896," unpublished manuscript in possession of its author, 5 Jan. 1996.

5. See Donna A. Barnes, *Farmers in Rebellion: The Rise and Fall of the Southern Farmers Alliance and People's Party in Texas* (Austin: University of Texas Press, 1984), regarding the problems created by the nomination of Bryan.

6. The lone exception is Gene Clanton, *Populism: The Humane Preference in America, 1890–1900* (Boston: Twayne Publishers, 1991), which I have drawn on for some material for this segment about the 1896 national convention. John Hicks republished all the Alliance platforms, as well as the Omaha platform, but not this 1896 document, in an appendix.

7. Clanton, *Humane Preference.* See especially the chapter entitled "Shallows and Miseries" for more extensive coverage of the 1896 election and its aftermath.

8. LeRoy Ashby, *William Jennings Bryan: Champion of Democracy* (Boston: Twayne Publishers, 1987), 65–72; Robert Durden, *Climax of Populism: The Election of 1896* (Lexington: University Press of Kentucky, 1965), 126 ff.

9. *Congressional Record,* 54th Cong., 2nd sess., 12 Jan. 1897, 723.

10. Ibid., 14 Jan. 1897, 791.

11. Ibid., 3 Mar. 1897, 2751.

12. Ibid., 14 Dec. 1896, 233–34.

13. *Emporia Gazette*, 5 Nov. 1896. See also Clanton, *Kansas Populism,* 197; Clanton, *Humane Preference,* 161.

14. Davis to Butler, 20 Mar. 1897, Butler Papers, Southern Historical Collection, Chapel Hill, N.C.

15. Kali S. Williard to Butler, 8 Apr. 1897, ibid.

16. James Hogan to Butler, 15 Apr. 1897, ibid.

17. *Congressional Record,* 55th Cong., 1st sess., 15 Mar. 1897, 12–13, 18.

18. Ibid., 22 Mar. 1897, 137.

19. Greene was replaced in a special election by William Neville, who was then reelected in 1900; as I have indicated, Neville merits the title of the last Populist. The district in Nebraska that elected Greene and Neville to Congress for three terms from 1897 to 1903 surely must qualify as the most genuinely Populist area in the nation. Greene's home was in Kearney; Neville's in North Platte. This is a distinction that the

area should be proud to acknowledge, no matter where the area stands today, politically speaking.

20. *Congressional Record,* 55th Cong., 1st sess., 22 Mar. 1897, 143–47.

21. Ibid., 23 Mar. 1897, 202–3.

22. Ibid., 24 Mar. 1897, 252–53. Regarding the context vital to California and the Pacific Northwest, see David B. Griffiths's extensively researched and detailed study *Populism in the Western United States, 1890–1900,* 2 vols. (Lewiston/Queenston/Lampeter, 1988).

23. *Congressional Record,* 55th Cong., 1st sess., 25 Mar. 1897, 271–72. See also William Joseph Gaboury, *Dissension in the Rockies: A History of Idaho Populism* (New York: Garland Publishing, 1988).

24. *Congressional Record,* 55th Cong., 1st sess., 25 Mar. 1897, 273–75.

25. Ibid., 308–10.

26. Ibid., 26 Mar. 1897, 381.

27. Ibid., 31 Mar. 1897, 550.

28. Ibid., 557. Edwin Reed Ridgely prepared a speech for this debate that he ultimately managed to insert in the appendix. This Kansas Populist represented the state's southeastern corner, an area whose political radicalism years ago drew the attention of the noted Kansas historian James Malin. Crawford County of Ridgely's district, which encompassed his residence in Pittsburg, would in 1912 distinguish itself by becoming the only county unit in the nation to cast its presidential vote for Eugene Debs; it also was home base for the *Appeal to Reason* and occasionally for Debs in his capacity as an editorial writer for that famous Socialist weekly. Perhaps being a crossover area between the North and the South—in addition to having a significant coal mining industry, commingled with a large element of agrarian radicalism—accounted for the area's unusual political stance. In his speech, Ridgely denounced the tariff as an unjust system of taxation that he insisted needed to be replaced by a graduated tax in order to "meet the present current expenses of the Government, including all State and local taxes." He said that he "would [also] largely increase our public improvement fund; and with this I would put every man in the land, who applied, at work on public improvements at such liberal wages as would compel our factory and mine owners to materially advance present wages or lose their operatives." His comments ended with this remark: " 'The greatest good to the greatest number' should be our motto, rather than the protection and enrichment of the few, and the enslavement of the many, as is now the tendency" (ibid., 19 July 1897, 445 ff).

29. Ibid., 30 Mar. 1897, 464 ff.

30. Ibid., 5 Apr. 1897, 577.

31. Ibid., 11 May 1897, 995.

32. Ibid., 4 June 1897, 1494–95.

33. Ibid.,15 July 1897, 2619.

34. Ibid.

35. Ibid., 2609–12.

36. Ibid., 2612–25.

37. Perhaps Jeffrey Ostler, *Prairie Populism: The Fate of Agrarian Radicalism in Kansas, Nebraska, and Iowa, 1880–1892* (Lawrence: University Press of Kansas, 1993), might discover in this segment some additional insights as to why Populism was strong in Kansas and Nebraska and weak in Iowa. The contests between Allen and Gear are

especially pertinent to answering that question. One might also better appreciate the point made by C. Vann Woodward many years ago when he noted that the Populists were a long way from having a monopoly on conspiracy theories.

38. *Congressional Record,* 55th Cong., 1st sess., 24 July 1897, 2974–76.

39. Ibid., 15 May 1897, 1201–2.

40. Ibid., 1 June 1897, 1393.

41. Ibid., 24 July 1897, 2965.

CHAPTER SEVEN. "COME OUT ON THE SIDE OF ETERNAL JUSTICE AND HUMAN LIBERTY"

1. James H. Ferriss to Butler, 7 Dec. 1897, Butler Papers, Southern Historical Collection, Chapel Hill, N.C.

2. *Congressional Record,* 55th Cong., 2nd sess., 8 Dec. 1897, 40.

3. Ibid., 5 Jan. 1898, 369.

4. Ibid., 19 Jan. 1898, 763–64.

5. Ibid., 20 Jan. 1898, 793; emphasis added.

6. Ibid., 802–4.

7. Ibid., 5 Jan. 1898, 311–12.

8. Ibid., 7 Jan. 1898, 427–30.

9. Ibid., 11 Jan. 1898, 512. See Walter Nugent, *Crossings: The Great Transatlantic Migrations, 1870– 1914* (Bloomington: Indiana University Press, 1992), for an excellent discussion of the subject of immigration; his chapter "United States of America" was especially helpful in putting this remarkable movement of humanity in perspective.

10. *Congressional Record,* 55th Cong., 2nd sess., 13 Jan. 1898, 583.

11. Ibid., 17 Jan. 1898, 689. To be paired is, by arrangement, to join the votes, pro and con, of absent members.

12. Ibid., 20 and 24 Jan. 1898, 803, 951.

13. See also John Higham, *Strangers in the Land: Patterns in American Nativism, 1860–1925* (New Brunswick, N.J.: Rutgers University Press, 1955), in particular as regards the antiradical component of nativism; and Nugent, *Crossings.* Maldwyn Allen Jones's *American Immigration* (Chicago: University of Chicago Press, 1960), 247–77, is a good example of the problem some have had in accounting for the voting pattern on the question of immigration restriction. I devoted so much space to the issue of immigration restriction because the Populist position has been so badly misrepresented on the issue; the same can be said for their position regarding intervention in Cuba.

14. *Congressional Record,* 55th Cong., 2nd sess., 7 Jan. 1898, 427–30.

15. Ibid., 17 Jan. 1899, 695.

16. Ibid., 22 Jan. 1898, 889–91.

17. Ibid., 16 Feb. 1898, 1760.

18. Ibid., 3 Mar. 1898, 258–60.

19. Ibid., 14 Mar. 1898, 2809.

20. Ibid.

21. Ibid., 19 Mar. 1898, 3010–12. Several months later, Charles Barlow, speaking in opposition to a move to extend the due date by ten years on money owed by a defaulting

railroad, stated that "private ownership of public utilities must be a thing of the past." He also stated: "My personal views on railroads are well known. I believe the only solution of the transportation question is the absolute Government ownership and operation of the railroads" (ibid., 6 July 1898, 6725). With the record of the performance of the Populists in the 55th Congress on this question, it is difficult to comprehend how anyone could conclude that they rarely had anything to say about their call for government ownership of the railroads. Regarding that, see Karel D. Bicha, *Western Populism: Studies on Ambivalent Conservatism* (Lawrence, Kans.: Coronado Press, 1976).

22. *Congressional Record,* 55th Cong., 2nd sess., 22 Jan. 1898, 871 ff.

23. Ibid., 3 Feb. 1898, 1397–99.

24. Ibid., 1407.

25. Quoted in C. Vann Woodward, *Tom Watson: Agrarian Rebel* (New York: Oxford University Press, 1963), 334–35.

26. One casualty by heat exhaustion was incurred in the naval battle that occurred in Manila Bay.

27. *Congressional Record,* 55th Cong., 2nd sess., 17 Feb. 1898, 1819.

28. Ibid; R. Hal Williams, *Years of Decision: American Politics in the 1890s* (New York: John Wiley and Sons, 1978), 138 ff.

29. *Congressional Record,* 55th Cong., 2nd sess., 7 Mar. 1898, 2556–57.

30. Ibid., 8 Mar. 1898, 2604.

31. Ibid., 2606.

32. Ibid., 1 Apr. 1898, 3465 ff.

33. Ibid., 31 Mar. 1898, 3410.

34. Ibid., 5 Apr. 1898, 3545 ff.

35. Ibid., 7 Apr. 1898, 3690–91.

36. Regarding the Populist position on financing the war, see James Gunn's comments, ibid., 22 Apr. 1898, 430–37; Edwin Ridgely, 27 Apr. 1898, appendix, 746–49; John Bell, 27 Apr. 1898, 4308–9; William Greene, 27 Apr. 1898, 4323–24; Freeman Knowles, 27 Apr. 1898, 4323–24; Curtis Castle, 18 Apr. 1898, appendix, 349 ff; William Vincent, 23 Apr. 1898, 4388; Jerry Simpson, 23 Apr. 1898, 4395–4400; Jeremiah Botkin, 28 Apr. 1898, 4400–4405; Samuel Maxwell, 29 Apr. 1898, 4406, 4459–60; Marion Butler, 2 May 1898, 4492–93; and William Allen, 25 May 1898, 5182.

37. Ibid., 19 Apr. 1898, 4459–60.

38. Williams, *Years of Decision,* 142; Nell Irvin Painter, *Standing at Armageddon: The United States, 1877–1919* (New York: W. W. Norton, 1987), 144 ff.

39. The yeas in the House were from Botkin, Kelley, Knowles, McCormick, Peters, Ridgely, Skinner, and Simpson; the nays were cast by Bell, Fowler, Howard, Martin, Maxwell, Shuford, and Stark; Barlow, Castle, Greene, Gunn, Sutherland, and Vincent did not vote. Ridgely reported that Vincent, who was absent, would likely have voted yea. The big surprise was the vote of Jerry Simpson for Hawaiian annexation. The day before he left Congress for good, he explained that vote while speaking on behalf of a government-owned cable to the islands: "Mr. Speaker, in the last session of this Congress I voted for the annexation of the Hawaiian Islands. I did so because I was persuaded that we ought to have those islands as a military necessity. Lying as they do on the great highway between America and Asia, nearly halfway between the two continents, the argument was offered that it was necessary to have those islands as a military station, as a great naval station."

He went on to make the same kind of argument regarding a cable to the islands; in these, his last extended remarks, Simpson also made one last pitch for public ownership of public instrumentalities (*Congressional Record,* 55th Cong., 3rd sess., 3 Mar. 1899, 2900; see also 6 July 1898, 6712). Allen had earlier called several times for annexation of Hawaii; he obviously had given the matter some thought and reversed his course, seeing annexation as the first step toward imperialism.

40. Ibid., 13 June 1898, 5832; emphasis added. Two of Bell's colleagues, Edwin Ridgely and Freeman Knowles, also spoke later on the annexationist side of the debate. Anticipated advantages to be derived from trade and military bases seemed to have been at the core of their decision (ibid., 5988–89).

41. Ibid., 6018.

42. Ibid., 6 July 1898, 6702.

43. Ibid., 27 June 1898, 6352–53.

CHAPTER EIGHT. THE ROAD TO EMPIRE, 1898–1903

1. *Congressional Record,* 55th Cong., 2nd sess., 25 May 1898, 5181.

2. Ibid., 4 and 10 June 1898, 5541, 5751, 5755, 5753–56. Interpreters have been quite at odds over the meaning of Populism since the advent of the movement, especially as it involves the question of socialism. Since the 1950s, the divergence has been quite remarkable. In various accounts, Populists have been portrayed as retrogressive capitalists, as crypto-socialists, and as neither capitalists nor socialists. Two contemporary, nonacademic, and conflicting interpretations by anti-Populists are those of Charles S. Gleed, "The True Significance of Western Unrest," *Forum* 16 (Oct. 1893): 251–60, and Frank Basil Tracy, "Rise and Doom of the Populist Party," *Forum* 16 (Oct. 1893): 240–50. Frank L. McVey, "The Populist Movement," *Economic Studies* 1 (Aug. 1896), and Frederick Emory Haynes, "The New Sectionalism," *Quarterly Journal of Economics* 10 (Apr. 1896), were the first scholarly treatments; both viewed the movement as socialistic. Another contemporary work that also saw the movement as socialistic, one that should be much more widely disseminated to enhance our understanding of anti-Populism and its latter-day ideological descendants, is that by George A. Sanders, *Reality: or Law and Order vs. Anarchy and Socialism: A Reply to Edward Bellamy's Looking Backward and Equality* (Cleveland: Burrows Brothers, 1898). Richard Hofstadter, in the *The Age of Reform: From Bryan to F.D.R.* (New York: Vintage, 1955), with Karel D. Bicha as his most active apparent disciple, presented the Populists as retrogressive capitalists; Norman Pollack, *The Populist Response to Industrial America: Midwestern Populist Thought* (Cambridge: Harvard University Press, 1962), saw them as incipient socialists; Lawrence Goodwyn, *Democratic Promise: The Populist Moment in America* (New York: Oxford University Press, 1976), and Bruce Palmer, *"Man over Money": The Southern Populist Critique of American Capitalism* (Chapel Hill: University of North Carolina Press, 1981), placed them somewhere in the twilight zone between the two; the views of the last two are similar to my own. More recently, Pollack published two more books on the subject wherein he drastically revised his earlier view, seconding—without acknowledging the revision—the interpretation of Clanton, Goodwyn, and Palmer; see Pollack's *The Just Polity: Populism, Law, and Human Welfare* (Urbana: University of Illinois Press, 1987) and *The Humane*

Economy: Populism, Capitalism, and Democracy (New Brunswick, N.J.: Rutgers University Press, 1990). My views were developed for a paper delivered and distributed in manuscript form at the Organization of American Historians in April 1973 and subsequently published as "Populism, Progressivism, and Equality: The Kansas Paradigm," *Agricultural History* 51 (July 1977): 559–81; in " 'Hayseed Socialism' on the Hill: Congressional Populism, 1891–1895," *Western Historical Quarterly* 15 (Apr. 1984); and even more so in *Populism: The Humane Preference in America, 1890–1900* (Boston: Twayne Publishers, 1991). Professor Bicha has denied any affinity for the views of the 1950s revisionists. Regarding that, as well as some other vital information concerning Bicha's findings at the state level, see Peter H. Argersinger, "Ideology and Behavior: Legislative Politics and Western Populism," *Agricultural History* 58 (Jan. 1984): 43–58, and K. D. Bicha, "Some Observations on 'Ideology and Behavior: Legislative Politics and Western Populism,' " and "Argersinger's Reply," ibid., 59–69. In addition to his book *Western Populism: Studies in an Ambivalent Conservatism* (Lawrence, Kans.: Coronado Press, 1976), Bicha has had articles published in the *Journal of American History* (1967), *Agricultural History* (1973, 1976), *Pacific Northwest Quarterly* (1974), *Alberta Historical Review* (1967), and *Mid-America* (1977).

3. *Congressional Record,* 55th Cong., 3rd sess., 9 Jan. 1899, 493–99.
4. Ibid., 10 Jan. 1899, 528.
5. Ibid., 11 Jan. 1899, 562.
6. Ibid., 19 Jan. 1899, 783–89.
7. Ibid., 24 Jan. 1899, 992.
8. Ibid., 25 Jan. 1899, 1055.
9. Ibid., 26 Jan. 1899, 1117.
10. Ibid., 1124.
11. Ibid., 1126–28.
12. Ibid., appendix, 90 ff. Castle, incidentally, went on to make some rather prophetic predictions about the cost of the war and a standing army should the nation persist in what would later be called a "double standard of international morality." The terminology here—"a dual definition of liberty"— is absolutely uncanny to anyone familiar with the work of Henry Steele Commager. See the latter's classic essay, truly a monument of our historical literature, "The Defeat of America," *New York Times Review of Books,* 5 Oct. 1972, 7–13. The phrase "double standard of international morality" was coined by Commager in a 1946 essay entitled "Where Are We Headed," *Atlantic Monthly* 177 (Feb. 1946): 54–58.
13. *Congressional Record,* 55th Cong., 3rd sess., 26 Jan. 1899, 1145.
14. Ibid., 27 Jan. 1899, appendix, 230–33.
15. Ibid., 30 Jan. 1899, 1264–65.
16. Ibid., appendix, 224–25.
17. Ibid., appendix, 145.
18. Ibid., 28 and 30 Jan. 1899, 1216–20, 1280–82; see also Richard E. Welch, Jr., *Imperialists vs. Anti-Imperialists: The Debate over Imperialism in the 1890's* (Itasca, Minn.: F. E. Peacock Publishers, 1972), 72–86.
19. *Congressional Record,* 55th Cong., 3rd sess., 31 Jan. 1899, 1317.
20. Ibid., 1334–35.
21. Ibid., 2 Feb. 1899, 1389.

22. Ibid., 3 Feb. 1899, 1422.

23. Ibid., 4 Feb. 1899, 1445 and 6 Feb. 1899, 1482.

24. Ibid., 6 Feb. 1899, 1483.

25. Ibid., 1491.

26. Ibid., 1490.

27. Richard E. Welch, Jr., *Response to Imperialism: The United States and the Philippine-American War, 1899–1902* (Chapel Hill: University of North Carolina Press, 1979), 18; R. Hal Williams, *Years of Decision: American Politics in the 1890s* (New York: John Wiley and Sons, 1978), 147.

28. *Congressional Record,* 55th Cong., 3rd sess., 6 Feb. 1899, 1486.

29. Welch, *Response to Imperialism*, 42.

30. *Congressional Record,* 55th Cong., 3rd Sess., 24 Feb. 1899, 2329.

31. Ibid., 25 Feb. 1899, 2407–8. The goodwill toward Simpson continued to the end. On 23 January 1899, he even received a tribute from Wisconsin Republican John James Jenkins. In it, this exchange took place: "JENKINS: I felt very bad when I read in the newspapers that my distinguished friend from Kansas was retired. / SIMPSON: I felt bad myself. [Laughter.] / JENKINS: I think my friend from Kansas is a very valuable man here. I have no objection to having here men of different minds and opinions" (ibid., 947). For an interesting look at the last three years of Simpson's life, see Elvis E. Fleming, " 'Sockless' Jerry Simpson: The New Mexico Years, 1902–1905," *New Mexico Historical Review* (Jan. 1994): 49–69. The thrust of Fleming's investigation, as I read it, is that Simpson continued to be as popular as ever and that he was the same old Jerry who had earned Champ Clark's tribute as "one of the friends of human freedom." If he went to New Mexico hoping to get rich "selling the overpriced lands of the Santa Fe Railroad," as was asserted by one historian years ago, Simpson may have been disappointed; when he died, his estate was appraised at $10,000. Appropriately enough, Fleming closed his article with these lines: "The satisfaction which he derived from helping people find new homes in the Pecos Valley made a fitting finale to his life's work."

32. *Congressional Record,* 55th Cong., 3rd Sess., 1 Mar. 1899, 2617 ff.

33. Ibid., 2671.

34. President George Herbert Walker Bush, more than anyone else in our time, used the word history in precisely the way I mentioned.

35. *Congressional Record,* 56th Cong., 1st sess., 7 Feb. 1900, 1609.

36. For a fairly representative sample of Beveridge's arguments, see his speech in *Congressional Record*, 56th Cong., 1st sess., 29 Mar. 1900, appendix, 279 ff. His first major speech on this subject was delivered in Boston on 27 April 1898 before entering the Senate.

37. Ibid., 23 Jan. 1900, 1053.

38. Ibid., 9 Jan. 1900, 714.

39. Welch, *Response to Imperialism,* 101. See also J. Morgan Kousser, *The Shaping of Southern Politics: Suffrage Restriction and the Establishment of the One-Party South* (New Haven: Yale University Press, 1974), and Nell Irvin Painter, *Standing at Armageddon: The United States, 1877–1919* (New York: W. W. Norton, 1987), 220–22, 227–29, 230.

40. See especially the ghastly stories reported in the *Springfield (Mass.) Weekly Republican,* 28 Apr. 1899.

41. Jacqueline Jones Royster, ed., *Southern Horrors and Other Writings: The Anti-Lynching Campaign of Ida B. Wells, 1892–1900* (Boston: Bedford Books, 1997), 10.

42. *Congressional Record,* 56th Cong., 1st sess., 16 Jan. 1900, 847–48.

43. Ibid., 6 Feb. 1900, 1544.

44. Ibid., 23 Feb. 1900, 2151. White's figures are higher than any I have ever encountered. One has to wonder whether the unreported figures could possibly have been so large.

45. Quoted in Francis Butler Simkins, *Pitchfork Ben Tillman, South Carolinian* (Gloucester, Mass.: Peter Smith, 1964), 5.

46. *Congressional Record,* 57th Cong., 1st sess., 22 and 28 Feb. 1902, 2079–83, 2206–7. The suspension vote was fifty-four yeas, twelve nays, and twenty-two not voting. A few voted nay, wanting no punishment for McLaurin and an even greater one for Tillman. For the record, the other two senators censured were Republicans—one in the late 1920s for corrupt practices, and the other Senator Joseph R. McCarthy, who, in 1954, after nearly four years of roughshod investigative tactics and right-wing political crusading in the name of cold war anticommunism, would be "condemned" by most of his colleagues.

47. Ibid., 56th Cong., 1st sess., 6 Feb. 1900, 1589–90.

48. Ibid., 57th Cong., 1st sess., 10 Feb. 1902, 1500.

49. Ibid., 15 Apr. 1902, 1002.

50. Ibid., 4147–50.

51. Ibid., 22 May 1902, 5798; emphasis added.

52. Ibid., 23 June 1902, 7269.

53. Theodore Roosevelt, *Independent*, 21 Dec. 1899, 3401–5, reprinted in Welch, *Imperialists vs. Anti-Imperialists,* 115–21.

54. Quoted in David Haward Bain, *Sitting in Darkness: Americans in the Philippines* (New York: Penguin Books, 1986), 183.

55. *Congressional Record,* 56th Cong., 1st sess., 14 Dec. 1899, 425.

56. Ibid., 31 May 1900, appendix, 359–65; O. Gene Clanton, *Kansas Populism: Ideas and Men* (Lawrence: University Press of Kansas, 1969), 226.

57. *Congressional Record,* 56th Cong., 1st sess., 5 June 1900, 6666.

58. Ibid., 57th Cong., 1st sess., 25 Mar. 1902, 3241. See *McCray v. United States* (1904).

59. Clanton, *Kansas Populism,* 237.

60. Ibid., 243; Clanton, "Populism, Progressivism, and Equality," 579.

61. We should note that Sinclair was commissioned by a former Populist, Julius Wayland, on behalf of *Appeal to Reason,* published in Girard, Kansas, to undertake this study; the novel was also serialized in the socialist weekly before appearing in book form.

62. Upton Sinclair's comment was made in an open letter written to one of his millionaire friends; it has been modified slightly for use here. His actual words, penned in 1939, were: "It is hard to get any man to understand an argument when his living depends upon his not understanding it." See also *The Jungle,* with an afterword by Robert B. Downs (New York: New American Library Edition, 11th Printing), 343–44.

EPILOGUE

1. O. Gene Clanton, *Kansas Populism: Ideas and Men* (Lawrence: University Press of Kansas, 1969), 197 ff.

2. Quoted in *Advocate and News* (Topeka), 23 Mar. 1898, 3; emphasis added.

3. Lawrence Goodwyn, *Democratic Promise: The Populist Moment in America* (New York: Oxford University Press, 1976), 539.

4. See "The Business Point of View," in Julius W. Pratt's *Expansionists of 1898: The Acquisition of Hawaii and the Spanish Islands* (Baltimore: Johns Hopkins University Press, 1936) and "Business, Labor, and the Influence of Economic Self-Interest," in Richard E. Welch, Jr., *Response to Imperialism: The United States and the Philippine-American War, 1899–1902* (Chapel Hill: University of North Carolina Press, 1979).

5. Thomas J. McCormick, *China Market: America's Quest for Informal Empire, 1893-1901* (Chicago: Quadrangle Books, 1967).

6. *Congressional Record,* 56th Cong., 1st sess., 26 Feb. 1900, 2500.

7. Christopher Lasch, "The Anti-Imperialists, the Philippines, and the Inequality of Man," *Journal of Southern History* 24 (Aug. 1958), reprinted in Thomas G. Paterson, ed., *American Imperialism and Anti-Imperialism* (New York: Thomas Y. Crowell, 1973), 110-17.

8. George H. Nadel and Perry Curtis, eds., *Imperialism and Colonialism* (New York: Macmillan, 1964), 1. I am reminded here of Joseph Conrad's statement in *The Heart of Darkness:* "The conquest of the earth, which mostly means the taking it away from those who have a different complexion or slightly flatter noses than ourselves, is not a pretty thing when you look into it much."

9. William Peffer, *Americanism and the Philippines* (Topeka: Crane and Company, 1900).

10. Peffer's history of Populism was recently made available in book form thanks to Peter H. Argersinger. With his superb introductory essay and textual annotation, we now have a valuable memoir by a leading Populist to add to our understanding of the movement. See William A. Peffer, *Populism: Its Rise and Fall* (Lawrence: University Press of Kansas, 1992).

11. Ibid., 182, 189,188.

12. *Congressional Record,* 56th Cong., 2nd sess., 29 Jan. 1901, 1634-38.

13. *Advocate* (Topeka), 17 Mar. 1897.

14. *Congressional Record,* 57th Cong., 1st sess., 16 Apr. 1902, 4210.

15. Lasch, "The Anti-Imperialists," 110-17. This transformation continued into our time and in my judgment, more than any other single factor produced the death of liberalism as we knew it. In a recent and highly perceptive book review, John Patrick Diggins raised a crucial question when he asked: Although there are many who see the absence of "morality" from "liberal political discourse" as a positive development, "by denying liberalism a moral dimension, are we not again allowing ourselves to be betrayed? The founding of politics on moral absolutes did not trouble Abraham Lincoln, and it did much to help the antislavery cause. For all the worries of well-meaning and serious observers . . . about the excesses of moralism in politics, the real sin is cynicism, the betrayal of conviction to ambition" ("Unnatural Bedfellows," *New York Times Book Review,* 7 May 1995, 24).

16. Gene Clanton, *Populism: The Humane Preference in America, 1890–1900* (Boston: Twayne Publishers, 1991), 166.

Bibliographical Note

For extensive lists of materials, primary and secondary, pertinent to this subject, see the bibliographical essays contained in Gene Clanton, *Populism: The Humane Preference in America, 1890–1900* (Boston: Twayne Publishers, 1991), and Robert C. McMath, Jr., *American Populism: A Social History* (New York: Hill and Wang, 1993). See also this book's notes for a fairly comprehensive listing of the various secondary works that have proven to be most relevant to this study.

On the subject of congressional Populism, the literature is not extensive. Hortense Marie Harrison, "The Populist Delegation in the Fifty-Second Congress, 1891–1893" (master's thesis, University of Kansas, 1933), and Richard N. Kottman, "An Analysis of the People's Party Delegation in Congress, 1891–1897" (master's thesis, University of Iowa, 1954), are the pioneer studies. Subsequently, Myron C. Scott, "A Congressman and His Constituents: Jerry Simpson and the Big Seventh" (master's thesis, [Fort Hays] Kansas State College, 1959), and Karel D. Bicha, "Jerry Simpson: Populist Without Principles," *Journal of American History* 54 (Sept. 1967): 291–306, have appeared. See also Bicha's chapter on congressional Populism in *Western Populism: Studies in an Ambivalent Conservatism* (Lawrence, Kans.: Coronado Press, 1976). At about the same time, Peter H. Argersinger published *Populism and Politics: William Alfred Peffer and the People's Party* (Lexington: University of Kentucky Press, 1974). See also the chapter entitled "No Rights on This Floor: Third Parties and the Institutionalization of Congress" in *The Limits of Agrarian Radicalism: Western Populism and American Politics* (Lawrence: University Press of Kansas, 1995). To this list add Gene Clanton, " 'Hayseed Socialism' on the Hill: Congressional Populism, 1891–1895," *Western Historical Quarterly* (Apr. 1984): 139–62.

As the notes illustrate, the *Congressional Record* has served as the primary source for this book. That record proved to be extensive and even more rewarding than I had hoped. The official index, it was discovered rather quickly, could not be relied upon to provide the necessary leads to important statements placed on the record. It was necessary to work through the mountain of material disposited on the record day after day, beginning with the Fifty-second and ending with the the Fifty-seventh Congress. This time-consuming endeavor has yielded the dividends that constitute this study. It will, I trust, enable future researchers to go beyond what has been done here. In particular it should enable scholars to make even more extensive use of private collections, as well as to engage in more comprehensive vote analysis. Some of that has been done here. The most important collections of materials for this study are contained at Chapel Hill, North Carolina, in the Southern Historical Collection, among them the Tom Watson and Marion Butler papers, both of which were carefully examined. Butler's papers are especially useful and merit even more extensive exploration. There are, of course, other collections that should add considerable insight. For example, the Richard Franklin Pettigrew papers housed in Washington, D.C., would likely prove most helpful. And there are, of course, also those papers of various key senators and representatives who served during the Populist years as members of the Republican or Democratic parties.

Index